mediate

**Student's Book**

New

# Headway

English Course

John and Liz Soars

# CONTENTS

## LANGUAGE INPUT

# SKILLS DEVELOPMENT

| Reading | Speaking | Listening | Writing (in the Workbook) |
|---|---|---|---|
| 'People, the great communicators' – the many ways we communicate p11 | Information gap – Joy Darling p8<br>Discussion – who are your ideal neighbours? p12<br>Roleplay – exchanging information about two neighbours p12 | Neighbours – Steve and Mrs Snell talk about each other as neighbours (jigsaw) p12 | Informal letters<br>A letter to a penfriend WB p9 |
| 'Living in the USA' – three people talk about their experiences (jigsaw) p18 | Information gap – people's lifestyles p16<br>Exchanging information about immigrants to the USA p18 | 'You drive me mad (but I love you)!' – what annoys you about the people in your life? p20 | Linking words<br>*but, however* WB p14<br>Describing a person WB p15 |
| 'The burglars' friend' p22<br>Newspaper stories p24<br>A short story – 'The perfect crime' p26 | Information gap – Zoë's party p25<br>Telling stories<br>*fortunately/unfortunately* p25 | A radio drama – 'The perfect crime' p26 | Linking words<br>*while, during,* and *for* WB p20<br>Writing a story 1 WB p21 |
| 'The best shopping street in the world' – Nowy Świat, in Poland p34 | Town survey – the good things and bad things about living in your town p32<br>Discussion – attitudes to shopping p34 | 'My uncle's a shopkeeper' p33<br>Buying things p36 | Filling in forms WB p26 |
| | | | |
| 'Hollywood kids – growing up in Los Angeles ain't easy' p42 | What are your plans and ambitions? p39<br>Being a teenager p42 | A song – *You've got a friend* p44 | Writing a postcard WB p32 |
| 'A tale of two millionaires' – one was mean and one was generous p50 | Information gap – comparing cities p48<br>Discussion – the rich and their money p50 | Living in another country – an interview with a girl who went to live in Sweden p49 | Relative clauses 1<br>*who/that/which/where* WB p37<br>Describing a place WB p37 |
| Celebrity interview from *Hi! Magazine* with the pop star and the footballer who are in love p58 | Mingle – Find someone who … p55<br>Roleplay – interviewing a band p57<br>Project – find an interview with a famous person p58 | An interview with the band *Style* p57 | Relative clauses 2<br>*who/which/that* as the object WB p41<br>Writing a biography WB p42 |

# LANGUAGE INPUT

## SKILLS DEVELOPMENT

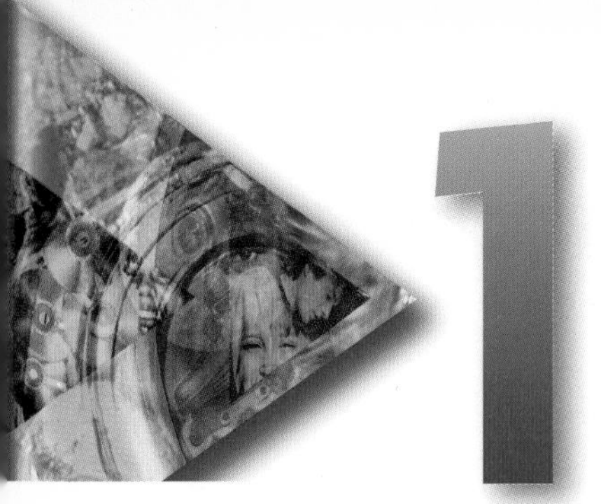

# 1 Getting to know you

**Tenses • Questions • Using a bilingual dictionary • Social expressions 1**

**STARTER** 

**1** Match the questions and answers.

| | |
|---|---|
| Where were you born? | A year ago. |
| What do you do? | Three times a week. |
| Are you married? | In Thailand. |
| Why are you learning English? | Because I need it for my job. |
| When did you start learning English? | I'm a teacher. |
| How often do you have English classes? | No, I'm single. |

**2** Ask and answer the questions with a partner.

## TWO STUDENTS

### Tenses and questions

**1** **T 1.1** Read and listen to Maurizio. Then complete the text, using the verbs in the box.

| | | | |
|---|---|---|---|
| 'm enjoying | 'm going to work | live | started |
| 'm studying | come | can speak | went |

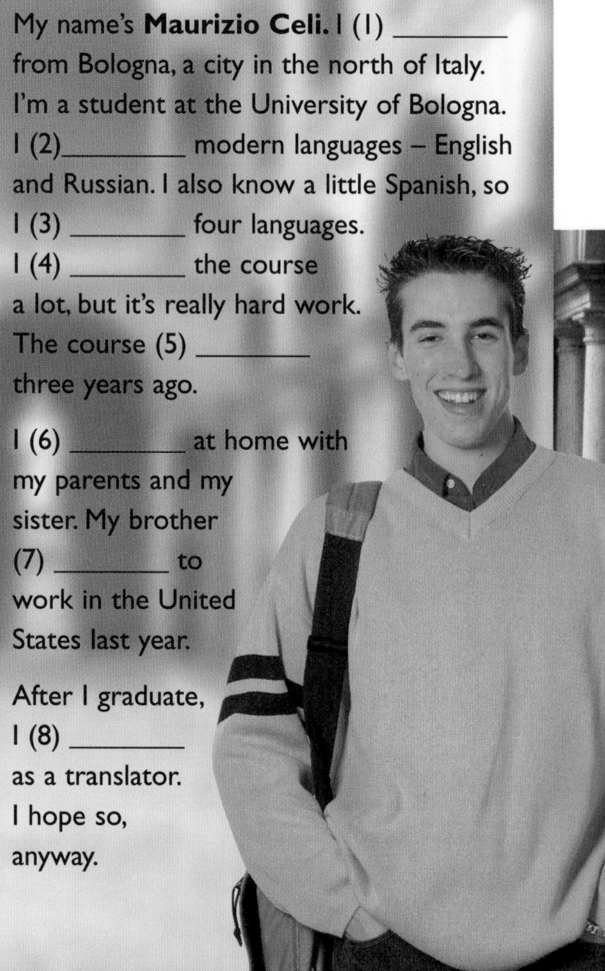

My name's **Maurizio Celi.** I (1) ________ from Bologna, a city in the north of Italy. I'm a student at the University of Bologna. I (2)________ modern languages – English and Russian. I also know a little Spanish, so I (3) ________ four languages. I (4) ________ the course a lot, but it's really hard work. The course (5) ________ three years ago.

I (6) ________ at home with my parents and my sister. My brother (7) ________ to work in the United States last year.

After I graduate, I (8) ________ as a translator. I hope so, anyway.

**2** Complete the questions about Carly.

1 ***Where does she*** come from?
2 ____________ live?
3 ____________ live with?
4 What ____________ studying?
5 ____________ enjoying the course?
6 How many ____________ speak?
7 ______ did her course start?
8 What ____________ after she graduates?

**T 1.2** Listen to Carly, and write the answers to the questions.

**3** Complete the questions to Carly.

1 'Which ***university do you go*** to?'
'I don't go to a university. I study at home.'
2 '____________ a job?'
'Yes, I do. A part-time job.'
3 'What ____________ at the moment?'
'I'm writing an essay.'
4 '____________ to England?'
'Fifteen years ago.'
5 '____________ name?'
'Dave.'
6 '____________?'
'He's an architect.'

## GRAMMAR SPOT

1 Find examples of present, past, and future tenses in the texts about Maurizio and Carly.
2 Which tenses are the two verb forms in these sentences? What is the difference between them?
He lives with his parents.
She's living with an English family for a month.
3 Match the question words and answers.

| | |
|---|---|
| What . . . ? | Because I wanted to. |
| Who . . . ? | Last night. |
| Where . . . ? | $5. |
| When . . . ? | A sandwich. |
| Why . . . ? | By bus. |
| How many . . . ? | In New York. |
| How much . . . ? | Jack. |
| How . . . ? | The black one. |
| Whose . . . ? | It's mine. |
| Which . . . ? | Four. |

▶▶ **Grammar Reference 1.1 and 1.2 p129**

# PRACTICE

## Talking about you

**1** Ask and answer questions with a partner.

- Where . . . live?
- . . . have any brothers or sisters?
- What . . . like doing at the weekend?
- Where . . . go for your last holiday?

Make more questions. Use some of the question words in the Grammar Spot on p7. Ask your teacher some of the questions.

**2** In groups, ask and answer the questions.

- Do you like listening to music?
- What sort of music do you like?
- What are you wearing?
- What is your teacher wearing?
- What did you do last night?
- What are you doing tonight?

**3** Write a paragraph about you. Use the text about Maurizio to help you.

## Getting information

**4** Your teacher will give you some information about Joy Darling, a postwoman. You don't have the same information. Ask and answer questions.

**Student A**

Joy Darling started working as a postwoman . . . (*When?*). She drives a van because she delivers letters to a lot of small villages.

*When did she start working as a postwoman?*

*Because she delivers letters to a lot of small villages.*

**Student B**

Joy Darling started working as a postwoman thirty years ago, when she was 22. She drives a van because . . . (*Why?*).

*Thirty years ago.*

*Why does she drive a van?*

## Check it

**5** Choose the correct verb form.

1 Maria *comes / is coming* from Chile.
2 She *speaks / is speaking* Spanish and English.
3 Today Tom *wears / is wearing* jeans and a T-shirt.
4 *Are you liking / Do you like* black coffee?
5 Last year she *went / goes* on holiday to Florida.
6 Next year she *studies / is going to study* at university.

# VOCABULARY
## Using a bilingual dictionary

**1** Look at this extract from the Oxford Portuguese Minidictionary.

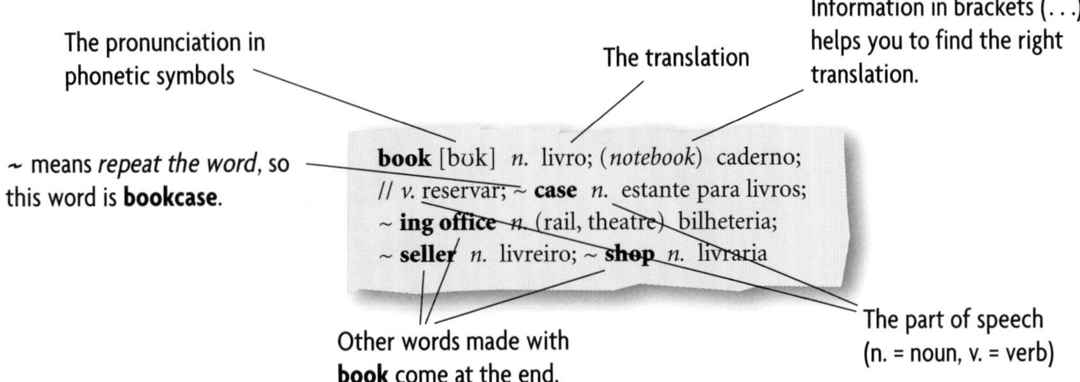
**book** [bʊk] *n.* livro; (*notebook*) caderno; // *v.* reservar; ~ **case** *n.* estante para livros; ~ **ing office** *n.* (rail, theatre) bilheteria; ~ **seller** *n.* livreiro; ~ **shop** *n.* livraria


**2** What are these words? Write *noun, verb, adjective, adverb, preposition,* or *past tense.*

| | | |
|---|---|---|
| bread ________ | beautiful ________ | on ________ |
| hot ________ | in ________ | came ________ |
| write ________ | never ________ | eat ________ |
| quickly ________ | went ________ | letter ________ |

**3** These words have more than one meaning. Write two sentences that show different meanings. Use a dictionary.

| | Sentence 1 | Sentence 2 |
|---|---|---|
| book | *I'm reading a good book.* | *I booked a room at a hotel.* |
| kind | | |
| can | | |
| mean | | |
| flat | | |
| play | | |
| train | | |
| ring | | |

**T 1.3** Listen to some sample answers.

**4** What are the everyday objects in the pictures? Look around the room you are in. Find five things you don't know the words for in English. Look them up in a dictionary.

# READING
## Communication

**1** How many different ways can people communicate?

**2** Your teacher will give you some ideas to communicate, but you can't use words! Mime to your partner, and your partner has to guess what they are.

**3** Read the text quickly and match the headings to the paragraphs.

A **HISTORY** OF COMMUNICATION

**HOW** WE COMMUNICATE

COMMUNICATION **TODAY**

DIFFERENCES BETWEEN **PEOPLE** AND **ANIMALS**

**4** Match the pictures on p11 to each of the four ancient societies in paragraph three.

**5** Read the text again and answer the questions.

1 Which animals are mentioned? What can they do?
2 What is special about human communication? What can *we* do?
3 Which four forms of media are mentioned in the last paragraph?
4 What is good and bad about information technology today?

### What do you think?

- What can animals do that people can't?
- How do *you* like to communicate?
- What is happening in information technology now?

# PEOPLE

## the great communicators

We can communicate with other people in many different ways. We can talk and write, and we can send messages with our hands and faces. There is also the phone (including the mobile!), the fax, and e-mail. Television, film, painting, and photography can also communicate ideas.

Animals have ways of exchanging information, too. Bees dance and tell other bees where to find food. Elephants make sounds that humans can't hear. Whales sing songs. Monkeys use their faces to show anger and love. But this is nothing compared to what people can do. We have language – about 6000 languages, in fact. We can write poetry, tell jokes, make promises, explain, persuade, tell the truth, or tell lies. And we have a sense of past and future, not just present.

Communication technologies were very important in the development of all the great ancient societies:

- Around 2900 BC, paper and hieroglyphics transformed Egyptian life.
- The ancient Greeks loved the spoken word. They were very good at public speaking, drama, and philosophy.
- The Romans developed a unique system of government that depended on the Roman alphabet.
- In the 14th century, the printing press helped develop new ways of thinking across Europe.

Radio, film, and television have had a huge influence on society in the last hundred years. And now we have the Internet, which is infinite. But what is this doing to us? We can give and get a lot of information very quickly. But there is so much information that it is difficult to know what is important and what isn't. Modern media is changing our world every minute of every day.

a

b

c

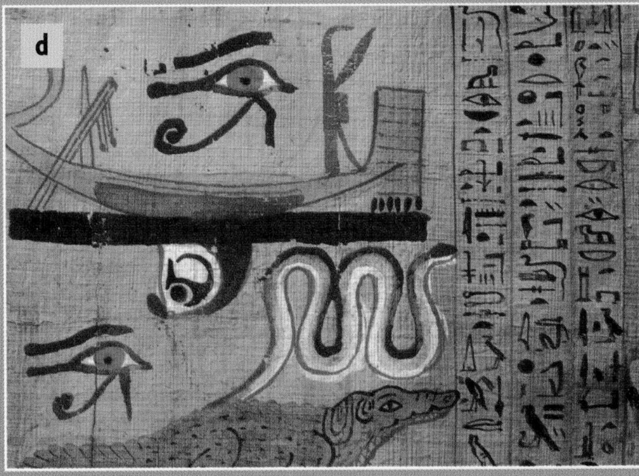

d

## LISTENING AND SPEAKING

### Neighbours

**1** Who are your ideal neighbours? Complete the questionnaire on the right, then discuss your answers with a partner.

**My ideal neighbours are people who . . .**

| | Yes | No |
|---|---|---|
| . . . say hello when I see them. | ☐ | ☐ |
| . . . I never see. | ☐ | ☐ |
| . . . have parties and invite me. | ☐ | ☐ |
| . . . are very quiet. | ☐ | ☐ |
| . . . often come round for a cup of coffee. | ☐ | ☐ |
| . . . come round to borrow things. | ☐ | ☐ |
| . . . make themselves at home in my house. | ☐ | ☐ |

**2** 'Good walls make good neighbours'. What does this mean? Do you agree?

**3** You will hear Mrs Snell and her new neighbour, Steve, talking about each other.

Work in two groups.

**T 1.4** **Group A** Listen to Mrs Snell.

**T 1.5** **Group B** Listen to Steve.

**4** Answer the questions.

1. When did Steve move into his new flat?
2. Is it a large flat?
3. What's his job? Is it a good job?
4. Does he work long hours?
5. What does he wear for work?
6. Who is staying with Steve at the moment?
7. What time did Steve's party end?
8. How many people came to the party?
9. What is Steve doing tonight?
10. Why doesn't Mrs Snell want to speak to Steve?

Compare your answers with a partner from the other group. What are the differences?

### Roleplay

Work in groups of three.

**Student A** You are Steve.
**Student B** You are Mrs Snell.
**Student C** You are another neighbour. You have invited them to your flat for coffee.

Continue the conversation below. Talk about these things.

- Steve's job
- Steve's sister
- the party

| | |
|---|---|
| **Neighbour** | Do you two know each other? |
| **Steve** | Well, we met a few days ago. |
| **Mrs Snell** | But we didn't introduce ourselves. I'm Mrs Snell. |
| **Steve** | Pleased to meet you. |
| **Neighbour** | Steve works in advertising, you know . . . |

### What do you think?

- What do you understand by the words 'generation gap'?
- Write down three things that young people think about older people and three things that older people think about young people. In groups, compare ideas.

# EVERYDAY ENGLISH
## Social expressions 1

**1** We use certain expressions in different social situations.

*I'm sorry I'm late!*

*Don't worry. Come and sit down.*

Match the expressions and responses. When do we use these expressions?

| | |
|---|---|
| How are you? | Sleep well! |
| Hello, Jane! | Yes. Can I help you? |
| How do you do? | Good morning! |
| See you tomorrow! | Fine, thanks. |
| Good night! | Pleased to meet you, Ela. |
| Good morning! | Not at all. Don't mention it. |
| Hello, I'm Ela Paul. | Thanks. |
| Cheers! | Same to you! |
| Excuse me! | That's very kind. Thank you. |
| Bless you! | Bye! |
| Have a good weekend! | How do you do? |
| Thank you very much indeed. | Hi, Peter! |
| Make yourself at home. | Cheers! |

**T 1.6** Listen and check. Practise saying them.

**2** Test a partner. Say an expression. Can your partner give the correct response?

**3** With your partner, write two short conversations that include some of the social expressions. Read your conversations to the class.

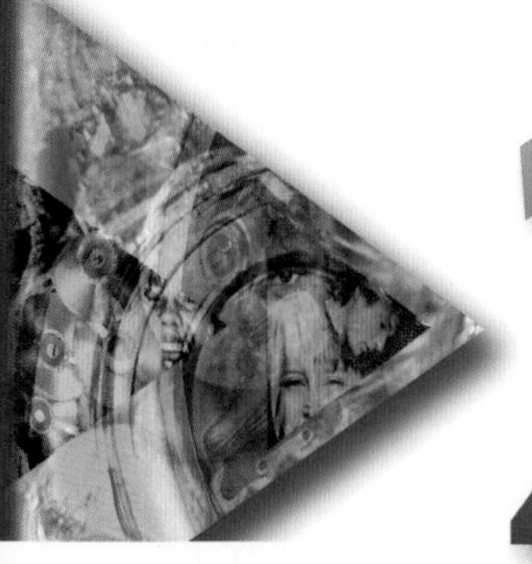

# 2 The way we live

**Present tenses • *have/have got* • Collocation – daily life • Making conversation**

**STARTER** 

These flags all belong to English-speaking countries. Write the name of the country.

1 ______________

2 ______________

3 ______________

4 ______________

5 ______________

6 ______________

The United States
Canada
Australia
New Zealand
South Africa
Scotland

## PEOPLE AND PLACES

### Present tenses and *have/have got*

**1** Read the texts. Match a country from the Starter with a text and a photograph. Complete the texts with the words from the boxes.

**a** ☐ exports enjoy immigrants huge

This country has quite a small population, just 16 million, but the country is ____ . The people are mainly of European descent, but there are also aborigines and a lot of south-east Asian ____ . People live in towns on the coast, not so much inland, because it is so hot. They live a lot of their lives outdoors, and ____ sports, swimming, and having barbecues. This country ____ wine and wool – it has more than 60 million sheep!

**b** ☐ favourite variety has only

This is the second biggest country in the world, but it has a population of ____ 30 million. It is so big that there is a ____ of climates. Most people live in the south because the north is too cold. It is famous for its beautiful mountains and lakes – it ____ more lakes than any other country. Their ____ sports are baseball and ice hockey.

**c**  elephants grows black climate

This country has a population of about 45 million. Of these, 76 per cent are ____ and 12 per cent white. It has a warm ____ . Either it never rains, or it rains a lot! It is the world's biggest producer of gold, and it exports diamonds, too. It ____ a lot of fruit, including oranges, pears, and grapes, and it makes wine. In the game reserves you can see a lot of wildlife, including lions, ____ , zebras, and giraffes.

2 **T 2.1** Listen to three people describing the other countries. Match a country from the Starter with a description and a photograph.

d ☐ e ☐ f ☐

3 Close your books. Remember three facts about each country.

## GRAMMAR SPOT

1 What tense are all the verb forms in texts a–c? Why?
2 Look at the sentences. Which refers to *all time*? Which refers to *now*?
   She has three children.
   She's having a shower.
3 Is *have* or *have got* used in texts a–c? And in d and e? Is *have got* more formal or informal?

▶▶ **Grammar Reference 2.1–2.4 p130**

4 Give some similar facts about your country.

# PRACTICE

## Talking about you

**1** Practise the forms of *have* and *have got* in the question, negative, and short answer.

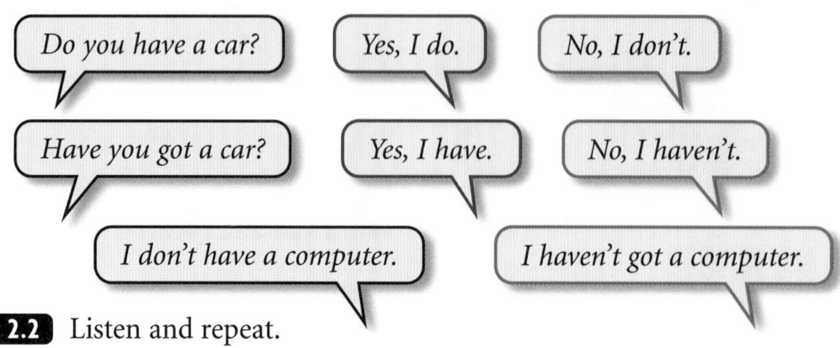


**T 2.2** Listen and repeat.

**2** Ask and answer about these things with a partner, using *have* or *have got*:

- a computer
- a stereo
- a camera
- a bicycle
- a credit card
- a Walkman
- a mobile phone
- a pet
- brothers and sisters
- your parents/a holiday home
- your sister/a car
- your brother/a motorbike

## Getting information

**3** Work with a partner.
**Student A** Look at this chart.
**Student B** Look at the chart from your teacher.

| Name and age | Town and country | Family | Occupation | Free time/ holiday | Present activity |
|---|---|---|---|---|---|
| **Mike**, 26 | | | | | |
| **Lucy**, 38 | | | | | |
| **Nicole**, 15 | Texas, the United States | two brothers and a dog! | student at high school | • listens to music<br>• Florida or Mexico | getting ready to go out |
| **Jeff**, 54, and **Wendy**, 53 | Melbourne, Australia | one daughter and three grandchildren | He . . . office. She . . . hairdresser. | • tennis, swimming<br>• Bali every summer | having a barbecue in the back yard |

Write questions to find the information about the people in your chart.

**Town/country** • Where does he . . . from?
**Family** • . . . married? • Has he got . . . ?
• Does she have . . . ? • How many . . . ?
**Occupation** • What . . . do?
**Free time/holiday** • What does she . . . in her free time?
• Where . . . go on holiday?
**Present activity** • What . . . doing at the moment?

**T 2.3** Listen and compare.

**4** Ask and answer questions with your partner to complete your chart.

5 Think of questions to ask about free time and holiday activities.

- What do you do in your free time?
- What do . . . at the weekend?
- . . . any sports?
- Do you like . . . ?
- Where . . . holiday?
- Do . . . winter holiday?

Stand up! Ask two or three students your questions. Use short answers when necessary. Find out who has the most hobbies and holidays.

*No, I don't.*

## Check it

6 Tick (✓) the correct sentence.

1 ☐ Where you go on holiday?
  ☐ Where do you go on holiday?

2 ☐ Do you have any children?
  ☐ Do you have got any children?

3 ☐ I'm Hans. I'm coming from Germany.
  ☐ I'm Hans. I come from Germany.

4 ☐ This is a great party! Everyone is dancing.
  ☐ This is a great party! Everyone dances.

5 ☐ I don't have a mobile phone.
  ☐ I no have a mobile phone.

6 ☐ Jack's a policeman, but he doesn't wear a uniform.
  ☐ Jack's a policeman, but he no wear a uniform.

7 ☐ 'Where is José?' 'He's sitting by the window.'
  ☐ 'Where is José?' 'He sits by the window.'

8 ☐ I'm liking black coffee.
  ☐ I like black coffee.

# VOCABULARY

## Daily life

1 Match the verbs and nouns.

| | |
|---|---|
| have<br>wash<br>watch<br>talk | a film on TV<br>to my friends<br>my hair<br>breakfast |

| | |
|---|---|
| make<br>listen<br>relax<br>do | to music<br>my homework<br>a cup of tea<br>on the sofa |

| | |
|---|---|
| have<br>clear up<br>do<br>have/put | posters on the wall<br>the mess<br>a shower<br>the washing-up |

| | |
|---|---|
| cook<br>go<br>put on<br>read | magazines<br>a meal<br>make-up<br>to the toilet |

**T 2.4** Listen and check.

2 Match the activities from exercise 1 with the correct room.

**Kitchen**

______________________
______________________
______________________
______________________

**Bathroom**

______________________
______________________
______________________
______________________

**Living room**

______________________
______________________
______________________
______________________

**Bedroom**

______________________
______________________
______________________
______________________

3 Do you like where you live? Choose your favourite room. What do you do in that room?

***I like my bedroom a lot because I've got lots of posters on the walls. I listen to music and do my homework . . .***

***I like my living room. The walls are white, and I love the big, comfortable sofa . . .***

4 Describe your favourite room to a partner. Don't say which room it is. Can your partner guess?

# READING AND SPEAKING
## Living in the USA

**1** Close your eyes and think of the United States. Write down the first five things you think of.

*The Empire State Building*
*Cheeseburger and fries*

Compare your list with other students.

**2** Read the introduction to the magazine article. Then work in three groups.
**Group A** Read about Roberto.
**Group B** Read about Endre.
**Group C** Read about Yuet Tung.

**3** Answer the questions.
1. Why and when did he/she come to the US?
2. What does he/she do?
3. What does he/she like about living in the US?
4. What was difficult at the beginning?

**4** Find a partner from each of the other two groups. Compare the three people.

**5** Answer the questions with your group.
1. What do the people have in common?
2. Are they all happy living in the US?
3. Who has other members of their family living there?
4. Do they all have children?
5. Who married someone from their own country?
6. What do Roberto and Endre like about the US?
7. What do they say about their own country?
8. Do they like the people?
9. What do they say about Americans and their cars?

### What do you think?

- What do you like best about living in your country? What would you miss if you lived abroad?
- Do you know any foreigners living in your country? What do they like about it? What do they find different?

# LIVING IN

**The people of the United States are nearly all immigrants, or descendants of immigrants. It is a young country, and much of the population has relatives who live in other parts of the world.**

**But how do they find the US when they first arrive? What do they think of the people, the culture, the way of life?**

**Jamie Peterson spoke to three of them.**

# THE USA

**Roberto Solano**
aged 24, from Mexico

**Endre Boros**
aged 45, from Hungary

**Yuet Tung**
aged 31, from Hong Kong

**Roberto** came from Acapulco to New York ten years ago. At first he missed everything – the sunshine, the food, his girlfriend. But now he has a successful business with his three brothers and his sister. They run a soccer store in New Brunswick. Roberto's girlfriend is now his wife, and they have two children who go to American schools.

When asked why he came to the US, Roberto says without hesitation, 'Because I want to work hard and be successful.' He certainly works hard. He's at the store all day, then works as a driver in the evening. 'That's why I like America,' he says. 'You can be what you want.'

'When I first came here, I didn't speak the language, and it was winter. It was so cold! There was snow! Now nearly all my family are here, not only in New York, but also in California, and in Texas. We meet about once a month and have a huge Mexican meal that takes about five hours! We're all happy here.'

**Endre** is a mathematician at Rutgers University, New Jersey. He came from Budapest thirteen years ago. 'I had an opportunity to come here for two years.' After a year, his wife came to join him, and since then they've had a daughter, so they decided to stay.

'At first it was very strange. Everything is so big here,' he says. 'I started to feel happy when I bought a car. Now I go everywhere by car. In Hungary, we only use the car at weekends, but here your car is part of your life. Nobody walks anywhere.'

How does he find the people? 'Very friendly. The first question everybody asks you is "Where are you from?" People talk to you here, they start conversations. I like the fact that there are people from all over the world.'

What about the way of life? 'The thing I like best is the independence. Nobody tells me what to do. Here you can do what you want, so you learn to make decisions for yourself. I feel in control.'

**Yuet Tung** is her Chinese name, but in English she's known as Clara. She came to the US eight years ago and studied fine art. Now she works on Madison Avenue for a publisher. She married a Vietnamese American three years ago, and they live in Long Island. They don't have any children yet.

What does she think of living in New York? 'It's very similar to Hong Kong. It's a busy city, very exciting, and people walk very fast! I like the stores here. They're huge, and it's cheaper than Hong Kong. But you need a car here. In Hong Kong everyone uses public transportation, because it's good and it's cheap. At first I hated driving here, but it's OK now.'

What does she like best? 'The space. Here I live in a house with a yard. In Hong Kong it is so crowded. And the people are friendly. When I go jogging, everyone says "Hi!" And the food is from every country in the world.'

# LISTENING AND SPEAKING

## You drive me mad (but I love you)!

Dave and Alison

Mike and Carol

**1** Complete these sentences about the people in your life. Tell a partner.

- My mother/father drives me mad when she/he . . .
- I hate it when my boyfriend/girlfriend . . .
- I don't like people who . . .
- It really annoys me when friends . . .

**2** Choose one person in your life. What annoying habits does he/she have?

Does he/she . . . ?
- always arrive late
- talk too loudly
- leave things on the floor

Is he/she . . . ?
- untidy
- always on the phone
- never on time

What annoying habits do *you* have? Discuss with your partner.

**3** You are going to listen to a radio programme called *Home Truths*. Two couples, Carol and Mike, and Dave and Alison, talk about their partner's annoying habits. Look at the pictures below. What are their annoying habits?

**T 2.5** Listen and write the correct names under each picture below.

**4** Are these sentences true (✓) or false (✗)? Correct the false sentences.

1 Carol and Mike never watch television.
2 Mike doesn't listen when his wife speaks to him.
3 Carol makes the decisions in their house.
4 Mike shouts at his wife when she's driving.
5 Dave never does any jobs at home.
6 Dave is bad at his job.
7 Alison tidies up Dave's mess.
8 Alison is very organized.

### What do you think?

**1** Do men or women typically complain about their partners doing these things?

- watching sport on TV
- driving badly
- taking a long time to get ready
- not tidying things away

**2** What do you think men are generally better at? What are women better at?

# EVERYDAY ENGLISH
## Making conversation

1 **T 2.6** Listen to two conversations. Maria and Jean-Paul are foreign students in Britain. Their teachers are trying to be friendly. Which conversation is more successful? Why?

2 Obviously, it is impossible to tell someone how to have a conversation, but here are some things that help.

- Ask questions.
- Show that you're interested.
- Don't just answer *yes* or *no*.
- Try to add a comment of your own.
- Don't let the conversation stop.

Find examples of these in the tapescripts on p119.

3 Match a line in **A** with a reply in **B** and a further comment in **C**.

| A | B | C |
|---|---|---|
| 1 What a lovely day it is today! | I'm enjoying it. | Was it a good game? |
| 2 It's very wet today. | Yes, no problems. | That's very kind of you. |
| 3 How are you today? | I'm very well, thanks. | We had a pub lunch and went for a walk. |
| 4 Did you have a nice weekend? | No, I missed it. | The plane was a bit late, but it didn't matter. |
| 5 How are you finding living in London? | Thank you. | Makes you feel miserable, doesn't it? |
| 6 Did you have a good journey? | Thank you very much. | I got it in Paris last year. |
| 7 Did you watch the football yesterday? | Yes. | How about you? |
| 8 What a lovely coat you're wearing! | Yes, it was lovely. | It was a bit strange at first, but I'm getting used to it. |
| 9 If you have any problems, just ask me for help. | Mm. Horrible. | Beautiful, isn't it? |

**T 2.7** Listen and check. Practise the conversations with a partner.

4 Think of three questions to ask someone about each of these subjects.

- job • home • free time • last holiday

5 Invent a new name and background for yourself.

*My name's James Bond. I'm a spy. I have homes in London, Moscow, and Beijing …*

Stand up! You're all at a party. Try to make some friends.

# 3 It all went wrong

**Past tenses • Word formation • Time expressions**

**STARTER** 

Here are the past tense forms of some irregular verbs. Write the infinitives.

| | | | | | | | |
|---|---|---|---|---|---|---|---|
| 1 _______ | were | 4 _______ | told | 7 _______ | took | 10 _______ | could |
| 2 _______ | saw | 5 _______ | said | 8 _______ | gave | 11 _______ | made |
| 3 _______ | went | 6 _______ | had | 9 _______ | got | 12 _______ | did |

## THE BURGLARS' FRIEND

### Past Simple

**1** **T 3.1** Read and listen to the newspaper article. Why was Russell the burglars' friend?

# The burglars' friend

IT was 3 o'clock in the morning when four-year-old Russell Brown woke up to go to the toilet.

**His parents were fast asleep in bed**

His parents were fast asleep in bed. But when he heard a noise in the living room and saw a light was on, he went downstairs.

There he found two men. They asked him his name, and told him they were friends of the family.

Unfortunately, Russell believed them. They asked him where the video recorder was. Russell showed them, and said they had a stereo and CD player, too.

The two men carried these to the kitchen. Russell also told them that his mother kept her purse in a drawer in the kitchen, so they took that. Russell even gave them his pocket money – 50p.

They finally left at 4 a.m. They said, 'Will you open the back door while we take these things to the car, because we don't want to wake Mummy and Daddy, do we?' So Russell held the door open for them. He then went back to bed.

His parents didn't know about the burglary until they got up the next day. His father said, 'I couldn't be angry with Russell because he thought he was doing the right thing.'

Fortunately, the police caught the two burglars last week.

**2** Write the past forms of these irregular verbs from the article.

| | | | |
|---|---|---|---|
| wake | ______ | leave | ______ |
| hear | ______ | hold | ______ |
| find | ______ | think | ______ |
| keep | ______ | catch | ______ |

**3** **T 3.2** You will hear some sentences about the story. Correct the mistakes.

Russell woke up at 2 o'clock.

*He didn't wake up at 2.00! He woke up at 3.00.*

**4** Write the questions to these answers.

1 Because he wanted to go to the toilet.
**Why did he wake up?**
2 They were in bed.
3 Because he heard a noise and saw a light on.
4 Two.
5 They told him they were friends of the family.
6 In a drawer in the kitchen.
7 50p.
8 At 4 a.m.
9 The next day. *(When ... find out about ... ?)*
10 Last week.

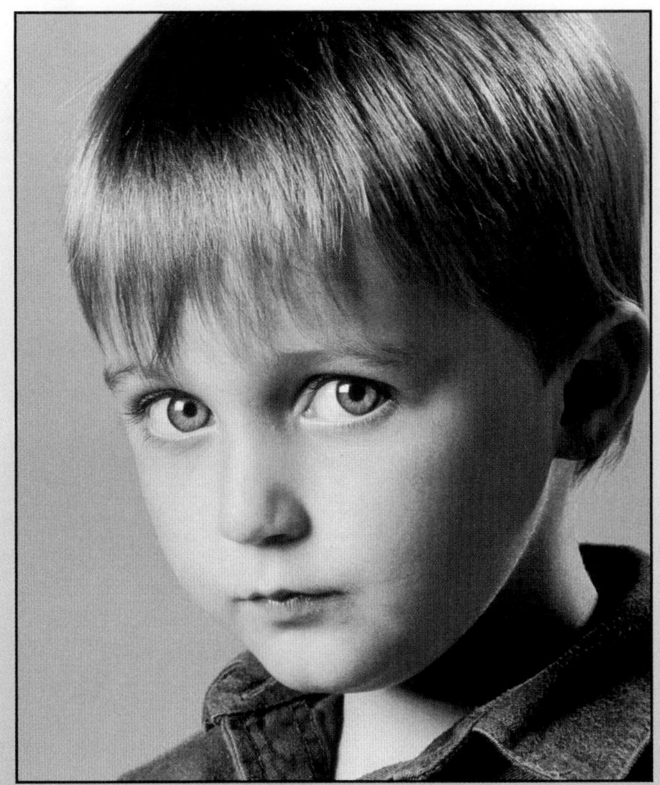

**Russell, 4, made thieves feel at home**

## GRAMMAR SPOT

1 What tense are nearly all the verbs in the article? Why? How do we form the question and negative?

2 Write the Past Simple of these verbs.

a ask ______
show ______
want ______
walk ______
start ______

b try ______
carry ______

c like ______
believe ______
use ______

d stop ______
plan ______

**T 3.3** Listen and repeat.

3 How is the regular past tense formed?
How is the past tense formed when the verb ends in a consonant + *y*?
When do we double the final consonant?

**There is a list of irregular verbs on p143.**

**▶▶ Grammar Reference 3.1 p131**

# PRACTICE

## Making connections

**1** Match the verb phrases. Then make sentences using both verbs in the past. Join the sentences with *so*, *because*, *and*, or *but*.

***I broke a cup, but I mended it with glue.***

| | |
|---|---|
| break a cup | answer it |
| feel ill | mend it |
| make a sandwich | wash my hair |
| have a shower | laugh |
| lose my passport | be hungry |
| call the police | go to bed |
| run out of coffee | buy some more |
| forget her birthday | find it |
| phone ring | say sorry |
| tell a joke | hear a strange noise |

**T 3.4** Listen and compare your answers.

## Talking about you

**2** Ask and answer these questions with a partner. Make more questions, using the Past Simple.

What did you do . . . ?
- last night
- last weekend
- on your last birthday
- on your last holiday

# NEWSPAPER STORIES

## Past Continuous

**1** Complete the newspaper articles with the Past Simple of the verbs in the boxes.

| have can steal give say |
|---|

| break hear come leave go |
|---|

**a**

# Hands up, I've got a burger!

**Last Tuesday a man armed with just a hot hamburger in a bag (1) ________ $1,000 from a bank in Danville, California.**

Police Detective Bill McGinnis (2) ________ that the robber entered the Mount Diablo National Bank at about 1.30 p.m. and (3) ________ the teller a note demanding $1,000. He claimed that he (4) ________ a bomb in the bag. The teller said she (5) ________ smell a distinct odour of hamburger coming from the bag. Even so, she handed the money to the man. He dropped the bag with the hamburger. He escaped in a car.

Police Detective Bill McGinnis

**b**

# Teenage party ends in tears

When Jack and Kelly Harman (1) ________ away on holiday, they (2) ________ their teenage daughter alone in the house. Zoë, aged 16, wanted to stay at home. Her parents said she could have some friends to stay. However, Zoë decided to have a party. Things started to go wrong. Forty uninvited guests arrived. They (3) ________ furniture, smashed windows, and stole jewellery.

When Mr and Mrs Harman (4) ________ the news, they (5) ________ home immediately.

Zoë Harman, 16, home alone

**2** Match these phrases to the articles. Where exactly does each phrase go in the story?

... because she was revising for exams.

As he was running out of the bank,

Everyone was having a good time when suddenly ...

... that was waiting for him outside.

... and some of them were carrying knives.

... , who was wearing a mask, ...

**T 3.5** Listen and check. Practise the sentences that contain these phrases.

### GRAMMAR SPOT

1. What tense are all the verb forms in exercise 2? Why is this tense used?
2. How do we make questions and negatives?
3. Look at these sentences. What's the difference between them?

| When we arrived, | she made<br>she was making | some coffee. |
|---|---|---|

▶▶ **Grammar Reference 3.2 and 3.3 p132**

## PRACTICE

### Discussing grammar

**1** Choose the correct verb form.

1 I *saw / was seeing* a very good programme on TV last night.
2 While I *shopped / was shopping* this morning, I *lost / was losing* my money. I don't know how.
3 Last week the police *stopped / were stopping* Alan in his car because he *drove / was driving* at over eighty miles an hour.
4 How *did you cut / were you cutting* your finger?
5 I *cooked / was cooking* and I *dropped / was dropping* the knife.
6 When I *arrived / was arriving* at the party, everyone *had / was having* a good time.
7 *Did you have / Were you having* a good time last night?

**2** Complete the sentences with the verbs in the Past Simple or Past Continuous.

1 While I _______ (go) to work this morning, I _______ (meet) an old friend.
2 I _______ (not want) to get up this morning. It _______ (rain) and it was cold, and my bed was so warm.
3 I _______ (listen) to the news on the radio when the phone _______ (ring).
4 But when I _______ (pick) up the phone, there was no one there.
5 I _______ (say) hello to the children, but they didn't say anything because they _______ (watch) television.

### Getting information

**3** Your teacher will give you some more information about the teenage party, but you don't have all the information. Ask and answer questions.

**Student A**

Mr and Mrs Harman arrived home at . . . (*When?*)
Zoë was staying with friends.

*When did Mr and Mrs Harman arrive home?*

*She was staying with friends.*

**Student B**

Mr and Mrs Harman arrived home at 10.30 in the evening.
Zoë was staying . . . (*Where?*)

*At 10.30 in the evening.*

*Where was Zoë staying?*

### *fortunately/unfortunately*

**4** Continue this story around the class.

I went out for a walk.
**Unfortunately**, it began to rain.
**Fortunately**, I had an umbrella.
**Unfortunately**, it was broken.
**Fortunately**, I met a friend in his car.
**Unfortunately**, his car ran out of petrol.
**Fortunately**, . . .

**5** Tell similar stories around the class. Begin with these sentences.

- I lost my wallet yesterday.
- It was my birthday last week.
- We went out for a meal last night.
- I went on holiday to . . . last year.

# LISTENING AND READING
## A radio drama

**1** **T 3.6** Look at the pictures below and listen to a radio play called *The perfect crime.*

**2** Answer the questions.

1. What can you see in the pictures?
2. How did Alice feel about Henry at the beginning of the play?
3. What did her husband tell her?
4. Who is Kathy? Who is Bobby?
5. What did she say when he told her? Why did she decide to do this?
6. What did she do to him then?
7. How do you think she murdered him?
8. What was her explanation to the police?
9. Why were all the policemen thirsty?

**3** Read the story. What do you learn from the story that you didn't from the radio drama?

## The perfect crime

**Alice Jackson's** husband, Henry, was a man of habit. So it was that at exactly six o'clock in the evening she was in the kitchen getting a beer for him out of the fridge and watching him walk up the path.

She was smiling. Today the routine was going to be different. It was their tenth wedding anniversary, and some friends were coming round for drinks at 8.00. There was a big ice statue of a couple kissing in the middle of the table in the living room, with twenty glasses waiting for the guests. Alice was looking forward to the evening.

She was very happy. She had a beautiful baby sleeping upstairs, a lovely home, and a husband who she adored.

Henry opened the door and came into the kitchen. She turned round to kiss him and give him his beer.

'Sit down,' Henry said. 'I've got something to say.'

Alice had no idea that in the next two minutes her whole life was going to change.

'I'm sorry,' he said. 'And it's our anniversary, as well. But it's just that Kathy and I are in love. Bobby won't miss me, he's too young.'

She didn't believe her ears. She was in a dream.

'I'll get ready for the party,' she said.

She walked into the living room. When she returned, Henry was standing with his back to her, drinking his beer. She was carrying something heavy. He turned. 'What on earth ... ?' These were Henry Jackson's last words. His wife hit him over the head.

At first he didn't move, then he fell to the floor.

Suddenly Alice began to think very clearly. She took the ice statue back to the living room, and phoned the police.

8

Then she turned up the central heating, and went upstairs to put on some make-up.

The police came quickly.

'Is he all right?' she asked.

'He's dead.'

Alice screamed. 'No, no, not Henry! My Henry! Oh Henry!' Through her tears she told how she put the baby to bed, and came downstairs to find Henry on the kitchen floor.

'Burglars,' said Detective Parry.

They took her into the living room.

'Sit down, Mrs Jackson. Sergeant Taylor, get Mrs Jackson a drink. A brandy with some ice. Phew! It's hot in this room. I hope you understand, Mrs Jackson, that we have to search the house immediately. We must find the murder weapon.'

The room was getting hotter. Suddenly an arm fell off the ice statue onto the table. It was melting. Sergeant Taylor went to the statue and picked up the melting arm. He broke it into bits and put some into Alice's brandy.

'Phew! Can I have a glass of water, Mrs Jackson? It's so hot in here.'

'I think we all need one,' said the detective. 'And with ice.' They were all very hot and thirsty.

Alice's friends arrived. 'Poor Alice! Poor Henry!' They cried, and they tried to comfort her.

'Oh, thank you, thank you,' sobbed Alice. 'Please ... stay and have a drink. Help yourselves.'

They all had drinks – gin and tonic, whisky – and they all had ice. The statue was now nearly a pool of water on the floor.

'I wonder what the burglar hit him with,' said one guest.

'Who knows?' said another, taking a sip of her drink.

Alice heard this conversation, and smiled into her brandy.

9

Based on *Lamb to the Slaughter* by Roald Dahl: see note on p144

**4** Are these sentences true (✓) or false (✗)? Correct the false sentences.

1 Alice was waiting for her husband because she wanted to kill him.
2 She was happy because it was her anniversary.
3 She didn't know what he was going to tell her.
4 Henry said that he was in love with someone else.
5 She thought for a long time about how to murder Henry.
6 She turned up the central heating because the room was cold.
7 After she murdered him, Alice was very clever in her behaviour.
8 Alice hid the murder weapon.

## What do you think?

- At the beginning and the end of the play, Alice was smiling. Why?
- Why do you think she did it?
- Do you think it was the perfect crime? Do you think she got away with the murder? Why/Why not?

## Language work

**5** Give the past form of these verbs from the story. Be careful with the pronunciation.

| | | | |
|---|---|---|---|
| adore | ______ | phone | ______ |
| open | ______ | scream | ______ |
| turn | ______ | take | ______ |
| walk | ______ | pick | ______ |
| hit | ______ | try | ______ |
| fall | ______ | sob | ______ |

## Speaking

**6** Retell the story in your own words around the class.

# VOCABULARY

## Nouns, verbs, and adjectives

**1** Look at these common noun and adjective suffixes. They are used to form different parts of speech.

| **nouns** | *-ation -ion -ness -ity -ence -sion -ment* |
|---|---|
| **adjectives** | *-ous -y -tific -ly -ful -less -ial* |

Complete the charts below and mark the stress. There are some spelling changes.

| Noun | Verb |
|---|---|
| *communi'cation* | co'mmunicate |
| ___________ | dis'cuss |
| ___________ | 'govern |
| invi'tation | ___________ |
| ___________ | de'velop |
| ___________ | ex'plain |
| edu'cation | ___________ |
| ___________ | de'cide |
| ___________ | en'joy |
| ___________ | 'organize |
| im'provement | ___________ |
| ___________ | em'ploy |

| Noun | Adjective |
|---|---|
| 'science | ___________ |
| friend | ___________ |
| ___________ | 'happy |
| ___________ | 'different |
| 'danger | ___________ |
| use | ___________ |
| help | ___________ |
| ___________ | 'special |
| care | ___________ |
| noise | ___________ |
| 'industry | ___________ |
| am'bition | ___________ |

**2** Complete the sentences with one of the words from exercise 1.

1 My English _______ a lot after I lived in London for a month.
2 I have two _______ in life. I want to be rich, and I want to be famous.
3 'I'm going to work hard from now on.' 'That's a very good _______.'
4 There are many _______ between my two children. They aren't similar at all.
5 Thank you for your advice. It was very _______ .
6 I like Italian people. They're very kind and _______ .
7 The United Nations is an international _______ .
8 I asked the teacher for help, but unfortunately, I didn't understand his _______ .
9 Motor racing is a very _______ sport.
10 Fish soup is a _______ of this area. You must try it.
11 I'm having a party on Saturday, and I'd like to _______ you.
12 This is the _______ part of my town. There are lots of factories and businesses.

## Making negatives

**3** We can make adjectives and verbs negative by using these prefixes.

| **adjectives** | *un- im- in- il-* |
|---|---|
| **verbs** | *un- dis-* |

Complete the sentences, using a word from the box and a prefix.

| pack possible agree tidy fair like appear employed legal polite |
|---|

1 Don't go into my bedroom. It's really __________ .
2 I can't do maths. For me, it's an __________ subject.
3 I don't __________ fish. I just prefer meat.
4 It's very __________ to ask someone how much they earn.
5 When we arrived at the hotel, we __________ our suitcases.
6 I was __________ for two years. Then I got a job in an office.
7 'I think learning languages is stupid.' 'I __________ . I think it's a good idea.'
8 The thief stole my bag, ran into the crowd and __________ . I never saw him again.
9 Cannabis is an __________ drug in many countries.
10 You gave her more money than me! That's __________ !

# EVERYDAY ENGLISH

## Time expressions

**1** There are two ways of saying dates. What are they?

8/1/98     16/7/85     25/11/02

**T 3.7** Listen and check.

Look at the same dates in written American English. What's the difference?

1/8/98     7/16/85     11/25/02

**T 3.8** Listen and check.

**2** Practise these dates. They are in British English.

4 June   5 August   31 July   1 March   3 February
21/1/1988   2/12/1996   5/4/1980   11/6/1965   18/10/2000   31/1/2005

**T 3.9** Listen and check.

What days are national holidays in your country?

**3** Complete these time expressions with *at*, *on*, *in*, or no preposition.

| | | |
|---|---|---|
| ___ six o'clock | ___ Saturday | ___ 1995 |
| ___ last night | ___ December | ___ the weekend |
| ___ Monday morning | ___ summer | ___ two weeks ago |
| ___ the evening | ___ yesterday evening | ___ January 18 |

▶▶ **Grammar Reference 3.4 p132.**

**4** Ask and answer the questions with a partner.

1 Do you know exactly when you were born?

*I was born at two o'clock in the morning on Wednesday, the twenty-fifth of June, 1979.*

2 When did you last … ?

- go to the cinema
- play a sport
- give someone a present
- have a holiday
- watch TV
- go to a party
- do an exam
- see a lot of snow
- clean your teeth
- catch a plane

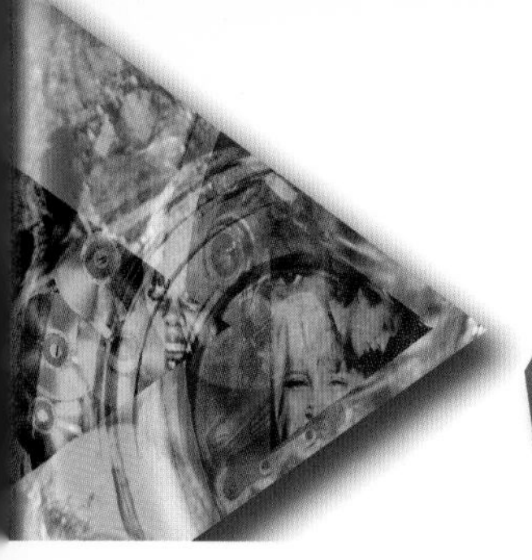

# 4 Let's go shopping!

***much/many* • *some/any* • *a few, a little, a lot of* • Articles • Shopping • Prices**

**STARTER** 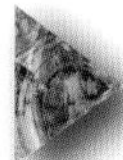

Play the alphabet game with things you can buy. Continue around the class.

**A** Yesterday I went shopping and I bought an **a**pple.
**B** Yesterday I went shopping and I bought an **a**pple and some **b**read.
**C** Yesterday I went shopping and I bought an **a**pple, some **b**read, and a **c**ar.
**D** Yesterday . . .

## THE WEEKEND SHOP

### Quantity

**1** Sarah and Vicky are two students who share a flat. It is Saturday morning, and Sarah has written a shopping list.

**T 4.1** Read and listen to their conversation.

**V** It says here *milk*. How much milk do we need?
**S** Two pints.
**V** And eggs? How many eggs?
**S** A dozen.
**V** And what about potatoes? How many potatoes?
**S** A kilo's enough.
**V** And butter? How much?
**S** Just one packet.

**GRAMMAR SPOT**

Can we count milk (one milk, two milks) ?
Can we count eggs (one egg, two eggs) ?
When do we say *How much . . . ?*
When do we say *How many . . . ?*

▶▶ **Grammar Reference 4.1 p133**

**2** Match these quantities with the shopping list.

| | |
|---|---|
| a bottle of red | six cans |
| just one white loaf | six pork ones |
| 200g of Cheddar | four big ones |
| four packets | |

Continue the conversation with a partner.

3 **T 4.2** Read and listen to the rest of the conversation.

**V** Do we need anything else?
**S** Let's have a look. We've got some apples, but there aren't any grapes. And there isn't any coffee, but we've got some tea.
**V** Is there any orange juice left, or did somebody finish it?
**S** There's a little, but there isn't much, so we need some more.
**V** And vegetables? Have we got many vegetables?
**S** Well, I can see a few carrots, but there aren't many onions.
**V** Oh, and don't forget we need a lot of crisps. My nephews are coming tomorrow!
**S** Right, then. I think that's everything. Let's go! By the way, how much money have you got?

## GRAMMAR SPOT

1 Find seven count nouns (CNs) and four uncount nouns (UNs) in the conversation.

2 Tick (✓) the correct columns.

| We use . . . | with CNs | with UNs | in positive sentences | in questions | in negative sentences |
|---|---|---|---|---|---|
| some | ✓ | ✓ | ✓ | ✓(sometimes) | ✗ |
| any | | | | | |
| much | | | | | |
| many | | | | | |
| a lot/lots of | ✓ | ✓ | ✓ | ✓ | ✓ |
| a few | | | | | |
| a little | | | | | |

3 Look at the forms of *something/someone*, etc. The rules are the same as for *some* and *any*. Find two examples in the conversation in exercise 3.

| some<br>any | + | thing<br>one/body<br>where |
|---|---|---|

**Grammar Reference 4.1 p133**

# PRACTICE

## Discussing grammar

**1** Complete the sentences with *some* or *any*.

1 Have you got _____ brothers or sisters?
2 We don't need _____ olive oil.
3 Here are _____ letters for you.
4 I need _____ money.
5 Is there _____ petrol in the car?

**2** Complete the sentences with *much* or *many*.

1 Have you got _____ homework?
2 We don't need _____ eggs. Just half a dozen.
3 Is there _____ traffic in your town?
4 I don't know _____ students in this class.
5 How _____ people live in your house?

**3** Complete the sentences with *a little*, *a few*, or *a lot of*.

1 I have _____ close friends. Two or three.
2 He has _____ money. He's a millionaire.
3 'Do you take sugar in coffee?' 'Just _____ . Half a spoonful.'
4 'Have you got _____ CDs?' 'Hundreds.'
5 I'll be ready in _____ minutes.
6 She speaks good Spanish, but only _____ Russian.

## Questions and answers

**4** Look at Sarah and Vicky's bathroom. Ask and answer questions with a partner about these things:

- make-up
- shampoo
- towels
- toothbrushes
- toothpaste
- toilet paper
- hairbrushes
- soap
- bottles of perfume

## *something/someone/somewhere*

**5** Complete the sentences with the correct word.

| | | |
|---|---|---|
| some<br>any<br>every<br>no | + | thing<br>one/body<br>where |

1 'Did you meet _________ nice at the party?'
'Yes. I met _________ who knows you!'

2 'Ouch! There's _________ in my eye!'
'Let me look. No, I can't see _________ .'

3 'Let's go _________ hot for our holidays.'
'But we can't go _________ that's too expensive.'

4 'I'm so unhappy. _________ loves me.'
'I know _________ who loves you. Me.'

5 I lost my glasses. I looked _________ , but I couldn't find them.

6 'Did you buy _________ at the shops?'
'No, _________ . I didn't have any money.'

7 I'm bored. I want _________ interesting to read, or _________ interesting to talk to, or _________ interesting to go.

8 It was a great party. _________ loved it.

**T 4.3** Listen and check.

## Town survey

**6** Work in groups. Talk about the good things and bad things about living in your town. Make a list. Compare your list with the class.

Good things

There are a lot of cafés and restaurants.

There are some good shops.

We can go on lots of walks.

Bad things

But we haven't got any good clubs.

There aren't many . . .

There's only one . . .

There isn't anywhere that we can . . .

# MY UNCLE'S A SHOPKEEPER
## Articles

**T 4.4** Read and listen to the text.

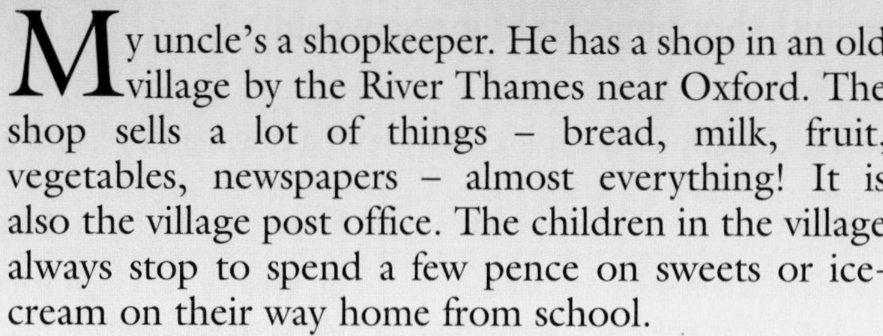

My uncle's a shopkeeper. He has a shop in an old village by the River Thames near Oxford. The shop sells a lot of things – bread, milk, fruit, vegetables, newspapers – almost everything! It is also the village post office. The children in the village always stop to spend a few pence on sweets or ice-cream on their way home from school.

My uncle doesn't often leave the village. He hasn't got a car, so once a month he goes by bus to Oxford and has lunch at the Grand Hotel with some friends. He is one of the happiest men I know.

**GRAMMAR SPOT**

1 Find examples of the definite article (*the*) and the indefinite article (*a/an*).

2 Find examples of when there is no article.

▶▶ **Grammar Reference 4.2 p133**

## PRACTICE

### Discussing grammar

**1** In pairs, find one mistake in each sentence.

1 He's postman, so he has breakfast at 4 a.m.
2 The love is more important than money.
3 I come to the school by bus.
4 I'm reading one good book at the moment.
5 'Where's Jack?' 'In a kitchen.'
6 I live in centre of town, near the hospital.
7 My parents bought the lovely house in the country.
8 I don't eat the bread because I don't like it.

**2** Complete the sentences with *a/an*, *the*, or nothing.

1 I have two children, _____ boy and _____ girl. _____ boy is twenty-two and _____ girl is nineteen.
2 Mike is _____ soldier in _____ Army, and Chloë is at _____ university.
3 My wife goes to _____ work by _____ train. She's _____ accountant. I don't have _____ job. I stay at _____ home and look after _____ children.
4 What _____ lovely day! Why don't we go for _____ picnic in _____ park?
5 'What did you have for _____ lunch?' 'Just _____ sandwich.'

# READING

## The best shopping street in the world

**1** Match a famous shopping street with a town, a store, and a product.

| Street | Town | Store | Product |
|---|---|---|---|
| Oxford Street | Milan | Guerlain | underwear and jumpers |
| Champs-Elysées | New York | Marks and Spencer | leather goods |
| Fifth Avenue | London | Gucci | jewellery |
| Via Montenapoleone | Paris | Tiffany's | perfume |

**2** Read the headline and the introduction of the newspaper article. Does anything surprise you? What do you want to find out when you read the article? Write some questions.

**3** Read the article quickly and answer the questions you have written.

What is the best summary of the article?

Nowy Świat is the best shopping street in the world because . . .
. . . so many Polish people go walking there.
. . . it is a pleasant place to shop and the shops are small.
. . . everything is very expensive and very exclusive.
. . . the shops sell quality goods that you can't buy anywhere else.

**4** Read the article again and answer the questions.

1 How do we know that Nowy Świat is the most popular shopping street?
2 Why is it such a nice place to go shopping?
3 What can you see in the photos that is described in the article?
4 Why don't many foreign people go to Nowy Świat?
5 Why are the things produced by Polish manufacturers so good?
6 What can you buy here? What can't you buy?
7 What is expensive? What isn't expensive?
8 What's good about *Café Blikle*?
9 What is special about the shops in Nowy Świat?

### Language work

Complete the sentences with different ideas from the article.

*In Nowy Świat, there are a lot of . . .* *There isn't any . . .*
*There aren't any/many . . .* *There are some . . .*

### What do you think?

- What are some of the famous brands and products that you can buy in many countries of the world? Think of clothes, food, cars . . . . Make a list. Work in groups and choose the most famous three. Compare your list with the class.
- What is the main shopping street in your town? What can you buy there that's special?
- Do you enjoy shopping? What do you like shopping for? What *don't* you like shopping for?

# The best shopping street in the world

No, it isn't Oxford Street, the Champs-Elysées, or even Fifth Avenue. A new survey shows that the most popular shopping street in the world is ... Nowy Świat. Where's that? In Warsaw, Poland, of course.

**by ANNE APPLEBAUM**

'If you're tired, stop at *Café Blikle*.'

'There are a lot of small, chic shops.'

A recent survey has shown that the busiest shopping street in the world is not in London, New York, or Paris, but in Warsaw. It's called Nowy Świat (pronounced /nɒvɪ ʃvɪət/), which means *New World*. An incredible 14,000 Poles walk down this main street every hour.

It is a lovely place to shop. The pavements are very wide. There are statues, palaces, attractive town houses, exclusive cafés, and high-class restaurants. The buildings aren't too tall. They look old, but in fact the whole city was rebuilt after World War II.

There aren't any billboards or neon lights. There isn't any loud music, and there aren't many tourists. People think that Polish shops have nothing to sell, so nobody comes shopping here. The world doesn't know about this paradise for shoppers – yet.

It is now possible to buy almost everything in Warsaw. There are a lot of shops from the West, but the interesting thing is that Polish manufacturers are now producing high quality goods. They are good because they are not mass produced for world consumption.

Nowy Świat has a lot of small shops, specialist shops, and chic shops. It hasn't got the huge department stores that sell the same things everywhere.

If you want an exquisite hand-made suit, Nowy Świat is the place to go. It isn't cheap. You will pay up to £1,000. For beautiful French baby clothes, go to *Petit Bateau*. You will pay £50 for a pair of blue jeans for a baby. A dress for a baby girl is about £90. At *Désa*, a famous antique shop, a desk costs £5,000, and a 19th century Russian icon is £200.

Not everything is expensive. At the shop *Pantera* you can buy leather goods – handbags, purses, coats, and belts. *Cepelia* specializes in folk art. There are also book shops and record shops. And there are a lot of small boutiques that sell men's and women's clothes that aren't too expensive.

If you're tired, stop at *Café Blikle*. This is a fashionable place to meet. You'll find a lively atmosphere, and a lot of well-known Poles. The frozen yoghurt and ice-creams are excellent, and its famous doughnuts are delicious.

It is possible to travel the world and find the same things for sale in every country. But Warsaw is different because its shops are unique – and they're in Nowy Świat.

# VOCABULARY AND LISTENING

## Buying things

**1** What can you buy or do in these places? Write two things for each place.
Compare your ideas with the class.

| a clothes shop | a chemist's | a café | a bank | a newsagent's |
|---|---|---|---|---|
| | | | | |

**2** **T 4.5** Listen to the conversations. Answer the questions.

1 Where are the conversations taking place? Choose from the places in exercise 1.
2 What does the customer want?
3 Can the shop assistant/cashier help?
4 How much does the customer pay?

**3** Complete these lines from the conversations. Look at the tapescript on p64 and check your answers.

1 **A** Hello. Can I help you?
**B** I _____________ , thanks.
. . .
**B** I'm looking for a jumper _____________ . Have you got _____________ ?
**A** I'll just have a look. _____________ are you?
**B** Medium.
**A** Here you are.
**B** That's great. _____________ ?
**A** Of course. The changing rooms are over there.
. . .
**B** I like it.
**A** It _____________ .
**B** How much is it?
**A** £39.99.
**B** OK. I _____________ .
**A** How would you like to pay?
**B** _____________ .

2 **A** ___________ help me? I'm looking for this month's edition of *Vogue*. Can you tell me ___________ ?
**B** Over there. Middle shelf. Next to *She*.

3 **A** Hello. I _____________ help me. I've got a bad cold and a sore throat. Can you _____________ ?
**B** OK. You can take these three times a day.
**A** Thank you. _____________ some tissues _____________ , please?
**B** Sure. _____________ ?
**A** No, that's all, thanks.

4 **A** Good morning. Can I have a _____________ , please?
**B** Espresso?
**A** Yes, please. Oh, and a doughnut, please.
**B** _____________ there aren't _____________ . We've got some delicious carrot cake, and chocolate cake.
**A** OK. Carrot cake, then.
**B** Certainly. Is _____________ ?
**A** Yes, thanks.
**B** _____________ , please.
**A** Thank you.

# EVERYDAY ENGLISH

## Prices and shopping

**1** Look at the way we write and say prices in British and American English. Practise saying them.

| **British English** | | **American English** | |
|---|---|---|---|
| **Written** | **Spoken** | **Written** | **Spoken** |
| £1 | a pound | $1 | a dollar |
| 50p | fifty p | 50¢ | fifty cents |
| £1.99 | one pound ninety-nine | 25¢ | a quarter |
| £16.40 | sixteen pounds forty | 10¢ | a dime |

**T 4.6** Listen to the conversations and write the numbers you hear.

**2** What's the exchange rate between sterling/US dollars and your currency?

*There are about five … to the dollar.*

In your country, how much is … ?

- a pair of jeans
- a hamburger
- a packet of cigarettes
- a litre of petrol

**3** Make conversations in these places with a partner. Use the ideas to help you.

**1 in a clothes shop**

a shirt/tie
What size are you?
small/medium/large
too small/too big
I'll have it, please.
I'll leave them, thanks.

**3 in a café**

a black/white coffee
an espresso/a cappuccino
a pot of tea
a sparkling/still mineral water
a piece of chocolate cake

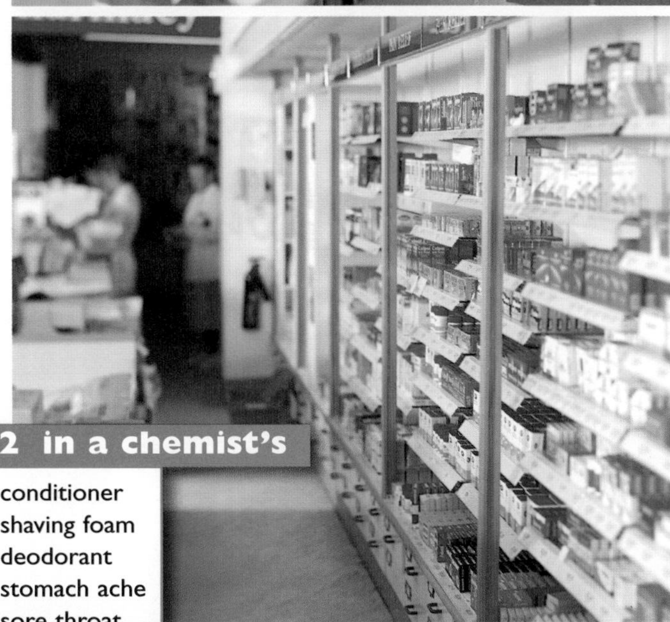

**2 in a chemist's**

conditioner
shaving foam
deodorant
stomach ache
sore throat

**4 in a post office**

some stamps
First or second class?
a letter/postcard to Japan
send this parcel to Mexico
buy some envelopes

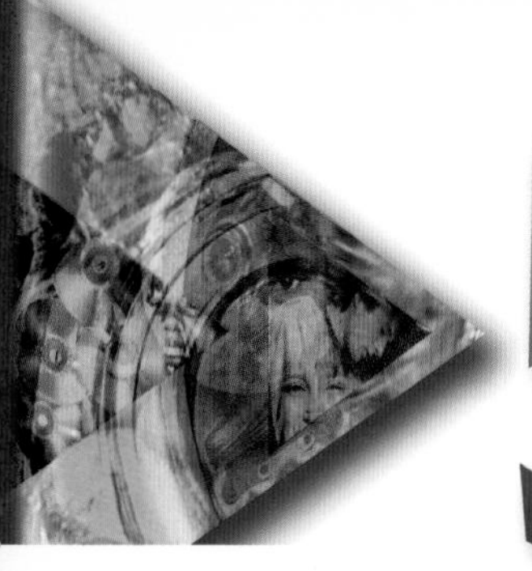

# 5 What do you want to do?

**Verb patterns 1 • Future forms • Hot verbs • How do you feel?**

**STARTER** 

Complete these sentences with ideas about you.

- One day I want to . . .
- I can . . . but I can't . . .
- Right now, I'd like to . . .
- Tonight I'm going to . . .
- I enjoy . . . because I like . . .

## HOPES AND AMBITIONS

### Verb patterns 1

**1** Match the people with their hopes and ambitions.

1 ☐ I'd like to have my own business, something like a flying school.
2 ☐ I'm going to be an astronaut and fly to Mars.
3 ☐ I'm looking forward to having more time to do the things I want to do.
4 ☐ I would love to have one of my plays performed on the London stage.
5 ☐ We hope to find work as we go round the world.
6 ☐ We're thinking of moving, because the kids will be leaving home soon.

**T 5.1** Listen and check.

**2** Complete the chart.

| | Ambitions/Plans | Reasons |
|---|---|---|
| Sean | | |
| Mel | | |
| Justin | | |
| Martyn | | |
| Amy | | |
| Alison | | |

**3** Underline the examples of verb + verb in exercise 1.

*I'd like to have my own business …*

Look at the tapescript on p120. Find more examples of verb + verb.

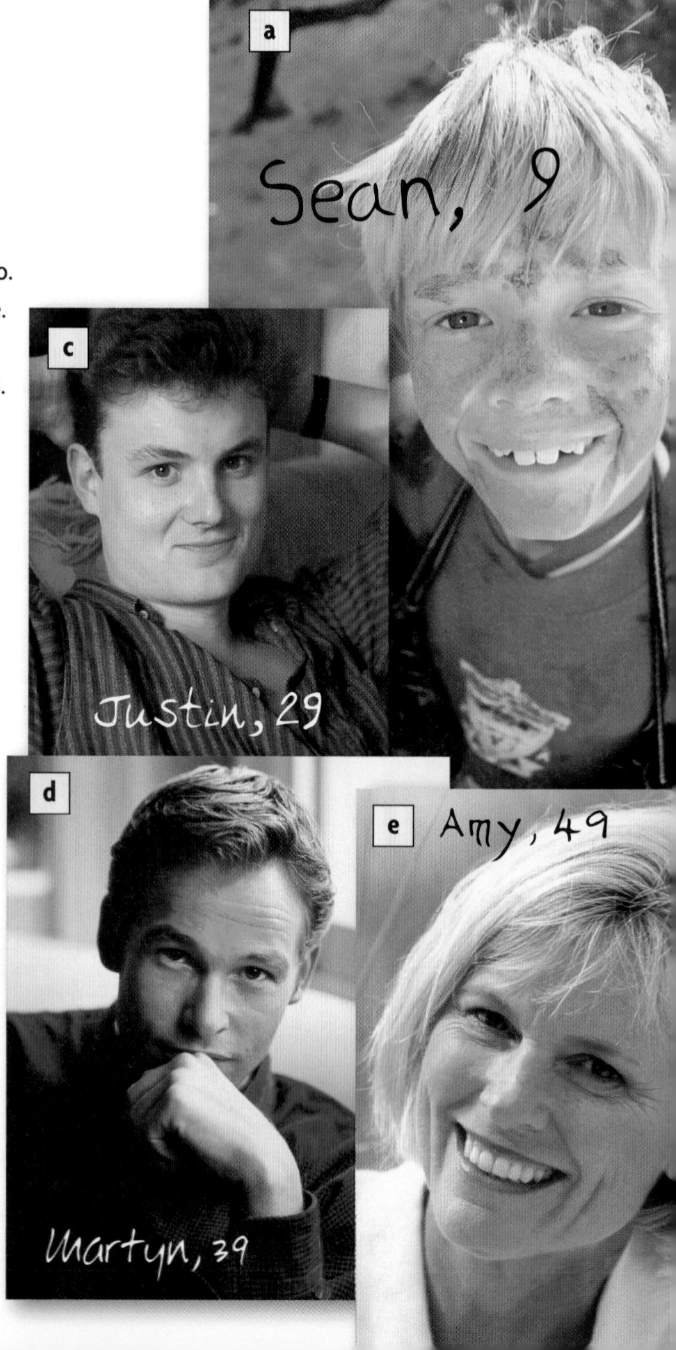

## GRAMMAR SPOT

1 Complete the sentences with the words *go abroad*. Put the verb *go* in the correct form.

I want *to go abroad*.
I'd like . . .
I can't . . .
I'm looking forward to . . .
I hope . . .
I enjoy . . .
I'm thinking of . . .
I'd love . . .

2 What's the difference between these sentences?

I like going to the cinema.
I'd like to go to the cinema tonight.

▶▶ **Grammar Reference 5.1 and 5.2 p134**

# PRACTICE

## Discussing grammar

**1** In these sentences, one or two verbs are correct, but not all three. Tick (✓) the correct verbs.

1 I _____ to live in a hot country.
a ☐ want b ☐ enjoy c ☐ 'd like
2 We _____ going to Italy for our holidays.
a ☐ are hoping b ☐ 're thinking of c ☐ like
3 I _____ go home early tonight.
a ☐ want b ☐ like c ☐ can
4 I _____ to see you again soon.
a ☐ hope b ☐ 'd like c ☐ 'm looking forward
5 Do you _____ learning English?
a ☐ want b ☐ enjoy c ☐ like
6 We _____ having a few days off soon.
a ☐ 're thinking of b ☐ 'd love to c ☐ 're looking forward to

Make correct sentences with the other verbs.

## Making questions

**2** Complete the questions.

1 **A** I hope to go to university.
**B** (What/want/study?) ______________________________
2 **A** One of my favourite hobbies is cooking.
**B** (What/like/make?) ______________________________
3 **A** I get terrible headaches.
**B** (When/start/get/them?) ______________________________
4 **A** We're planning our summer holidays at the moment.
**B** (Where/think/go?) ______________________________
5 **A** I'm tired.
**B** (What/like/do/tonight?) ______________________________

**T 5.2** Listen and check. What are **A**'s answers? Practise the conversations with a partner.

## Talking about you

**3** Ask and answer the questions with a partner.

- What do you like doing on holiday?
- Where would you like to be right now?
- Do you like learning English?
- Would you like to learn any other languages?
- Would you like to have a break now?

**4** Ask and answer questions about your plans and ambitions.

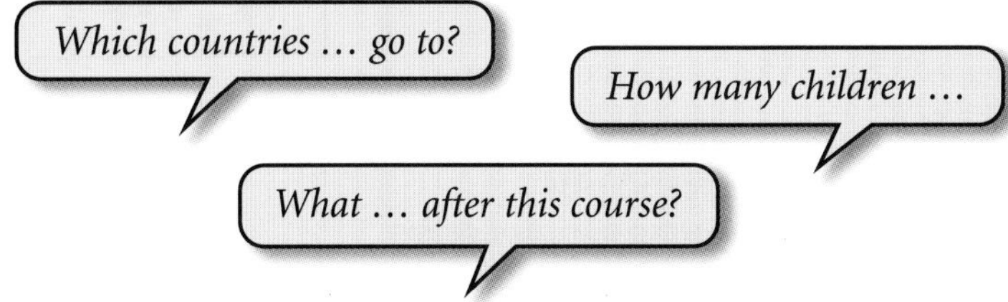

# FUTURE INTENTIONS
## *going to* and *will*

**1** Match the pictures and sentences.

1 ☐ They're going to watch a football match.
2 ☐ I'll pick it up for you.
3 ☐ She's going to travel round the world.
4 ☐ It's OK. I'll answer it.
5 ☐ Don't worry. I'll lend you some.
6 ☐ We're going out to have a meal.

**2** Add a line before and after the sentences in exercise 1.

**Before**

I haven't got any money.
What's Ali doing next year?
The phone's ringing.
Damn! I've dropped one.
What are you and Pete doing tonight?
What are the lads doing this afternoon?

**After**

Thank you. That's very kind.
I'm expecting a call.
Thanks. I'll pay you back tomorrow. I won't forget.
Lucky her!
Arsenal are playing at home.
It's my birthday.

**T 5.3** Listen and check. Practise the conversations with a partner.

### GRAMMAR SPOT

1 Notice the forms of *will*.
 **I'll** = short form
 I **won't** = negative short form

2 All the sentences in exercise 1 express intentions. Three intentions are spontaneous. Which are they?
Three of the intentions are premeditated. What happened **before** each one?

▶▶ **Grammar Reference 5.3 p134**

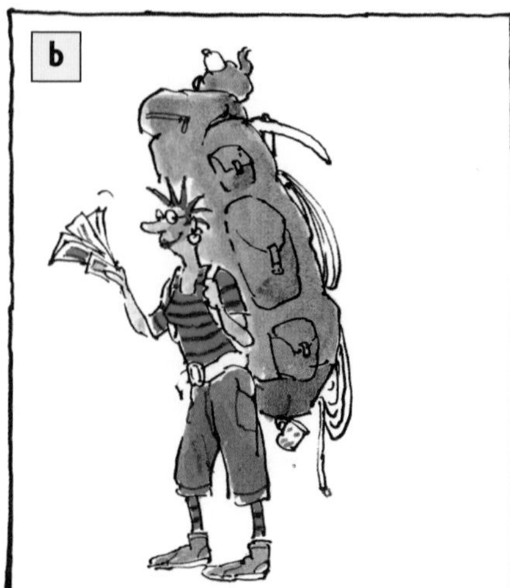

# PRACTICE

## Let's have a party!

**1** Your class has decided to have a party. Everyone must help. Say what you'll do.

*I'll bring the music.*

*I'll buy some crisps.*

**2** Your teacher didn't hear what you said. Listen to your teacher and correct him/her.

| **Teacher** | **You** |
|---|---|
| *Right. I'll bring some music.* | *No, **I'm** going to bring some music!* |
| *Oh, all right. Well, I'll buy some crisps.* | *No, no. **I'm** going to buy some crisps!* |

## Discussing grammar

**3** Choose the correct verb form.

1 'My bag is so heavy.'
'Give it to me. *I'll carry / I'm going to carry* it for you.'
2 I bought some warm boots because *I'll go / I'm going* skiing.
3 'Tony's back from holiday.'
'Is he? *I'll give / I'm going to give* him a ring.'
4 'What are you doing tonight?'
'*We'll see / we're going to see* a play at the theatre.'
5 You can tell me your secret. *I won't tell / I'm not going to tell* anyone.
6 Congratulations! I hear *you'll get married / you're going to get married.*
7 'I need to post these letters.'
'*I'll go / I'm going* shopping soon. *I'll post / I'm going to post* them for you.'
8 'Now, holidays. Where *will you go / are you going* this year?' 'We don't know yet.'

**4** **T 5.4** Close your books. Listen to the beginnings of the conversations. Complete them.

## Check it

**5** Correct these sentences.

1 What you want drink?
2 I have a Coke, please.
3 I can't to help you.
4 It's starting rain.
5 I'm looking forward to see you again soon.
6 I think to change my job soon.
7 Phone me tonight. I give you my phone number.
8 I see the doctor tomorrow about my back.

## Talking about you

**6** Talk to a partner about your plans for tonight, tomorrow, next weekend, your next holiday, Christmas …

*What are you doing/going to do tonight?*

*I'm going to stay at home and …*

*Where are you going … ?*

*I'm going to see …*

*I think I'll …*

# READING
## Hollywood kids

**1** What are some of the problems of being a teenager? Tick (✓) the boxes on the left.

☐ drugs ☐
☐ violence in the streets ☐
☐ they don't have enough money ☐
☐ their parents don't give them enough attention ☐
☐ they worry about how they look ☐
☐ they have no interests or ambitions ☐
☐ their parents want them to do well in life ☐
☐ they're too old to be children, but too young to be adults ☐

**2** Read the text about Hollywood kids. What are some of their problems? Tick (✓) the boxes on the right. Are there any differences?

**3** Are these sentences true (✓) or false (✗)? Correct the false sentences.

1 Everybody in Hollywood is rich and famous.
2 Hollywood kids don't lead ordinary lives.
3 They understand the value of what they have.
4 Trent Maguire is spoilt and ambitious.
5 The adults try hard to be good parents.
6 Amanda's mother listens to all her daughter's problems.
7 The kids are often home alone.
8 Their parents organize every part of their lives.
9 The kids don't want to be children.
10 All the kids complain about living in Hollywood.

**4** Answer the questions.

1 In what ways do Trent, Amanda, Emily, and Lindsey live unreal lives?
2 Does anything surprise you in what the kids say?
3 What are their ambitions?

### What do you think?

- Do you feel sorry for children in Hollywood? Is there anything about their lives that you would like?
- What is your opinion of their parents?
- Do teenagers around the world think the same as Hollywood kids?
- Do you think it is dangerous to have everything you want?

# Hollywood
## Growing up in

In Hollywood, everybody wants to be rich, famous, and beautiful. Nobody wants to be old, unknown, and poor. For Hollywood kids, life can be difficult because they grow up in such an unreal atmosphere. Their parents are ambitious, and the children are part of the parents' ambitions.

Parents pay for extravagant parties, expensive cars, and designer clothes. When every dream can come true, kids learn the value of nothing because they have everything. A 13-year-old boy, Trent Maguire, has a driver, credit cards, and unlimited cash to do what he wants when he wants. 'One day, I'll earn more than my Dad,' he boasts.

Parents buy care and attention for their children because they have no time to give it themselves. Amanda's mother employs a personal trainer, a nutritionist, a bodyguard/chauffeur, a singing coach, and a counsellor to look after all her 15-year-old daughter's needs.

Often there is no parent at home most days, so children decide whether to make their own meals or go out to restaurants, when to watch television or do homework. They organize their own social lives. They play no childhood games. They become adults before they're ready.

Hollywood has always been the city of dreams. The kids in L.A. live unreal lives where money, beauty, and pleasure are the only gods. Will children around the world soon start to think the same? Or do they already?

“Looks are very important in Hollywood. If you're good-looking, you'll go far. I want to be a beautician. You grow up really fast in L.A. Everyone is in a rush to be an adult, to be going to clubs. It's not cool to be a kid.” **Mijanou, aged 18**

# kids

## Los Angeles ain't easy

"I live in a hotel and when I come home from school, there are maybe 80 people who say 'Good day' to me. It's their job to say that. In the bathroom there are mirrors everywhere. I love looking at myself. I can spend five hours doing my hair and posing.
I'm going to be a model."

**Emily, aged 10**

"I've wanted to get my nose done since I was 12. My friends started having plastic surgery and liposuction during my freshman year of high school. My nose cost $10,000.
But it was worth it. It changed my life. I'm gonna get into the movies."

**Lindsey, aged 18**

"Everyone thinks Hollywood is so glamorous, but I have news for you. It is really dangerous growing up in L.A. People have guns. Sometimes I think I'm going crazy. I'm going to get out of here just as soon as I can." **Zavier, aged 18**

# VOCABULARY

## Hot verbs – *have, go, come*

**1** The verbs *have*, *go*, and *come* are very common in English. Look at these examples from the text on p42–3.

| have | go | come |
|---|---|---|
| ... they have no time ...<br>I have news for you. | You'll go far.<br>I'm going crazy. | Every dream can come true.<br>... come home from school ... |

**2** Put *have*, *go*, or *come* into each gap.

______ an accident
______ first in a race
______ out for a meal
______ and see me
______ shopping
______ a cold
______ wrong
______ a meeting
______ abroad

**3** Complete the sentences with the correct form of *have* (or *have got*), *go*, or *come*.

1 We're ______ a party next Saturday. Would you like ______ ?
2 I ______ a terrible headache. Can I ______ home, please?
3 You must see my new flat. ______ round and ______ a drink some time.
4 'I'm ______ out now, Mum. Bye!' 'OK. ______ a good time. What time are you ______ home?'
5 Hi, Dave. Pete ______ a shower at the moment. I'll just ______ and tell him you're here.
6 ______ on! Get out of bed. It's time ______ to school.
7 It's a lovely day. Let's ______ to the park. We can ______ a picnic.
8 I'm ______ skiing next week. ______ you ______ any ski clothes I could borrow?

# LISTENING

## You've got a friend

**1** Who says these things? Write 1, 2, or 3 in the boxes.

1 Your best friend
2 Your boyfriend/girlfriend
3 Your ex-boyfriend/girlfriend

☐ I'll love you forever.
☐ I'll never forget you.
☐ I'll always be there for you.
☐ I'll always remember the times we had together.
☐ I'll do anything for you.
☐ You'll never find anyone who loves you more than I do.

**2** Listen to the first verse of the song. Discuss these questions.

1 Do you think the man and woman live together?
2 Is it a close relationship?
3 What is the relationship between them now? What do you think it was in the past?

**3** **T 5.5** Listen and complete the song.

### You've got a friend, by Carole King

When you're down and troubled
And you need a ____________
And nothing, but ____________
Close your eyes and think of me
And soon I ____________
To brighten up even your darkest nights.
(Chorus)
You just call out my name,
and you know wherever I am
I ____________ to see you again.
Winter, spring, ____________
All you have to do is call
And I'll be there, yeah, yeah, yeah,
You ____________ .

If the sky above you
____________ and full of clouds
And that old north ____________
Keep your head together
And ____________
And soon I'll be knocking on your door.
Hey, ____________ that you've got a friend?
People can be so cold
____________ and desert you
Well they'll take your soul if you let them
Oh, yeah, but ____________ .
(Chorus)

# EVERYDAY ENGLISH

## How do you feel?

**1** Look at the photos. How do the people feel?

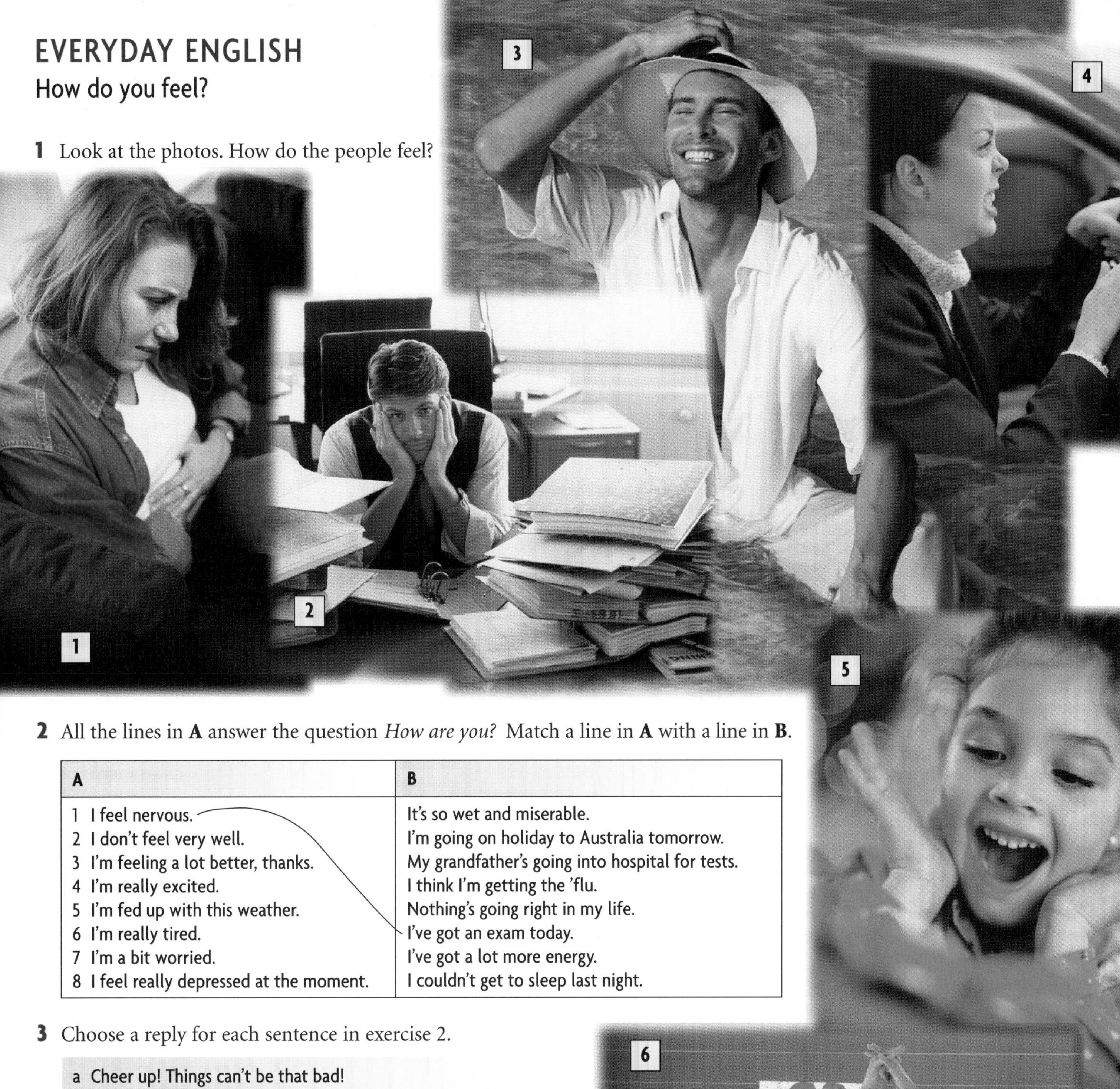


**2** All the lines in **A** answer the question *How are you?* Match a line in **A** with a line in **B**.

| A | B |
|---|---|
| 1 I feel nervous. | It's so wet and miserable. |
| 2 I don't feel very well. | I'm going on holiday to Australia tomorrow. |
| 3 I'm feeling a lot better, thanks. | My grandfather's going into hospital for tests. |
| 4 I'm really excited. | I think I'm getting the 'flu. |
| 5 I'm fed up with this weather. | Nothing's going right in my life. |
| 6 I'm really tired. | I've got an exam today. |
| 7 I'm a bit worried. | I've got a lot more energy. |
| 8 I feel really depressed at the moment. | I couldn't get to sleep last night. |

**3** Choose a reply for each sentence in exercise 2.

a Cheer up! Things can't be that bad!
b Why don't you go home to bed?
c I'm sorry to hear that, but I'm sure he'll be all right.
d I know. We really need some sunshine, don't we?
e Poor you! That happens to me sometimes. I just read in bed.
f That's great. Have a good time.
g That's good. I'm pleased to hear it.
h Good luck! Do your best.

**T 5.6** Listen and compare your answers.

**4** Make more conversations with a partner about these things:

- a wedding
- a visit to the dentist
- a letter from the bank
- a big project at work
- problems with teenage children

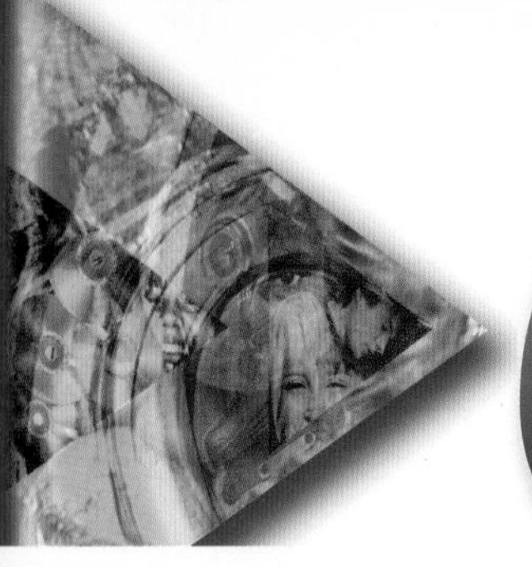

# 6 Tell me! What's it like?

*What ... like?* • Comparatives and superlatives • Synonyms and antonyms • Directions

**STARTER** 

1 What is the capital city of your country? What is the population? Is it an old or modern city?

2 Write down two things that you like about your capital and two things that you don't like. Tell the class.

*I like travelling on the buses in London but I don't like the Underground, it's too expensive.*

## WORLD TRAVEL
### What's it like?

**1** Read about Todd Bridges.

**2** What do you know about **Melbourne**, **Dubai**, and **Paris**? Where are they?

**3** **T 6.1** Listen to what Todd says about them. Write the adjectives he uses for each city. Compare with a partner.

**GRAMMAR SPOT**

1 Match the questions and answers.

| | |
|---|---|
| | It's beautiful. |
| Do you like Paris? | Yes, I do. |
| What's Paris like? | It's got lots of old buildings. |
| | No, I don't. |

2 Which question in 1 means: *Tell me about Paris.*

 Grammar Reference 6.1 p135

**4** Work with a partner. Ask and answer questions about the places Todd visited.

## TODD BRIDGES

**Todd Bridges** is only seventeen years old but he is already a successful tennis player. He comes from Chicago, USA, but he travels all over the world playing tennis. Last year he played in tennis championships in **Melbourne**, **Dubai**, and **Paris**.

# PRACTICE

## What's Chicago like?

**1** You are asking Todd about Chicago. Complete the questions with *is* or *are* and the correct words from the box.

| the restaurants | the people | the night-life | the buildings |
|---|---|---|---|

1 **You** What ***'s the weather*** like?
**Todd** Well, Chicago's called 'the windy city' and it really can be windy!

2 **You** What __________ like?
**Todd** They're very interesting. You meet people from all over the world.

3 **You** What __________ like?
**Todd** A lot of them are very, very tall. The Sears Tower is 110 storeys high.

4 **You** What __________ like?
**Todd** They're very good. You can find food from every country in the world.

5 **You** What __________ like?
**Todd** Oh, it's wonderful. There's lots to do in Chicago.

**2** **T 6.2** Listen and check. Practise with a partner.

**3** Ask and answer the same questions about the town or city you are in now.

# *BIG, BIGGER, BIGGEST!*

## Comparatives and superlatives

**1** Read the second part of the conversation with Todd. He compares the places he visited last year. Can you complete any of the sentences?

**MELBOURNE**

"Melbourne was interesting, but for me, Paris was ______ interesting ______ Melbourne, and in some ways Dubai was the ______ interesting of all because it was so different ______ any other place I know. It was also the ______, driest, and ______ modern. It was hot in Melbourne but not ______ hot ______ in Dubai. Dubai was ______ hotter! Melbourne is ______ older ______ Dubai but not ______ old ______ Paris. Paris was ______ oldest city I visited, but it has some great modern buildings, too. It was the ______ romantic place. I loved it."

**DUBAI** **PARIS**

**T 6.3** Listen and check.

## GRAMMAR SPOT

1 What are the comparative and superlative forms of the following adjectives? What are the rules?

a small
cold
near

b big
hot
wet

c busy
noisy
dry

d beautiful
interesting
exciting

2 These adjectives are irregular. What are the comparative and superlative forms?

| far good bad |
|---|

3 Adjectives also combine with *as . . . as*.
Melbourne isn't **as** cosmopolitan **as** Chicago.

▶▶ **Grammar Reference 6.2 p135**

**2** **T 6.4** Listen and repeat the sentences.

/hɒtə ðən/
This summer's hotter than last.

/əz hɒt əz/
It wasn't as hot as this last year.

**3** Practise these sentences with a partner.

It isn't as cold today as it was yesterday.
But it's colder than it was last week.
I'm not as tall as you, but I'm taller than Anna.
This car's more expensive than John's.
But it isn't as expensive as Anna's.

**T 6.5** Listen and check.

**4** Learn this poem by heart.

*Good, better, best.*
*Never, never rest*
*'til your good is better,*
*And your better best.*

# PRACTICE

## Comparing four capital cities

**1** Match the cities and the photographs. Of which countries are these the capital cities?

| Paris Beijing Stockholm Brasilia |
|---|

1

2

3

4

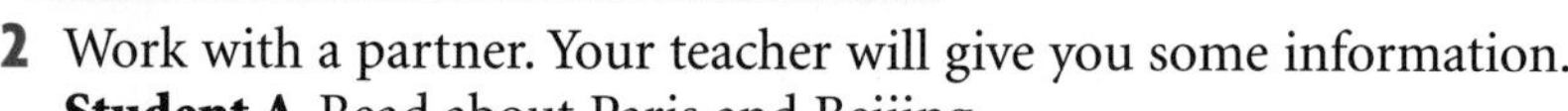

**2** Work with a partner. Your teacher will give you some information.
**Student A** Read about Paris and Beijing.
**Student B** Read about Stockholm and Brasilia.

Ask and answer these questions to find out about the other two cities.

- How old is it?
- How big is it?
- How many people live there?
- How hot/cold does it get?
- How wet is it?
- How far is it from the sea?

*How old is it?*

*It's very old. It was founded in …*

**3** Now compare the four cities.

*Beijing is bigger than Brasilia.*

*Paris is the oldest.*

**4** Compare some cities in your country.

## Conversations

**5** Work with a partner and continue these conversations.

1 **A** I moved to a new flat last week.
**B** Oh, really? What's it like?
**A** Well, it's bigger than my old one but it isn't as modern, and …

2 **A** I hear Sandy and Al broke up.
**B** Yeah. Sandy's got a new boyfriend.
**A** Oh, really? What's he like?
**B** Well, he's _____ than Al, and …

3 **A** We have a new teacher.
**B** Oh, really? What's she like?
**A** Well, I think she's the _____ teacher we've ever had …

4 **A** Is that your new car?
**B** Well, it's second-hand, but it's new to me.
**A** What's it like?
**B** Well, it's _____ than my old car …

Act out a conversation to the class. Whose is the longest?

**T 6.6** Listen and compare. Repeat the last lines.

## Check it

**6** Correct these sentences.

1 He's more older than he looks.
2 Jessica's as tall than her mother.
3 'What does New York like?' 'It's really exciting!'
4 Trains in London are more crowded that in Paris.
5 Oxford is one of oldest universities in Europe.
6 He isn't as intelligent than his sister.
7 This is more hard than I expected.
8 Who is the most rich man in the world?
9 Everything is more cheap in my country.
10 Rome was hotter that I expected.

# LISTENING AND SPEAKING

## Living in another country

**1** What do you know about Sweden? What is the country like? What are the people like? Discuss these statements about Sweden. Do you think they are true (✓) or false (✗)?

1 In winter there is only one hour of daylight.
2 Swedish people look forward to winter.
3 The houses are cold.
4 The houses are much better insulated than in Britain.
5 In parts of Sweden from May to July the sun never sets.
6 Londoners work longer hours than the Swedes.
7 Swedes always start work early in the morning.
8 Country cottages in Sweden are usually very luxurious.
9 All houses have a sauna.
10 The whole family like to sit in the sauna together.

**2** **T 6.7** You are going to listen to Jane Bland talking to her friend, Fran, about her life in Sweden. Jane comes from London, but three years ago she married a Swede and went to live and work in Stockholm. Listen and check your answers to exercise 1.

**3** Compare your country with what you learned about Sweden.

***In my country it gets dark at five o'clock in winter, and it's much warmer.***

## READING AND SPEAKING
### A tale of two millionaires

**1** Who are the richest people in your country? Where does their money come from? How do they spend their money?

**2** Match the verbs and nouns. Many of them are to do with money.

| Verbs | Nouns |
|---|---|
| buy | a bank account |
| spoil | poverty |
| wear | a thief |
| open | a will |
| live in | stocks and shares |
| inherit | a child |
| make | a leg |
| arrest | ragged clothes |
| invest | a lot of money from someone |
| amputate | a lot of money in something |

**3** You are going to read about two millionaires. One was very mean, the other very generous. First read *quickly* about Milton Petrie. Can you remember any examples of his kindness?

**4** Now read *quickly* about Hetty Green. Can you remember any examples of her meanness?

**5** Read one text more carefully, then answer the questions with a partner who read the other text.

1. When were Milton and Hetty born?
2. What were their parents like?
3. How did Milton and Hetty become so wealthy?
4. Who wore ragged clothes?
5. What was the meanest thing Hetty did?
6. Why did Milton like making a lot of money?
7. Who did they marry?
8. When did they die? How old were they?
9. Who left the most money? Who did they leave it to?

### What do you think?

Discuss these questions in small groups.

- How were Milton and Hetty's childhoods different?
- How did their childhoods affect them later?
- Why was Milton especially generous to policemen?
- Why did Hetty's daughter build a hospital?
- What was the kindest thing Milton did?
- Who had the happier life? Milton or Hetty?

# A tale of

Some millionaires

## Milton Petrie

**The Most Generous Man in the World**

Every morning, billionaire Milton Petrie walked from his New York apartment and bought a newspaper from the ragged old man on the street corner. One morning the man wasn't there. Petrie learned that he was very ill in the city hospital. Immediately he paid his hospital bill and later, when the man died, paid for his funeral.

**Milton with the model he helped**

# two millionaires

spend it and some save it. **Elizabeth Wilson** reports on one of each.

The old man was just one of many people that Milton Petrie helped with his money. Whenever he read about personal disasters in his newspaper Petrie sent generous cheques, especially to the families of policemen or firemen injured at work. He also sent cheques to a mother who lost five children in a fire, and a beautiful model, whose face was cut in a knife attack. It cost him millions of dollars, but he still had millions left. He said that he was lucky in business and he wanted to help those less fortunate than himself. 'The nice thing is, the harder I work, the more money I make, and the more people I can help.'

Milton Petrie died in 1994, when he was 92. His will was 120 pages long because he left $150 million to 383 people. His widow, Carroll, his fourth and last wife, said his generosity was a result of the poverty of his early years. His family were poor but kind-hearted. His father was a Russian immigrant who became a policeman, but he never arrested anyone, he was too kind. He couldn't even give a parking ticket.

## Hetty Green

### The Richest, Meanest Woman in the World

Henrietta (Hetty) Green was a very spoilt, only child. She was born in Massachusetts, USA, in 1835. Her father was a millionaire businessman. Her mother was often ill, and so from the age of two her father took her with him to work and taught her about stocks and shares. At the age of six she started reading the daily financial newspapers and she opened her own bank account.

Her father died when she was 21 and she inherited $7.5 million. She went to New York and invested on Wall Street. Hetty saved every penny, eating in the cheapest restaurants for 15 cents. She became one of the richest and most hated women in the world. She was called 'The Witch of Wall Street'. At 33 she married Edward Green, a multi-millionaire, and had two children, Ned and Sylvia.

Hetty's meanness was legendary. She always argued about prices in shops. She walked to the local grocery store to buy broken cookies (biscuits) which were much cheaper, and to get a free bone for her much-loved dog, Dewey. Once she lost a two-cent stamp and spent the night looking for it. She never bought clothes and always wore the same long, ragged black skirt. Worst of all, when her son Ned fell and injured his knee, she refused to pay for a doctor and spent hours looking for free medical help. In the end Ned's leg was amputated.

When she died in 1916 she left her children $100 million (worth $9.3 billion today). Her daughter built a hospital with her money.

# VOCABULARY AND PRONUNCIATION

## Synonyms

**1** We often use synonyms in conversation because we don't want to repeat words.

Complete the conversations, using an adjective of similar meaning from the box.

| fed up | generous | brilliant | messy | modern | wealthy |
|---|---|---|---|---|---|

1 'Mary's family is very rich.'
'Well, I knew her uncle was very ______ .'
2 'Look at all these new buildings!'
'Yes. Paris is much more ______ than I expected.'
3 'Wasn't that film wonderful!'
'Yes, it was ______ .'
4 'George doesn't earn much money, but he's so kind.'
'He is, isn't he? He's one of the most ______ people I know.'
5 'Ann's bedroom's really untidy again!'
'Is it? I told her it was ______ yesterday, and she promised to clean it.'
6 'I'm bored with this lesson!'
'I know, I'm really ______ with it, too!'

**2** **T 6.8** Listen and check. Listen again, paying particular attention to the stress and intonation. Practise the conversations with a partner.

## Antonyms

**3** We can also use antonyms in conversation to avoid repeating words.

Match the following adjectives with their *two* opposites in exercise 1.

| | | |
|---|---|---|
| interested | bored | fed up |
| horrible | ______ | ______ |
| mean | ______ | ______ |
| old | ______ | ______ |
| poor | ______ | ______ |
| tidy | ______ | ______ |

**4** Sometimes it is more polite to use *not very* and an opposite adjective.

| | |
|---|---|
| *Tom's so short.* | *Well, he's* ***not very tall.*** |
| *He always wears such dirty clothes.* | *They certainly* ***aren't very clean.*** |

Reply to these sentences. Be more polite.

1 London's such an expensive city.
2 Paul and Sue are so mean.
3 Their house is always so messy.
4 Their children are so noisy.
5 John looks so miserable.
6 His sister's so stupid.

**5** **T 6.9** Listen and check. Pay particular attention to the stress and intonation. Practise the conversations with your partner.

# EVERYDAY ENGLISH
## Directions

**1** Look at the map of Chesswood and find these things:
- a farm
- a wood
- a pond
- a path
- a hill
- a river
- a bridge
- a gate

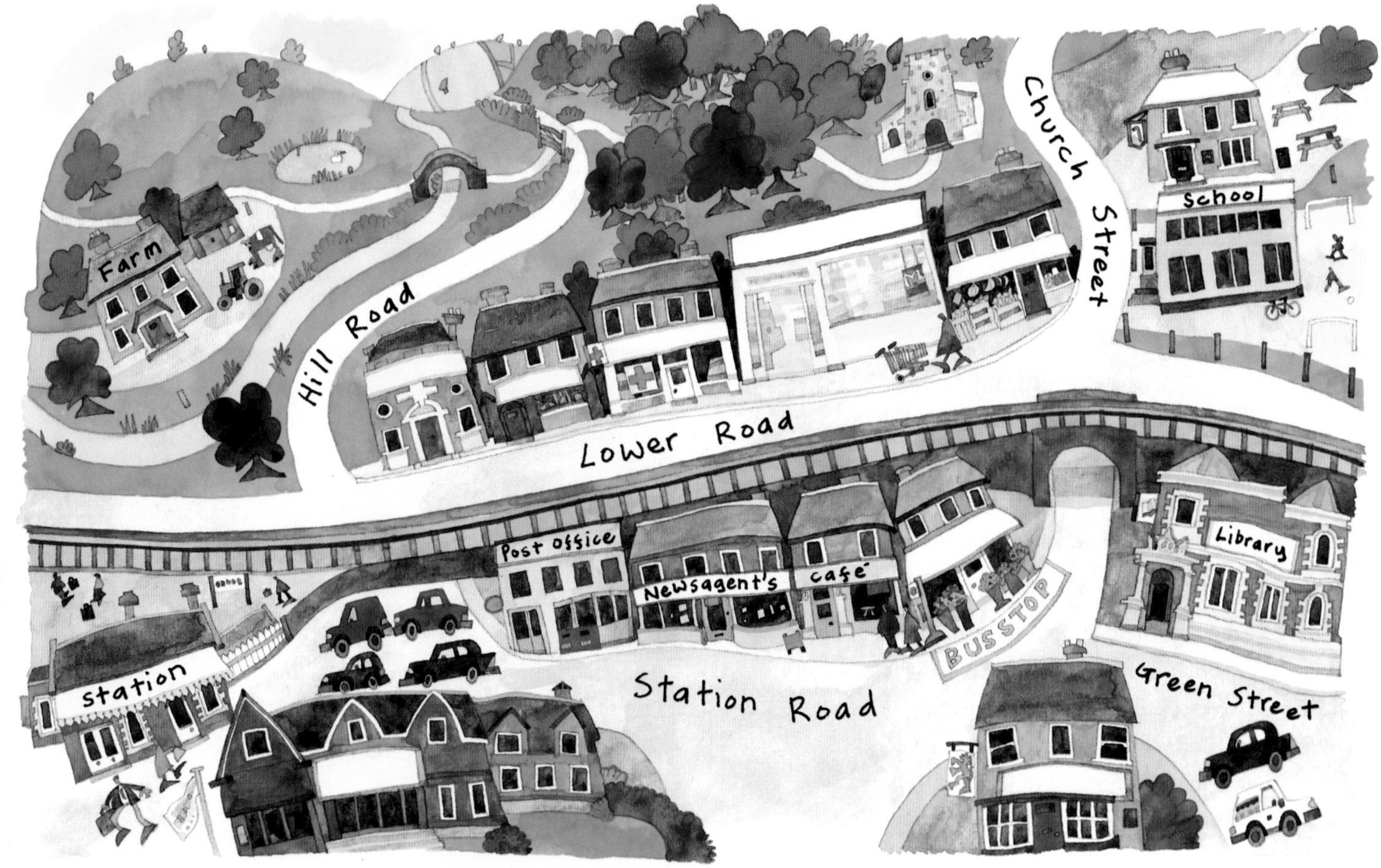

**2** Read these descriptions and add the places to the map.
1. The hotel is **opposite** the car park.
2. The bank is **on the corner of** Lower Road and Hill Road. It is **next to** the baker's.
3. The supermarket is **between** the chemist's and the greengrocer's.
4. There is a bus stop **in front of** the flower shop in Station Road.
5. There are two pubs. The Red Lion is in Station Road, **opposite** the flower shop **near** the railway bridge, and the Old Shepherd is in Church Street, **behind** the school.

**3** Ask and answer questions about the places on the map. Use the prepositions from exercise 2.

*Where's the library?*

*It's on the corner of Station Road and Green Street, opposite the flower shop.*

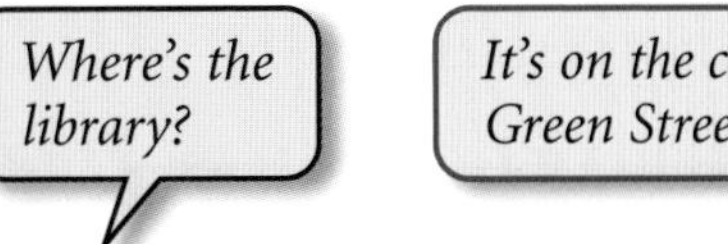

**4** Complete the directions from Chesswood farm to the church with the prepositions in the box. Look at the map to help you.

| up | down | over | past | through | out of (x2) | in(to) | across |
|---|---|---|---|---|---|---|---|

You go ______ the path, ______ the pond, ______ the bridge, and ______ the gate. Then you go ______ the road and take the path ______ the wood. When you come ______ the wood you walk ______ the path and ______ the church. It takes five minutes.

**T 6.10** Listen and check.

**5** Give your partner directions to get to your house from your school.

# 7 Famous couples

**Present Perfect • *for, since* • Adverbs, word pairs • Short answers**

**STARTER** 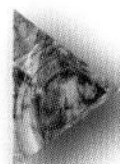

What is the Past Simple and the past participle of these verbs?

write be sell win have read do eat know break

## FAMOUS WRITERS

### Present Perfect and Past Simple

**1** Look at the photographs of two well-known English writers. How do you think they are related?

Complete the sentences with *He* or *She*.

1. _____ wrote novels about Victorian life. _____ writes novels about modern people and their relationships.
2. _____ wrote 47 novels, travel books, biographies, and short stories. _____ has written over twenty novels. _____ started writing in her thirties.
3. _____ has lived in the west of England for forty years. _____ lived in Ireland for eighteen years.
4. _____ has been married twice, and has two daughters. _____ married for the first time in 1966. _____ was married and had two sons.

**T 7.1** Listen and check. Practise the sentences.

**GRAMMAR SPOT**

1. Find examples of the Past Simple in sentences 1–4. Find examples of the Present Perfect.
2. Complete the rule. We make the Present Perfect with the auxiliary verb __________ + the __________ .
3. Why are different tenses used in these sentences?
   Anthony Trollope **wrote** forty-seven novels.
   Joanna Trollope **has written** twenty novels.

▶▶ **Grammar Reference 7.1 and 7.2 p136**

2 Put the verbs in the Present Perfect or Past Simple.

1 Anthony Trollope _______ (travel) to South Africa, Australia, Egypt, and the West Indies. Joanna Trollope _______ (travel) to many parts of the world.
2 She _______ (win) many awards, and several of her stories _______ (appear) on TV.
3 Her first book _______ (come) out in 1980. Since then, she _______ (sell) more than 5 million copies.
4 She _______ (go) to school in the south of England, and _______ (study) English at Oxford University, but she _______ (live) in the country for most of her life.
5 She writes her books by hand. She _______ (have) the same pen since 1995.

**T 7.2** Listen and check.

3 Here are the answers to some questions about Joanna. What are the questions?

1 For forty years.
2 English. *(... study ... ?)*
3 More than twenty.
4 Over five million.
5 In 1980.
6 Twice. *(How many times ... ?)*
7 Yes, two daughters. *(... children?)*
8 Since 1995.

**T 7.3** Listen and check.

# PRACTICE

## Discussing grammar

1 Choose the correct verb form.

1 *Have you ever been / Did you ever go* to a rock concert?
2 I *saw / have seen* The Flash last week.
3 I love rock and roll. I *like / have liked* it all my life.
4 The Flash's concert *was / has been* fantastic.
5 I *have bought / bought* all their records since then.
6 The Flash *have been / are* together for over fifteen years.

## Find someone who . . .

2 Your teacher will give you a card which begins *Find someone who ...* .

**Find someone who has been to China.**

Decide on the question, beginning *Have you ever ... ?* Stand up, and ask everyone in the class.

Ask questions to find out more.

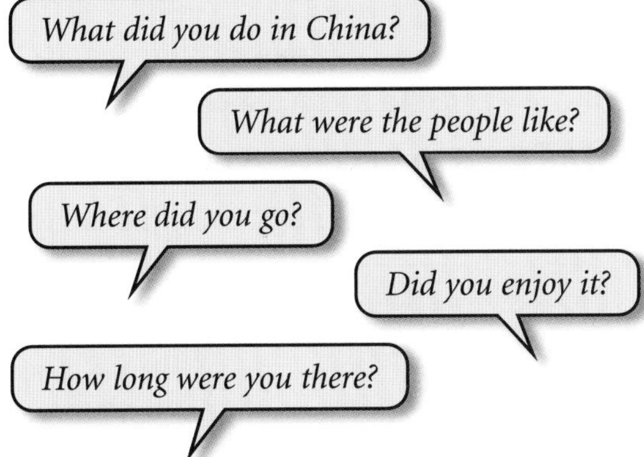


3 Report back to the class.

*No one has been to China.*

*Pierre and Sophie have been to China.*

## *for* and *since*

**4** Complete the time expressions with *for* or *since*.

1 _____ a year
2 _____ half an hour
3 _____ August
4 _____ nine o'clock
5 _____ I was a student
6 _____ a couple of days
7 _____ months
8 _____ 1999

**5** Match a line in **A** and **B** and a sentence in **C**. There is more than one answer.

| A | B | C |
|---|---|---|
| 1 I've known my best friend | from 1988 to 1996. | It's not bad. I quite like it. |
| 2 I last went to the cinema | for an hour. | I went camping with some friends. |
| 3 I've had this watch | two weeks ago. | We met when we were 10. |
| 4 We've used this book | since 1985. | I really need a cup of coffee. |
| 5 We lived in our old flat | since the beginning of term. | My Dad gave it to me for my birthday. |
| 6 We haven't had a break | for years. | We moved because we needed somewhere bigger. |
| 7 I last had a holiday | for three years. | The film was rubbish. |
| 8 This building has been a school | in 1999. | Before that it was an office. |

**T 7.4** Listen and check. Make similar sentences about you.

## Asking questions

**6** Complete the conversation.
What tenses are the three questions?

**A** Where _______ live, Olga?
**B** In a flat near the park.
**A** How long _______ there?
**B** For three years.
**A** And why _______ move?
**B** We wanted to live in a nicer area.

**T 7.5** Listen and check. Practise the conversation with a partner.

**7** Make more conversations, using the same tenses.

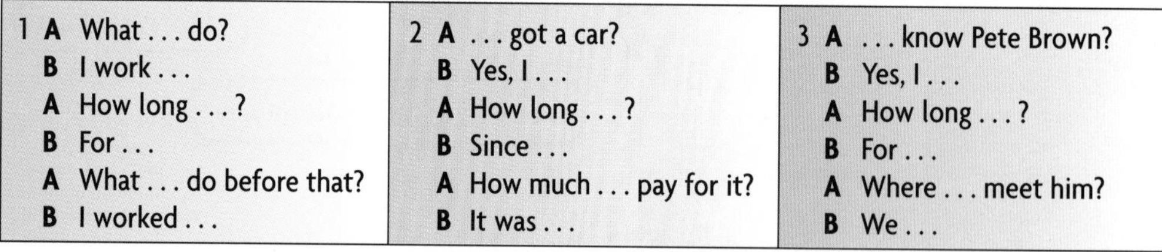

| 1 | 2 | 3 |
|---|---|---|
| **A** What . . . do? | **A** . . . got a car? | **A** . . . know Pete Brown? |
| **B** I work . . . | **B** Yes, I . . . | **B** Yes, I . . . |
| **A** How long . . . ? | **A** How long . . . ? | **A** How long . . . ? |
| **B** For . . . | **B** Since . . . | **B** For . . . |
| **A** What . . . do before that? | **A** How much . . . pay for it? | **A** Where . . . meet him? |
| **B** I worked . . . | **B** It was . . . | **B** We . . . |

**8** With a partner, ask and answer questions beginning *How long . . . ?*

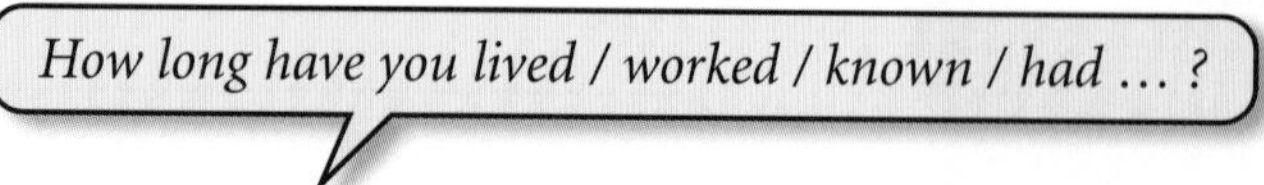


Then get some more information.

# LISTENING AND SPEAKING

## The band *Style*

**1** What kinds of music do you like? If you could meet your favourite bands or singers, what would you ask them?

**2** **T 7.6** Listen to an interview with two musicians, Suzie and Guy, from the band *Style*. Put **S** or **G** in columns 1 and 2. Put ✓ or ✗ in column 3.

| 1 What do they do in the band? | 2 Bands they have played with | 3 Places they have visited |
|---|---|---|
| ☐ guitar | ☐ UB40 | ☐ Holland |
| ☐ keyboards | ☐ Lionel Richie | ☐ Hungary |
| ☐ drums | ☐ Phil Collins | ☐ America |
| ☐ harmonica | ☐ Genesis | ☐ Sweden |
| ☐ vocalist | ☐ Happy Mondays | ☐ Japan |
| | ☐ Bon Jovi | ☐ Italy |
| | ☐ Ace | ☐ Australia |

Which bands have they played with? Which countries have they been to?

**3** Answer the questions.

1 Why do Suzie and Guy feel tired?
2 What have they done this year?
3 Have they had a good time?
4 What was special about the song *Mean Street*?
5 How many years have they been together?
6 Where do they want to go?
7 What jobs has Guy had? What about Suzie? *(She's worked … )*

### Language work

**4** Make sentences about Suzie and Guy with the phrases in the boxes.

| A | B |
|---|---|
| in April<br>in 1995<br>two years ago<br>when she left college | since 1997<br>about twenty-five<br>fifteen years<br>since he was 17 |

What tense are the verbs in the sentences from **A**? What about **B**?

**5** Ask and answer the questions.

- What/do/before forming *Style*?
- … be/to America?
- How/meet each other?
- How many records/make?

### Roleplay

**6** Some of you are members of a band. Others are journalists who are going to interview the band. Your teacher will give you some ideas. When you are ready, have the interview.

# READING

## Celebrity interview

**1** Which celebrities are in the news at the moment? Why are they in the news? What have they done?

**2** Look at the article from *Hi! Magazine*. Who is the couple in the interview? Are there magazines like this in your country? What sort of stories do they have?

**3** Read the article quickly and put these questions in the right place.

1. **Have there ever been times when you have thought 'This relationship isn't working'?**
2. **Terry, footballers are usually hard, but you seem very sensitive. Why is this?**
3. **You're both terribly busy in your separate careers. How do you find time to be together?**
4. **How did you two meet?**
5. **How do you find being superstars?**

**4** Read the article again and answer the questions.

1. Why are they famous?
2. They are both successful in their careers. What have they done?
3. In what ways are they normal people? What is not normal about their lives?
4. How do you know they're in love?
5. Was it love at first sight?
6. What is their attitude to newspapers and 'other people'?
7. Why do some people want them to split up?
8. In what way is Terry unusual for a footballer?

**5** Work in groups of three. Read the text aloud.

### Language work

**6** Choose the correct tense.

1. Donna and Terry *are / have been / were* together for two years.
2. They *like / have liked / liked* watching TV on Saturday night.
3. They *meet / have met / met* after a football match.
4. They *have lived / live / lived* in their new home since April.
5. Terry *is / has been / was* in love just once.

### Project

**7** Buy a magazine like *Hi!* and find an interview with a famous couple. Bring it into class and tell the class about it.

THE POP STAR AND THE FOOTBALLER

## DONNA FLYNN & TERRY WISEMAN

TALK TO *HI! MAGAZINE* ABOUT THEIR LOVE FOR EACH OTHER

**This is the most famous couple in the country. She is the pop star who has had six number one records – more than any other single artist. He has scored fifty goals for Manchester United, and has played for England over thirty times. Together they earn about £20 million a year. They invited *Hi! Magazine* into their luxurious home.**

______________________________?

**Donna:** A lot of the time since we've been together, one of us has been away. We really have to try hard to be together. We have both flown all over the world just to spend a few hours together.
**Terry:** Obviously, people say, 'Oh, you've got all this money, what are you going to spend it on?' But the best thing is that money buys us the freedom to be together.

______________________________?

**Donna:** It hasn't changed us. We are still the same people. Newspapers have told terrible stories about us, but it's all lies.
**Terry:** Our perfect Saturday night is sitting in front of the telly with a take-away. Our favourite programmes are *Blind Date* and *Friends*. You won't find photos of us coming out of pubs and clubs drunk, having spent the night with a whole load of famous people.

**Donna says: 'We are so totally in love. I'm the happiest I've ever been.'**

______________________________?

**Donna:** I went to one of his matches because I liked him and I wanted to meet him. It's funny, because I'm not really interested in football, so when I met him after the match, I didn't know what to say to him.
**Terry:** I'm very shy. We just looked at each other from opposite sides of the room. But I said to my mate, 'She's the one for me. I'm going to marry her one day.' Fortunately, she came to another game, and we started talking then.

______________________________?

**Donna:** Not really. Naturally, it's hard when you're away from each other, but in a way this has made us stronger. ▷

Donna and Terry have been together for just over two years. They have lived in their house since April. She says: 'He has good taste – but not as good as mine!'

A lot of people would love to see us split up. People have accused Terry of things …

**Terry:** Of course you have to be prepared to give and take in any relationship. There's a trust between us, and as long as that's there, we will last.

?

**Terry:** It's because this is the first time I've been in love. I think that when you meet the person that you want to spend the rest of your life with, you change. You become a softer person.

**Donna:** We mean the world to each other. Neither of us will do anything to spoil it. HI!

Terry says: 'She's the only woman I've ever loved.'

# VOCABULARY

## Adverbs

**1** Many adverbs end in *-ly*.

| slowly carefully usually |
|---|

Find some more examples in the text on p58–9.

**2** There are also many adverbs that don't end in *-ly*. Find these examples in the text.

| together hard still just of course |
|---|

**3** Complete the sentences with one of these adverbs.

| still<br>nearly<br>only<br>of course<br>together |
|---|

1 'Do you love me?' '________ I do. I adore you.'
2 I called Tom at 10.00 in the morning, but he was ________ in bed.
3 It's our anniversary today. We've been ________ for fifteen years.
4 Kate is very fussy about food. She ________ eats pasta and crisps.
5 She was very ill and ________ died, but fortunately, she got better.

**4** Complete the sentences with one of these adverbs.

| at last exactly too especially just |
|---|

1 I like all Russian novelists, ________ Tolstoy.
2 'I hate ironing.' 'Me, ________ . It's so boring.'
3 'Are you telling me that we have no money?' '________ . Not a penny.'
4 I met her on December 23, ________ before Christmas.
5 ________ I have finished this exercise. Thank goodness! It was so boring.

## Word pairs

**1** There are many idiomatic expressions which consist of two words joined by *and*. Here is an example from the text on p59.

*'Of course you have to be prepared to* ***give and take*** *in any relationship.'*

**2** Match the words.

| | | |
|---|---|---|
| ladies | | don'ts |
| fish | | pepper |
| now | | then |
| yes | | quiet |
| do's | and | down |
| up | | chips |
| peace | | sound |
| safe | | gentlemen |
| salt | | no |

**3** Complete the sentences with one of the expressions.

1 'Do you still play tennis?' 'Not regularly. Just ____ , when I have time.'
2 This is a pretty relaxed place to work. There aren't many ____ .'
3 Here you are at last! I've been so worried! Thank goodness you've arrived ____ .
4 'Do you like your new job?' '____ . The money's OK, but I don't like the people.'
5 Sometimes there are too many people in the house. I go into the garden for a bit of ____ .
6 Good evening, ____ . It gives me great pleasure to talk to you all tonight.
7 'How's your Gran?' '____ . There are good days, and then not such good days.'
8 'Here's supper. Careful! It's hot.' '____ ! Yummy!'

**T 7.7** Close your books. Listen to the beginnings of the conversations and complete them.

# EVERYDAY ENGLISH

## Short answers

**1** **T 7.8** Listen to the conversations. What's the difference between them? Which sounds more polite?

> **!**
> 1 When we answer *Yes/No* questions, we often repeat a subject and the auxiliary verb. *Yes* or *No* on its own sounds impolite. Complete these short answers.
>
> | | |
> |---|---|
> | Do you like cooking? | Yes, I ***do*** . |
> | Is it raining? | No, it ____ . |
> | Have you been to France? | Yes, I ____ . |
> | Are you good at chess? | No, I ____ . |
> | Can you speak Spanish? | Yes, I ____ . |
>
> 2 It also helps a conversation if you can add more information.
>
> Do you like cooking? Yes, I do, actually, especially Italian food.

**2** Complete the short answers. Continue with a line from the speech bubbles.

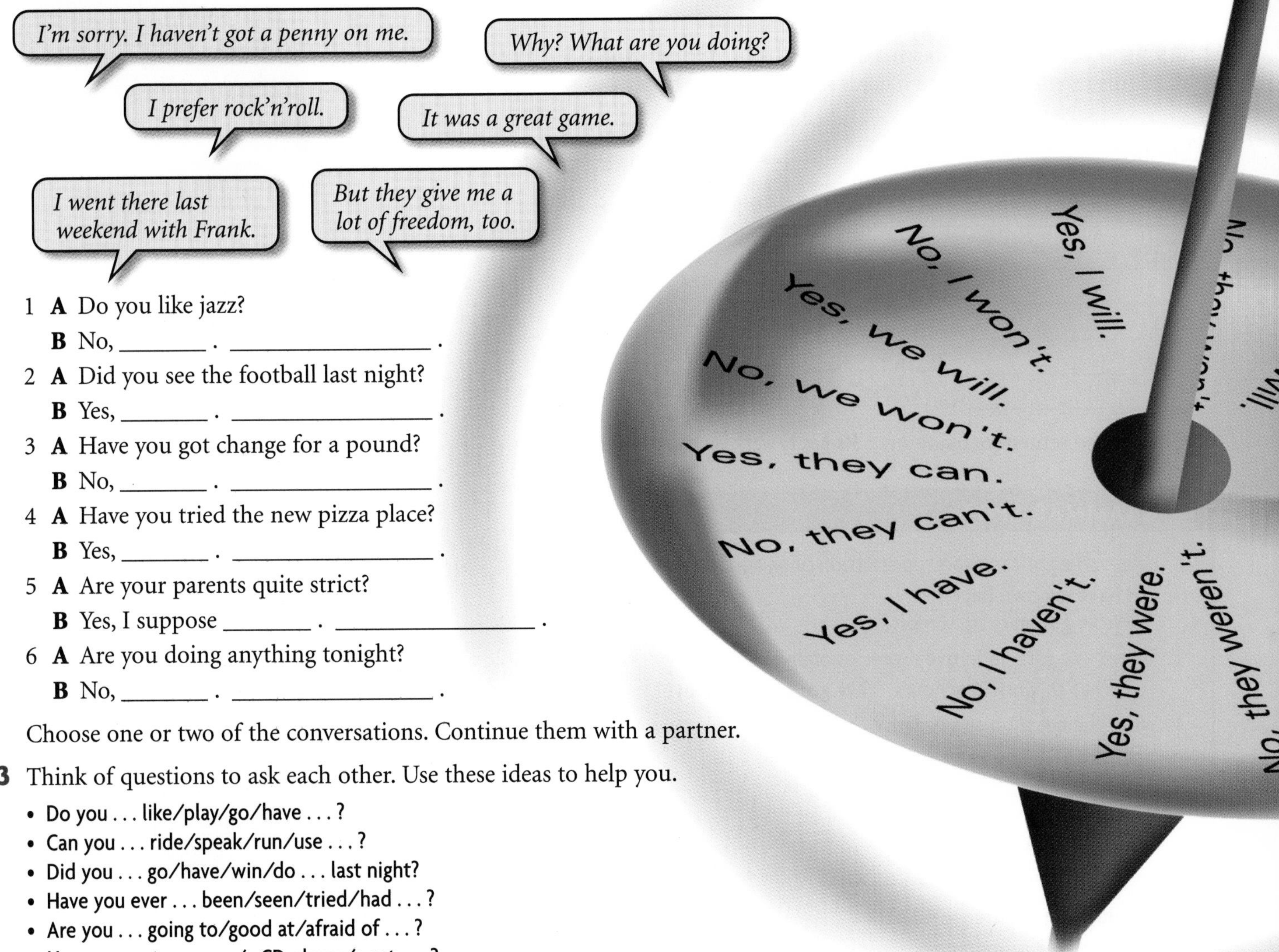


1 **A** Do you like jazz?
  **B** No, ________ . ____________________ .

2 **A** Did you see the football last night?
  **B** Yes, ________ . ____________________ .

3 **A** Have you got change for a pound?
  **B** No, ________ . ____________________ .

4 **A** Have you tried the new pizza place?
  **B** Yes, ________ . ____________________ .

5 **A** Are your parents quite strict?
  **B** Yes, I suppose ________ . ____________________ .

6 **A** Are you doing anything tonight?
  **B** No, ________ . ____________________ .

Choose one or two of the conversations. Continue them with a partner.

**3** Think of questions to ask each other. Use these ideas to help you.

- Do you . . . like/play/go/have . . . ?
- Can you . . . ride/speak/run/use . . . ?
- Did you . . . go/have/win/do . . . last night?
- Have you ever . . . been/seen/tried/had . . . ?
- Are you . . . going to/good at/afraid of . . . ?
- Have you got . . . a car/a CD player/a cat . . . ?

**4** Stand up and ask your questions. Use short answers in your replies.

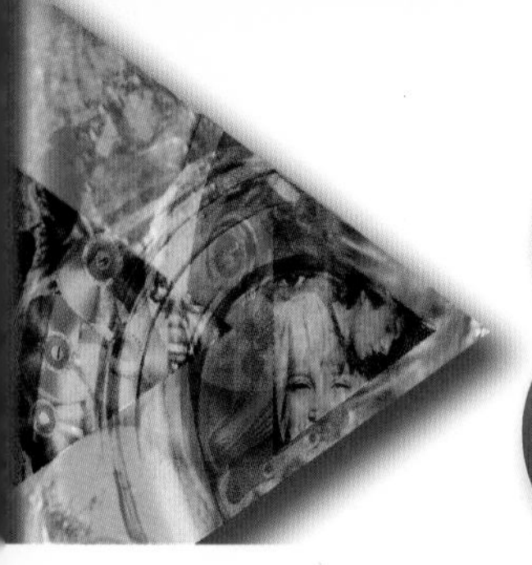

# 8 Do's and don'ts

***have (got) to*** • ***should/must*** • **Words that go together** • **At the doctor's**

**STARTER** 

What's true for you? Make sentences about your life.

**I have to . . .** **I don't have to . . .**

- get up early every morning
- pay bills
- go to school
- work at the weekend
- do the housework

## WORK, WORK

### *have (got) to*

**1** **T 8.1** Listen to Steven talking about his job. What do you think his job is? Would you like his job? Why/Why not?

**2** Complete the sentences from the interview with words from the box.

| don't have to | have to | had to | Do you have to | didn't have to |
|---|---|---|---|---|

I _______________ work very long hours.
_______________ work at the weekend?
I _______________ do the washing-up.
We _______________ learn the basics.
I _______________ wait too long to get a job.

**3** Change the sentences using *he*. **He has to work very long hours.**

**GRAMMAR SPOT**

1 *have/have got* can express possession or an action.
I **have** my own flat.
We**'ve got** an exam tomorrow.

2 *have/have got* + infinitive expresses obligation.
He **has** to work long hours. I**'ve got** to go now. Bye!

3 Write the question and negative.
I have to get up early.
What time ____ you _______________ up?
I _______________ up early.
Put the sentence in the past.
Yesterday I _______________ up early.

▶▶ **Grammar Reference 8.1 p137**

**4** What are some of the other things Steven has to do?

# PRACTICE

## Pronunciation

**1** **T 8.2** Listen to these sentences. What are the different pronunciations of *have/has/had*?

1 ☐ I **have** a good job. ☐ I **have** to work hard.
2 ☐ He **has** a nice car. ☐ She **has** to get up early.
3 ☐ I **had** a good time. ☐ I **had** to take exams.

Put a–f in front of the sentences according to the pronunciation below.

a /hæz/ b /hæv/ c /hæd/
d /hæf/ e /hæs/ f /hæt/

**T 8.2** Listen again and repeat.

## Jobs

**2** Work with a partner. Choose one of the jobs from the box, but don't tell your partner. Ask and answer *Yes/No* questions to find out what the job is.

| shop assistant receptionist taxi-driver artist architect lawyer ambulance driver miner dancer soldier decorator detective vet mechanic dentist housewife farmer plumber firefighter |
|---|

| Do you . . . ? | Do you have to . . . ? |
|---|---|
| • work inside | • wear a uniform |
| • earn a lot of money | • use your hands |
| • work regular hours | • answer the phone |

*Do you work inside?*

*Yes, I do./No, I don't.*

**3** Which of the jobs *wouldn't* you like to do? Why?

**I wouldn't like to be a farmer because they have to work outside all year.**

## Talking about you

**4** In groups, discuss the questions. If you live at home with your parents, use the present tense. If you've left home, use the past tense.

1 What do/did you have to do to help in the house? What about your brothers and sisters?

2 Can/Could you stay out as long as you want?/wanted? Or do/did you have to be home by a certain time?

3 Do/Did you always have to tell your parents where you are/were going?

4 How strict are/were your parents? What do/did they let you do?

5 What do/did you argue about?

# PROBLEMS, PROBLEMS

## *should, must*

**1** Match the problems and suggestions on the right. What advice would *you* give?

**2** **T 8.3** Listen and complete the advice. Use the words from the box.

| shouldn't | should |
|---|---|
| must | don't think you should |

1 I think you ______________ talk to your boss.
2 You ______________ drink coffee at night.
3 I ______________ go to the wedding.
4 You ______________ go to the dentist.

Practise the conversations with a partner.

**3** Give advice to your friends.

- I'm overweight.
- I've got exams next week.
- My cat's ill.

- I'm always arguing with my parents.
- It's my parents' wedding anniversary soon.
- My car's making a funny noise.

### GRAMMAR SPOT

1 Which sentence expresses a suggestion?
Which sentence expresses strong obligation?
You should go on a diet.
You must go to the doctor's.

2 *Should* and *must* are modal verbs.
He **must** be careful.
You **shouldn't** drink and drive.
What **should** she do?
Do we add *-s* with *he/she/it*? Do we use *do/does* in the question and negative?

3 We can make a negative suggestion with *I don't think ...*
I don't think you should smoke so much.

►► Grammar Reference 8.2–8.4 p137

**Problems**

I'm working 16 hours a day.

I can't sleep.

My ex-boyfriend's getting married.

I've had a terrible toothache for weeks.

**Suggestions**

Don't drink coffee at night.

Go to the dentist.

Don't go to the wedding.

Talk to your boss.

# PRACTICE

## Grammar

**1** Make sentences from the chart.

| If you want to ... | | |
|---|---|---|
| learn English,<br>do well in life,<br>keep fit, | you have to<br>you don't have to<br>you should<br>you shouldn't | work hard.<br>do some sport.<br>learn the grammar.<br>go to university.<br>buy a dictionary.<br>smoke.<br>believe in yourself.<br>speak your language in class. |

## A trip to your country

**2** Someone is coming to stay in your country for six months. What advice can you give?

*You should bring warm clothes.*
*You have to have a passport.*
*You don't have to get a visa.*
*You must try our local speciality.*

Include advice about money, documents, clothes, health, accommodation, and food.

# LISTENING AND SPEAKING
## Holidays in January

**1** Do many people in your country go on holiday in winter? Where do they go? Where would you like to go for a winter holiday? Write a sentence and read it to the class.

***I'd like to go to . . . because . . .***

**2** **T 8.4** Listen to three people giving advice about visiting their country in the month of January. Complete the chart. Compare your answers with a partner.

| | Weather and clothes | Things to do, places to go | Food and drink |
|---|---|---|---|
| Silvia | | | |
| Fatima | | | |
| Karl | | | |

**3** Answer the questions.

1. Which countries are they talking about? How do you know?
2. Look at the photographs. Which country do they go with?
3. Who talked about sport? Which sport?
4. Who talked about money? What did he/she say?
5. Who suggested going on a boat trip? Where?
6. Which of these countries would you like to visit in January? Why?

### Speaking

**4** Put the words in the correct order to make questions.

1. weather / is / like / in / what / the / January?
2. take / clothes / what / should / I?
3. can / things / sort / of / what / do / I?
4. special / any / there / places / are / that / should / visit / I?
5. food / you / recommend / do / what?

**5** Work with someone from a different country, or choose another country you know. Ask and answer the questions.

## READING AND SPEAKING
### Problem page

**1** These problems come from a newspaper column where people write in with a problem, and other members of the public give their advice. Read the problems. What advice would you give?

**2** Match the readers' letters to these problems. There are two for each problem.

# DILEMMAS

with **Vanessa Goodman**

### THIS WEEK'S PROBLEMS

#### *Do I have to act my age?*

**Polly is 47**. She is single, and her children have left home. She is very successful in her career, and has a lot of friends, but she isn't satisfied. She longs to change her life. She wants to live abroad, paint, and write poetry, but her friends tell her she should stop being silly and act her age.

**a** ☐ ☐

#### *Must I be a slave to my mobile?*

**Jason's company** has bought him a mobile phone. They want him to keep it on all the time, so that they can contact him anywhere, anytime. He dislikes the idea of always being available, and he hates the way people use mobiles to have private conversations in public.

**b** ☐ ☐

#### *Should I throw my son out?*

**Sarah's 24-year-old son** lives at home, stays in bed till late, and watches TV all day. He buys and sells drugs. He's clever, but he dropped out of school. He's never had a job. His father wants to throw him out, but Sarah worries that he could get further into drugs and end up in prison.

**c** ☐ ☐

## Readers' advice

1 Children always need the support of their parents, whether they're four or 24. I think you should pay for him to get some qualifications, and when he's ready, ____ to find somewhere to live. Meanwhile, ____ him all the love that he needs.

**Jenny Torr**
Brighton

2 I decided to give it all up and change my life dramatically three years ago. Since then, ____ the most exciting three years of my life. It can be scary, but if you don't do it, you won't know what you've missed. I don't think ____ . Go for it.

**Mike Garfield**
Manchester

3 He's using you. I think ____ . It's time for him to go. Twenty-four is too old to be living with his parents. He's got to take responsibility for himself. And ____ about his drug-taking. Sometimes you have to be cruel to be kind.

**Tony Palmer**
Harrow

4 Why ____ it? He isn't their slave, they don't own him. And I also can't stand the way people use their mobiles in restaurants, on trains and buses. They think that the people around them are invisible and can't hear. ____ .

**Jane Sands**
London

5 I think ____ before she gives up her job and goes to live abroad. Does she think that the sun will always shine? If there is something in her life that makes her unhappy now, this will follow her. She should take her time ____ .

**Nigella Lawnes**
Bristol

6 ____ ! He should have a word with his company and come to an arrangement with them. Why can't he turn it off sometimes? Mobile phones are great, and if he's got one for free, _____ . They are one of the best inventions ever.

**Pete Hardcastle**
Birmingham

**3** Where do these lines go? Put a letter in the gaps.

a ... you should tell him to leave home.
b ... she should be very careful ...
c ... you should help him ...
d ... you should worry.
e He must keep it!
f ... before making a decision.
g It is so rude.
h ... he's very lucky.
i I have had...
j ... you must tell the police ...
k ... you've got to give ...
l ... should he accept ...

**T 8.5** Listen and check.

**4** Which letter writer ... ?

- suggests waiting
- thinks love is the answer
- has been adventurous
- thinks that employers shouldn't exploit their employees
- loves mobile phones
- suggests being tough

The readers make very different suggestions. Who do you agree with?

### What do you think?

- How old are children when they leave home in your country?
- What do you think of people who use mobile phones in public?
- Do you think older people should act their age? Why/Why not?
- 'You have to be cruel to be kind'. Can you think of an example?

### Roleplay

With a partner, choose a situation and roleplay the conversation.

- Polly and one of her friends
- Jason and his boss
- Sarah and her husband

### Group work

In groups, write a letter to a problem page.

Exchange your letters and write a reply. Try to express sympathy with the problem and give some explanation, as well as practical advice.

# VOCABULARY
## Words that go together

**1** Many verbs and nouns go together.

*tell a story*   *leave home*

Look at the chart on the right. Match a verb with a complement. They all appear in the letters and problems on p66–67.

Look at the letters again and check your answers.

| Verbs | Complements |
|---|---|
| live | being silly |
| write | your age |
| stop | abroad |
| act | responsibility |
| take | poetry |
| take | your job |
| stay | what you've missed |
| don't know | a word with someone |
| have to be | in bed |
| give up | your time |
| have | cruel to be kind |

**2** Close your books. Try to remember the sentences that include the phrases from the box.

**3** Two nouns can go together. There are no rules about spelling.

| post office   headache   horse-race |
|---|

The stress is usually on the first word.

Match the nouns to make new words.

| | |
|---|---|
| alarm | cream |
| car | glasses |
| traffic | table |
| credit | coat |
| ice | lights |
| sun | card |
| time | park |
| rain | clock |

| | |
|---|---|
| hair | case |
| sun | drier |
| ear | quake |
| sign | post |
| book | ring |
| rush | lighter |
| cigarette | set |
| earth | hour |

**T 8.6** Listen and check.

**4** Choose a word and give a definition to the class. Can they guess the word?

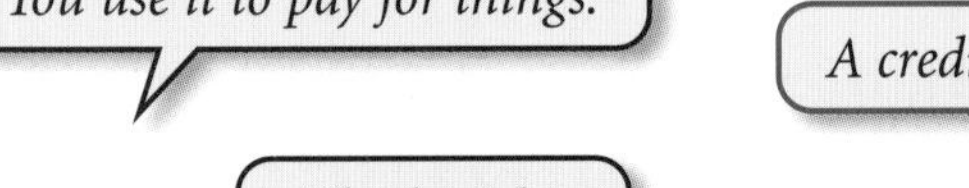

# EVERYDAY ENGLISH

## At the doctor's

**1** Complete the chart with an illness or a symptom.

| diarrhoea<br>food poisoning<br>'flu |
|---|

| It hurts when I walk on it.<br>My glands are swollen, and it hurts when I swallow.<br>I can't stop sneezing and my nose is runny. |
|---|

| Illnesses | Symptoms |
|---|---|
| I've got a cold. | |
| I've got __________ . | I've got a temperature, my whole body aches, and I feel awful. |
| I've twisted my ankle. | |
| I've got __________ . | I keep going to the toilet. |
| I've got a sore throat. | |
| I've got __________ . | I keep being sick, and I've got diarrhoea. |

What's the difference between these sentences?

*I feel sick.* *I was sick last night.*

**2** Put the sentences in the correct order.

- [1] I didn't feel very well.
- [ ] She took my temperature and examined me.
- [ ] After a few days, I started to feel better.
- [ ] I went to the surgery and saw the doctor.
- [ ] I went to the chemist's, paid for the prescription, and got some antibiotics.
- [ ] I phoned the doctor's surgery and made an appointment.
- [ ] She told me I had an infection.
- [ ] I explained what was wrong.
- [ ] She gave me a prescription.

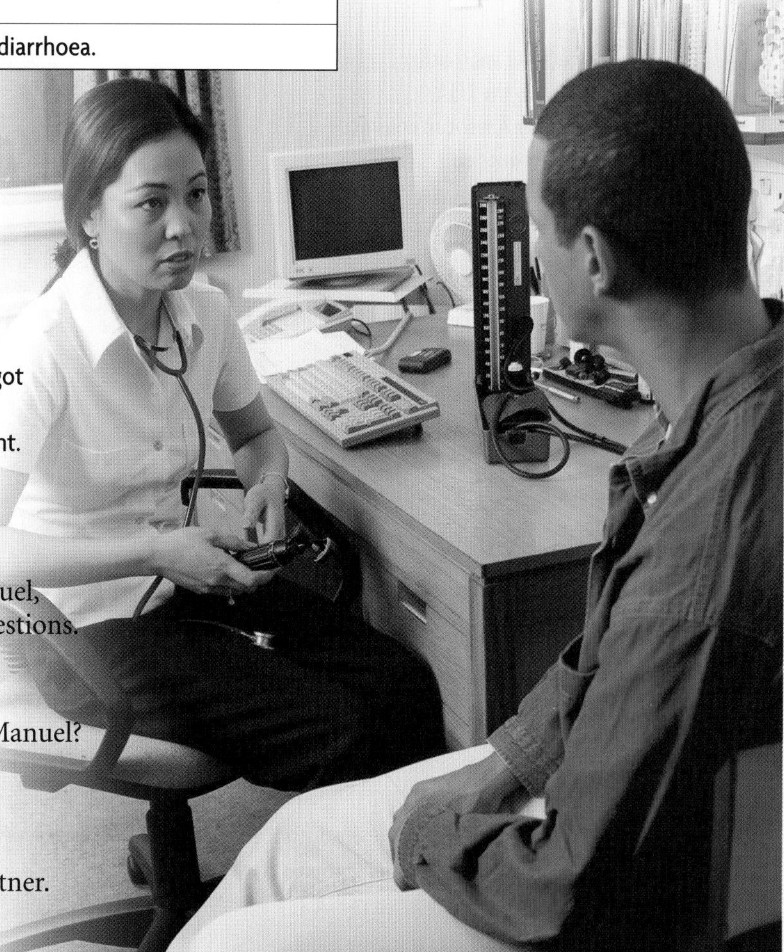

**3** **T 8.7** You will hear a conversation between Manuel, a student from Chile, and a doctor. Answer the questions.

1. What are Manuel's symptoms?
2. What questions does the doctor ask?
3. What does the doctor think is the matter with Manuel?
4. What does she prescribe?
5. What advice does she give him?
6. Does he have to pay for anything?

**4** Look at the tapescript on p124. Practise with a partner.

**5** Make similar conversations with other symptoms.

# 9 Going places

**Time clauses • *if* • Hot verbs • In a hotel**

**STARTER**

What do you think you will do if the weather is nice this weekend?
What will you do when you get home tonight?

## THE GAP YEAR

### Time and conditional clauses

**1** Clare and her friend Ally are having a gap year. Complete the sentences with phrases from the box below.

1 We're travelling round the world . . . [c]
2 We're going to leave . . . □
3 □ . . . we're going to learn to scuba dive on the Great Barrier Reef.
4 □ . . . we'll look after each other.
5 □ . . . we're going to the USA.
6 We can stay with my American cousins . . . □
7 Our parents will be worried . . . □
8 We'll stay in the States . . . □

a while we're in Los Angeles.
b If we get ill,
c before we go to university.
d until our visa runs out.
e When we're in Australia,
f as soon as we have enough money.
g if we don't keep in touch.
h After we leave Australia,

**T 9.1** Listen and check.

**2** Cover the box. Practise the sentences.

### GRAMMAR SPOT

1 Underline the words in the box that introduce the clauses, e.g. *while*
2 Which tense are all the verbs in the box? Do they refer to the present or the future?
3 What are the different future forms in Clare and Ally's sentences?
4 What's the difference between these sentences? Which one is sure? Which one is possible?
**When** I get home, I'll have something to eat.
**If** there isn't any food, I'll get a pizza.

▶▶ **Grammar Reference 9.1–9.3 p138**

## PRACTICE

### *when, as soon as*

**1** Complete the sentences with your ideas.

**T 9.2** Listen and compare your answers.

### *What if . . . ?*

**2** Look at these hopes for the future. Make sentences using *If … will …*

*If I don't go out so much, I'll do more work.*
*If I do more work, I'll …*

I don't go out so much
do more work
pass my exams
go to university
study medicine
become a doctor
earn a good salary.

I stop smoking
have more money
save some every week
be rich when I'm thirty
have my own business
make a lot of money
retire when I'm forty.

## What will you do?

**3** Work with a partner. One of you is going skiing for the first time. The other sees all the problems. Use these ideas to help you.

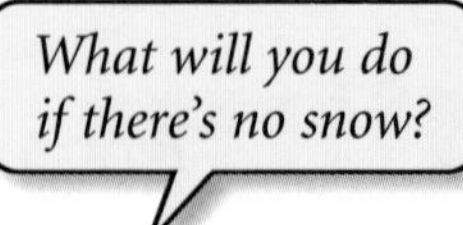

- don't like the food
- it rains
- don't learn to ski
- hurt yourself
- there's nothing to do in the evening
- don't make any friends
- lose your money
- get lost in a snowstorm

Make a similar conversation about going on safari for the first time.

## Discussing grammar

**4** Complete the sentences with *when*, *if*, *before*, or *until*.

1. I'll have a bath _____ I go to bed.
2. I'm coming to London tomorrow. I'll ring you _____ I arrive.
3. _____ it's a nice day tomorrow, we can go swimming.
4. Wait here _____ I get back.
5. _____ you have any problems, just ask for help.
6. I want to get home _____ it gets dark.
7. I'm going to have driving lessons _____ I pass my test.
8. Give me your address _____ you go home.

## When I get to New York . . .

**5** Put the verbs in brackets in the correct tense. Put *if*, *when*, *while*, or *as soon as* into each box.

**Paul** Bye, darling. Have a good trip to New York.

**Mary** Thanks. I *'ll ring* (ring) you [ as soon as ] I arrive at the hotel.

**Paul** Fine. Remember I _________ (go) out with Henry tonight.

**Mary** Well, [ ] you _________ (be) out [ ] I _________ (ring), I _________ (leave) a message on the answerphone so you'll know I've arrived safely.

**Paul** Great. What time do you expect you'll be there?

**Mary** [ ] the plane _________ (arrive) on time, I _________ (be) at the hotel about 10.00.

**Paul** All right. Give me a ring [ ] you _________ (know) the time of your flight back, and I _________ (pick) you up at the airport.

**Mary** Thanks, darling. Don't forget to water the plants [ ] I _________ (be) away.

**Paul** Don't worry. I won't. Bye!

**T 9.3** Listen and check.

## LISTENING AND SPEAKING

### Life in 2050

**1** Read this description of the airline of the future:

> *'There will be just two crew members, a pilot and a dog. The pilot's job is to feed the dog. The dog's job is to bite the pilot if he tries to touch anything.'*

What does this story say about life in the future?

**2** You will hear an interview with Michio Kaku, Professor of Theoretical Physics at City University, New York. He has written a book, *Visions*, which explains how science will revolutionize the 21st century.

He is asked these questions.

- Are you optimistic about the future?
- Are we ready for the changes that will come?
- Is world population going to be a big problem?
- What will happen to people who don't have computers?
- Will there be a world government?
- Will we have control of everything?
- What are your reasons for pessimism?

Discuss your opinions on these subjects.

**3** **T 9.4** Listen to the interview. Make notes on Michio Kaku's answers.

**4** Answer the questions.

1. What does Michio Kaku say will continue into the twenty-first century?
2. How do some people react to the new technology? What is his reaction?
3. Why will the population of the world stop increasing?
4. Why will we need a world government?
5. What are some of the things we will be able to control?
6. What examples does he give of the behaviour of 'stupid' people?

#### What do you think?

Michio Kaku obviously believes in the power of science. What isn't he so sure about? Do you agree?

# READING AND SPEAKING

## The world's first megalopolis

**1** Are these statements about China true or false?

- China is a communist country.
- One in five people in the whole world is Chinese.
- Chinese families can only have one child.
- Chinese people love tradition.
- Chinese people prefer bicycles to cars.
- The biggest city in the world is in China.

**2** Read the newspaper article about Pearl River City. Which of the subjects in exercise 1 are talked about?

**3** On the map find the following:

- Shenzhen
- Pearl River Estuary
- Guangzhou
- the Hopewell Highway

**4** Answer the questions.

1. Has this city got a name yet?
2. Why is it ugly? Why is it exciting?
3. What are some of the statistics about Shenzhen that make it a remarkable place?
4. In what ways is China changing? Why were Deng Xiaoping's words significant?
5. How are the people changing? Why do they want to own a car?
6. What does Shenzhen look like?
7. Why will this city be important in the 21st century?
8. What do these numbers refer to?

| | |
|---|---|
| 1982 | thousands |
| 3 million | six months |
| less than ten years | two hours |
| 40 million | four hours |

### What do you think?

- In groups, write what you think are the ten largest cities in the world. Compare your list with the class. Your teacher will tell you the answer.
- Make a list of some of the problems that these cities face. Decide which are the three most important problems. Compare your ideas with the class.

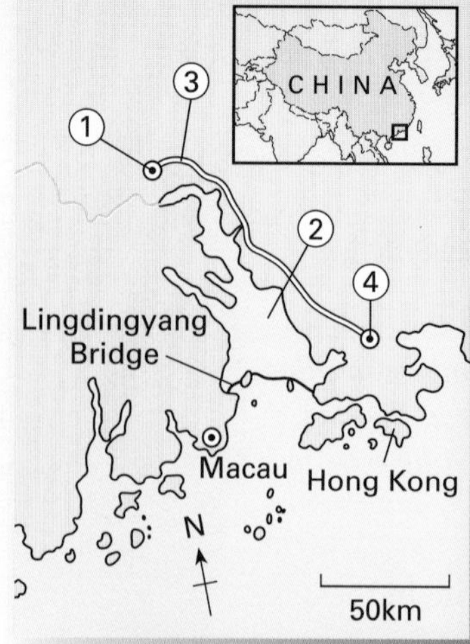


**To the north of Hong Kong, the world's biggest city is growing. It hasn't got a new name yet, but it will probably be called Pearl River City. Jonathon Glancey visits this ugly, exciting mess.**

# Megalopolis

The town of Shenzhen, just forty kilometres north of Hong Kong, is the world's biggest building site. In 1982 it was a fishing village with two main roads, fields, and a population of 30,000. Now it has a population of 3 million. It is growing at an incredible speed. It is spreading north towards Guangzhou (also known as Canton) and west towards Macau. The Chinese government hopes that in less than ten years this area will be the biggest city on earth, with a population of 40 million people.

China is changing. It is no longer a country where absolutely everything is owned and controlled by the state. Developers are welcome. As Deng Xiaoping, the Chinese leader, said in 1992, 'To get rich is glorious'. The old China of bicycles and Little Red Books is disappearing. A world of mobile phones and capitalism is arriving.

The Chinese people seem to welcome dramatic change. They don't worry about losing traditional ways of life. They want the new. As the posters on the sides of the highways shout, 'Development is the only way.'

Shenzhen is a shocking place, like nowhere else on earth that I have ever seen. It is a city with no boundaries and no centre. There are new concrete office blocks, factories, and housing blocks as far as the eye can see. Not just dozens of new buildings, nor even hundreds, but thousands. And it is all happening so fast. It takes just six months to design, build, and finish a 60-storey, air-conditioned skyscraper. As one architect said to me, 'If you move too slowly here, someone will walk over you.'

The new Hopewell Highway runs from Shenzhen to Guangzhou, and it takes just two hours to do the 123 kilometres. This superhighway will become the main street of a huge new city, as it gets bigger and bigger until the east meets the west, and the countryside in the middle disappears under concrete.

There will of course be more and more cars on the road. People don't want bicycles. If you have a car, it means you have made money. So the traffic will be like in Bangkok, where people spend four hours commuting every day. People eat and work in their car.

Pearl River City very nearly exists. It will probably be the world's First City, the greatest city on earth. It won't be beautiful, but its power, energy, and wealth will be felt in all corners of the world.

# VOCABULARY

## Hot verbs – *take*, *get*, *do*, and *make*

**1** The verbs *take*, *get*, *do*, and *make* are very common in English. Find these examples in the text about China:

| **get** rich   it **gets** bigger and bigger   you have **made** money<br>it **takes** two hours **to do** 123 kilometres |
|---|

**2** Here are some more examples.

**A** How long does it take you to get ready in the morning?
**B** It takes me about fifteen minutes.

**A** How long does it take you to get to school?
**B** I can get here in twenty minutes.

**A** Do you get tired in the evening?
**B** Yes. Especially if I've done a lot of homework.

**A** Do you make a lot of mistakes in English?
**B** Well, I do my best, but I still make a few mistakes.

Ask and answer the same questions with a partner.

**3** Put the words and phrases from the box in the correct column.

| some shopping   back home   two tablets a day   a cold<br>angry   sure   friends   up your mind   a photo<br>somebody out for a meal   me a favour   a reservation<br>on well with someone   a complaint   care |
|---|

| TAKE | GET | DO | MAKE |
|---|---|---|---|
| | | | |

**4** Complete the sentences with one of the verb phrases. Use the correct form of the verb.

1 I _________ while I was in town. I bought myself a new jumper.
2 'I don't know if I love Tom or Henry.' '_________ . You can't marry both of them.'
3 Bye-bye! See you soon. _________ of yourself.
4 Aachoo! Oh dear. I think _________ .
5 'Are the doors locked?' 'I think so, but I'll just _________ .'

**T 9.5** Listen and check.

**5** Discuss these questions with a partner.

- How long does it take to get from your school to the station? From your home to work?
- When did you last do someone a favour/make a complaint/take a photo/get angry?
- What time did you get home last night?
- Do you get on with your parents/your neighbours?
- Do you find it easy to make friends?
- Is your English getting better?

# EVERYDAY ENGLISH

## In a hotel

**1** What is the best hotel in your town? What facilities does the hotel have?

**2** Ask and answer questions with a partner about the Grand Hotel.

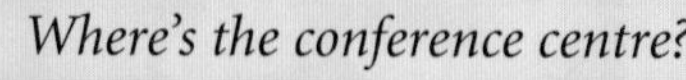


*On the second floor.*

**The Grand Hotel**

| | |
|---|---|
| Ground Floor | Reception<br>City Bar |
| First Floor | Dining Room<br>Buckingham Rooms |
| Second Floor | Conference Centre |
| Top Floor | Panorama Restaurant |
| Basement | Gym<br>Swimming pool |

**3** Put the lines from the telephone conversation between the receptionist and client in the right order.

**Receptionist** Hello, the Grand Hotel. Cathy speaking. How can I help you?
**Client** reservation / make / like / a / I'd / to / please

_______________________________________________ .

**Receptionist** Certainly. When is it for?
**Client** It's for two nights, the thirteenth and the fourteenth of this month.
**Receptionist** single / want / do / room / or / double / a / And / you / a

_______________________________________________ ?

**Client** A single, please.
**Receptionist** OK. Yes, that's fine. I have a room for you. And your name is?
**Client** Robert Palmer.
much / you / Can / it / tell / how / is / me

_______________________________________________ ?

**Receptionist** Yes. That's £95 a night. Can I have a credit card number, please?
**Client** Yes, sure. It's a Visa. 4929 7983 0621 8849.
**Receptionist** Thank you.
number / could / And / phone / I / have / a

_______________________________________________ ?

**Client** Uh huh. 01727 489962.
**Receptionist** That's fine.
forward / look / seeing / on / you / We / to / thirteenth / the

_______________________________________________ . Bye-bye.

**Client** Thanks a lot. Goodbye.

**T 9.6** Listen and check.

**4** With a partner, roleplay the conversation between Robert Palmer and the receptionist as he checks into the hotel.

*Good evening.*

*Hello. I have a reservation. My name's Robert Palmer.*

**5** Roleplay these conversations with your partner. Phone Reception from your room. Make these requests.

- You can't get the TV to work.
- You'd like an extra pillow.
- You'd like to order Room Service.
- You'd like a wake-up call at 7.00 tomorrow morning.

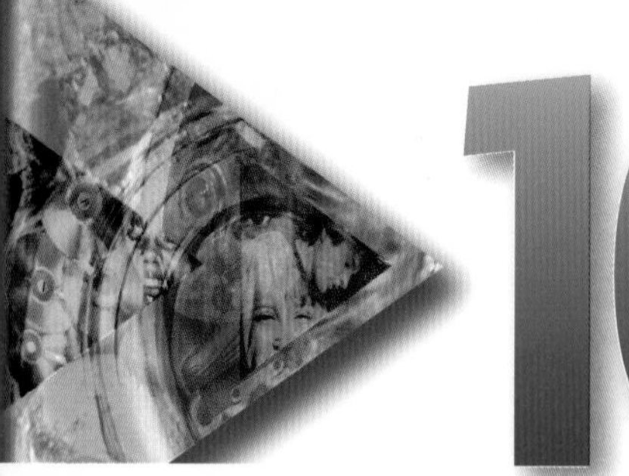

# 10 Scared to death

**Verb patterns 2 - *manage to, used to* • *-ed/-ing* adjectives • Exclamations**

**STARTER** 

1 What are these people afraid of? How do they feel?

2 What are you afraid of? Why?

## A WALK WITH DEATH

### Verb patterns and infinitives

1 Look at the photograph. Does the path look safe to you?

Read about Paul Lay's adventure. How did he feel at different times in the story?

2 Complete the text using these words.

| began to feel started aching<br>used to have went camping<br>decided to stand up |
|---|

**T 10.1** Listen and check.

3 Answer the questions.

1. What is Paul Lay's hobby?
2. What did he use to do with his father?
3. Does he go to the same place every year?
4. Is the King's Way in good condition?
5. Why couldn't he have a rest?
6. Why didn't he enjoy the walk?

# Don't look down

**Paul Lay dances with death in the mountains of southern Spain**

I have always enjoyed walking. When I was a boy, I used to go walking at weekends with my father. We (1) ______ and climbing together.

I try to visit a new place every year. Last year I decided to walk a path in Spain called *El Camino del Rey*, which means the King's Way. It is one of the highest and most dangerous footpaths in Europe. It used to be very safe, but now it is falling down.

I took a train to the village of El Chorro and started to walk towards the mountains. I was very excited. Then the adventure began.

The path was about three feet wide and there were holes in it. It (2) ______ a handrail, but not any more. I didn't know what to do – should I go on my hands and knees, or stand up? I (3) ______ and walk very slowly. At times the path was only as wide as my two boots. I stopped to have a rest, but there was nowhere to sit.

I (4) ______ very frightened. It was impossible to look down or look up. I was concentrating so hard that my body (5) ______ . There was no thrill of danger, no enjoyment of the view. I thought I was going to die.

I finally managed to get to the end. I was shaking, and I was covered in sweat from heat and fear. I fell to the ground, exhausted.

## GRAMMAR SPOT

1. Are these verbs followed by the infinitive or *-ing* in the text?
   enjoy try decide start begin manage
2. Find the examples of *used to* + infinitive.
   *Used to* expresses a past action which doesn't happen any more.
   *I **used to** play games with my brother, but now I don't.*
   Notice the pronunciation /juːst tʊ/.
3. Complete these examples from the text.
   I used to go __________ at weekends.
   I didn't know what __________ .
   I stopped __________ a rest.
   It was impossible __________ down.
   There was nowhere __________ .

▶▶ **Grammar Reference 10.1–10.4 p139**

# PRACTICE

## Discussing grammar

**1** Complete these sentences with the verb *ski* in the correct form.

1. I go ________ every winter.
2. I started ________ when I was six.
3. I tried ________ down the mountain, but it was too steep.
4. My instructor made me ________ down the steep mountain.
5. I enjoy ________ very much.
6. Dave used ________ when he was younger, but not any more.

**2** Choose the correct form.

1. I've decided *stop / to stop / stopping* smoking.
2. I managed *find / to find / finding* my passport.
3. Let's go *shop / to shop / shopping*!
4. Please let me *go / to go / going* to the party!
5. Would you like something *eat / to eat / eating*?
6. I need a recipe for a cake that's easy *make / to make / making*.

## When I was young, I used to ...

**3** **T 10.2** Listen to James talking about his childhood and his life now. Complete the chart. Write one sentence with *used to* for each question.

| | Life as a child |
|---|---|
| 1 What/do at the weekend? | |
| 2 What/do in the evening? | |
| 3 Where/go on holiday? | |
| 4 What sports/play? | |
| 5 What TV programmes/like? | |
| 6 What food/like? | |

James

Ask and answer the questions above with a partner about your life now and your life as a child.

*What do you do at the weekend?*

*I usually go shopping and ...*

*What did you do when you were a child?*

*I used to play with my friends and ...*

## Infinitives

**4** Why do you go to these places?

*Why do you go to the hairdresser's?*

*To have a haircut.*

- the post office
- a petrol station
- a bookshop
- the newsagent's
- the library
- the market

With your partner, ask and answer questions about more places.

**5** Make sentences with a line in **A**, a word in **B**, and an infinitive in **C**.

| A | B | C |
|---|---|---|
| 1 I'm hungry. I need | how | to say to you. |
| 2 I'm going to a posh party, but I don't know | anything | to talk to. |
| 3 My CD player's broken. Can you show me | where | to eat. |
| 4 Don't talk to me. I have | somebody | to wear. |
| 5 Do I turn left or right? I don't know | how much | to repair it? |
| 6 I'm bored. I haven't got | nothing | to do. |
| 7 'Can you get some meat?' 'Sure. Tell me | something | to go. |
| 8 I feel lonely. I need | what | to buy.' |

**T 10.3** Think of some replies. Then listen and compare your answers.

## Check it

**6** Choose the correct form.

1 I went to the shops *for to buy / for buy / to buy* some shoes.
2 Do you enjoy *dance / dancing / to dance*?
3 When I was young, I used *to go / go / going* ice-skating.
4 He told me he loves me. I didn't know what *say / to say / saying*.
5 When we were on holiday, we went *swim / to swim / swimming* every day.

## VOCABULARY
### -*ed*/-*ing* adjectives

**1** How can you describe the experiences below? Use an adjective from the box.

| frightening exciting surprising terrifying boring exhausting |
|---|

1 You get stuck in a lift.
2 You go on a 15-mile walk, then climb three mountains.
3 You go on the biggest roller coaster in the world.
4 You find a spider in the bath.
5 Someone shows you their holiday photos for hours and hours …
6 Your teacher says 'You're all such wonderful students that I won't give you any more homework.'

**2** How do the people in the photos feel?

***He's frightened.***

**T 10.4** Listen and practise the pronunciation of these words.

> **!**
> 1 -*ing* adjectives describe a situation, person, or thing.
> an **interesting** life
> a **boring** teacher
> an **exciting** film
>
> 2 -*ed* adjectives describe how people feel.
> I'm very **interested** in modern art.
> We were **bored** at the end of the lesson.
> She's **excited** about going on holiday tomorrow.

**3** Complete the sentences. Use one of these adjectives.

| | |
|---|---|
| excit-<br>frighten-<br>bor-<br>interest-<br>confus-<br>disappoint-<br>worry/worri-<br>surpris- | -ed<br><br>-ing |

1 'I met a famous film star today.' 'Really? How ________ !'
2 'I spent four hours going round a museum.' 'Was it ________ ?' 'No, it was ________ .'
3 'I haven't heard from my parents for two months.' 'You must be ________ .'
4 'Wow, Maria! What are you doing here?' 'Why are you so ________ to see me?'
5 I failed my exam. I worked really hard for it. I'm so ________ .
6 'A man started to follow me home last night.' 'Weren't you ________ ?'
7 My computer's broken, and I don't understand the manual. It's so ________ .

**T 10.5** Close your books. Listen to the beginnings of the lines. Complete them.

**4** What have you seen on television or in the cinema recently? What books have you read? What did you think of them? Tell a partner.

> *I read a spy novel. It was very exciting.*

> *I saw a horror film. I thought it was frightening.*

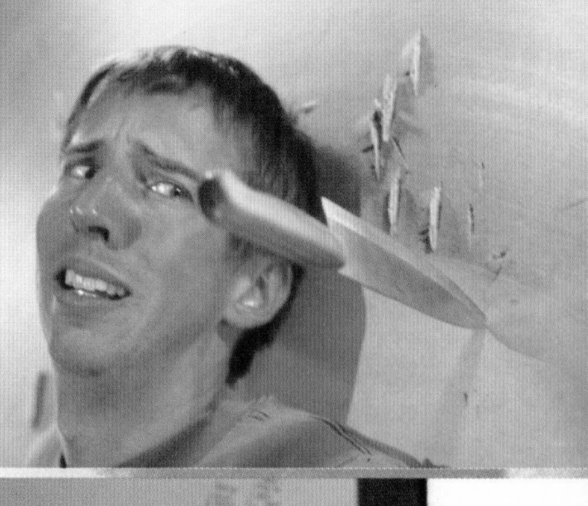

# READING AND SPEAKING

## Into the wild

**1** Describe what you can see in the photograph. Which country do you think it is? What makes life difficult for people who live here?

**2** Read the introductory paragraph and the words in **bold**. In pairs, decide whether these statements are true (✓) or false (✗).

- Chris McCandless died very young.
- He was killed by hunters.
- He didn't enjoy his life.
- He loved nature and a simple life.
- He wanted to die.
- He knew he was dying.

What do you want to know about Chris?

**3** Read to the line ending "… *Thank you!' his diary reads.*" and answer the questions.

1 Did Chris keep in touch with his parents? When did they last hear from him?
2 Why did he get rid of his car and burn his money?
3 What did he need? What didn't he need?
4 In what way was his life rich?

**4** Read to the line ending "… *I didn't know where he was.*" Choose the best answer.

1 Chris didn't get on with his father because his father
- ☐ had a lot of money.
- ☐ didn't let Chris work in the family business.
- ☐ tried to tell Chris what to do.

2 When the parents didn't hear from Chris,
- ☐ the police got in touch with them.
- ☐ they got in touch with the police.
- ☐ they did nothing.

3 In July 1992
- ☐ his mother dreamt that she heard Chris calling her.
- ☐ his mother is sure that she heard Chris calling her.
- ☐ Chris phoned his mother for help.

**5** Read to the end. Correct the mistakes in this summary.

Chris got the train to Alaska, and arrived in May, 1992. He lived in a bus, and there was a bed and a bath in it. He was very happy. There was lots to eat – small animals, and fruit and vegetables, which he grew himself.

After five months of living alone, he started to feel ill. He had no strength because he was eating poisonous plants, but he didn't know that this was the reason. He continued eating. He died of food poisoning.

He knew he was dying. He wrote a letter to his parents, and took a photo of himself. He seemed happy to die in these circumstances.

### What do you think?

- What was important to Chris? What wasn't important?
- What do you think he was trying to do?
- Why do young people feel the need to break away from their parents?

**In April 1992, Chris McCandless, a young man from a wealthy American family, hitchhiked to Alaska. Four months later, his dead body was found by a group of hunters. Jon Krakauer investigated the story.**

When Chris McCandless graduated from Emory University, Atlanta, in June 1990, he sent his parents a letter containing his final reports. His letter ended 'Say 'Hi' to everyone for me.'

No one in Chris's family ever heard from him again.

He drove west out of Atlanta, and invented a new life for himself with a new name. He left his car in some woods and burned all his money, because, as he wrote in his diary, **'I need no possessions. I can survive with just nature.'**

For the next two years, he hitched to various parts of the United States and

# Into the wild

Mexico. He wanted the freedom to go where he wanted and to work when he needed. For him, his life was very rich. '**God, it's great to be alive. Thank you! Thank you!**' his diary reads.

Chris came from a comfortable background. His father had a business which he ran efficiently, and he controlled his own family in a similar way. Chris and his father didn't get on. When his parents didn't hear from him for several months, they contacted the police, but they could do nothing. In July 1992, two years after Chris left Atlanta, his mother woke in the middle of the night. 'I could hear Chris calling me. I wasn't dreaming. He was begging, 'Mom! Help me!' But I couldn't help him because I didn't know where he was.'

**'I need no possessions. I can survive with just nature.'**

Chris's dream was to spend some time in Alaska, and this is where he went in April 1992. In early May, after a few days in the Alaskan bush, Chris found an old bus which hunters used for shelter. It had a bed and a stove. He decided to stay there for a while. '**Total freedom,**' he wrote. '**My home is the road.**'

However, reality soon changed the dream. He was hungry, and it was difficult to find enough to eat. He shot ducks, squirrels, birds, and sometimes a moose, and with these he ate wild potatoes, wild mushrooms, and berries. He was losing a lot of weight.

On July 30 he wrote, '**Extremely weak. Fault of potato seed. Can't stand up. Starving. Danger.**' It seems that Chris was eating a part of the wild potato plant that was poisonous. He couldn't get out of the bus to look for food. '**I am trapped in the wild,**' he wrote on August 5.

He became weaker and weaker as he was starving to death. His final note says, '**I have had a good life and thank the Lord. Goodbye and may God bless all!**'

Then he crawled into his sleeping bag and lost consciousness. He probably died on August 18. One of the last things he did was to take a photo of himself, one hand holding his final note, the other hand raised in a brave goodbye. His face is horribly thin, but he is smiling in the picture, and the look in his eyes says 'I am at peace.'

# LISTENING AND SPEAKING

## It was just a joke

**1** In Britain, your eighteenth birthday is important, because it is the birthday when you become an adult. Which birthdays are special in your country? What do people do?

**2** You will hear a boy called Jamie describing what he did on his friend's eighteenth birthday. It was just a joke, but it looked serious! Look at the pictures. What do you think happened? Check that you know these words.

| to kidnap | a balaclava | to tie up | a blindfold | a witness |
|---|---|---|---|---|

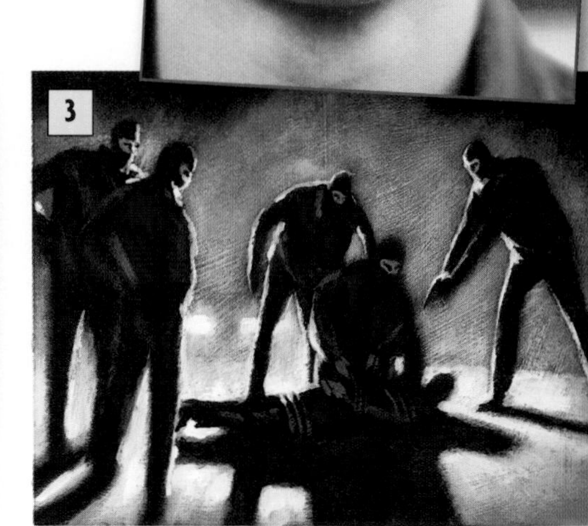

**3** **T 10.6** Listen to Jamie being interviewed. Does he tell the story in the same order as the pictures?

4 Answer the questions.

1 Identify these people in the pictures.

| Tom Jamie Dave Andrew the witness |
|---|

2 Imagine who says these lines in the story.

- I've had a really good idea for Tom's birthday!
- Lie on the ground! Don't move!
- Please let me go!
- Send the police immediately!
- Come and help. This looks really serious.
- Happy birthday, dear Tom!
- You *****s! I thought you were my friends!
- I knew it was you from the beginning!
- Excuse me, gentlemen. Can I just ask you a few questions?
- I think we have a bit of a confession to make.

### Roleplay

With a partner, roleplay one of these conversations and retell the story.

- Tom talking to his girlfriend
- the witness talking to the emergency services
- Jamie talking to the policeman

# EVERYDAY ENGLISH

## Exclamations with *so* and *such*

**1** **T 10.7** Read and listen to the sentences.

*Tom was scared. He was very scared. He was so scared!*

Do you think this use of *so* is more written or spoken? What effect does it have?

**2** Look at the sentences. When do we use *so*, *such a(n)*, *such*, *so many*, and *so much*?

We were all *so worried*!
Mike's *such an idiot*!
It was *such a good idea* of Jamie's!
He has *such crazy friends*!
We had *such awful weather* on holiday!
There are *so many places* I want to go to!
I've got *so much work*!

**3** Complete the sentences in **A** with *so*, *such a*, *such*, *so many*, or *so much*. Then match them with the sentences in **B**.

| A | B |
|---|---|
| 1 Their house is ________ mess! | I could eat a horse. |
| 2 There were ________ people at the party! | I don't know where it's all gone. |
| 3 I'm ________ hungry! | You really didn't have to. |
| 4 Jane and Pete are ________ nice people! | She understands every word I say. |
| 5 I've spent ________ money this week! | There was nowhere to dance. |
| 6 A present! For me? You're ________ kind! | Thank you so much for inviting us. |
| 7 We've had ________ nice time! | But I can't stand their kids. |
| 8 Molly's ________ clever dog! | I don't know how they live in it. |

**T 10.8** Listen and check. Practise the exclamations.

**4** What can you say … ?

- at the end of a long journey

- when you finish an interesting book with a sad ending
- as you go round a friend's new flat
- at the end of a wonderful meal
- in a row with your boyfriend/girlfriend
- at the end of a great English lesson

# 11 Things that changed the world

**Passives • Verbs and nouns that go together • Notices**

**STARTER** 

1 Make true sentences from the chart.
2 What is made and grown in your country?

| | | | |
|---|---|---|---|
| Champagne<br>Whisky<br>Rice<br>Rolls Royce cars<br>Nikon cameras<br>Coffee<br>Pineapples | is<br>are | made in<br>grown in | Japan.<br>France.<br>England.<br>Hawaii.<br>Brazil.<br>China.<br>Scotland. |

## SOLD WORLDWIDE

### Passives

**1** Do you drink Coca-Cola? Do you think these facts about Coca-Cola are true (✓) or false (✗)?

1 ☐ 1.6 billion gallons are sold every day.
2 ☐ Coca-Cola is drunk in every country in the world.
3 ☐ It was invented in the USA.
4 ☐ It is nearly 100 years old.

Read the story of Coca-Cola and check your ideas.

## Things go better with Coca-Cola

**Coca-Cola is enjoyed all over the world.**

1.6 billion gallons are sold every year, in over one hundred and sixty countries. The drink was invented by Dr John Pemberton in Atlanta as a health drink on 8 May 1886, but it was given the name Coca-Cola by his partner, Frank Robinson, because it was originally made from the coca plant. In the first year, only nine drinks a day were sold.

The business was bought by a man called Asa Candler in 1888, and the first factory was opened in Dallas, Texas, in 1895. Coca-Cola is still made there. Billions of bottles and cans have been produced since 1895, but the recipe is still kept secret!

Diet Coke has been made since 1982, and over the years many clever advertisements have been used to sell the product. It is certain that Coca-Cola will be drunk far into the twenty-first century.

## GRAMMAR SPOT

1 Nearly all the verb forms in the text about Coca-Cola are in the passive. The passive is formed with the verb *to be* and the past participle.

Champagne **is made** in France.
Pineapples **are grown** in Hawaii.

2 Read the text again and write the passive verb forms under these headings.

| Present Simple | Past Simple | Present Perfect | *will* Future |
|---|---|---|---|
| is enjoyed | was invented | have been produced | |

3 What is the main interest of the text? Dr John Pemberton? Frank Robinson? Coca-Cola?

When we are more interested in the object of the active sentence, we use the passive.

**Active:** Dr John Pemberton invented Cola-Cola.
**Passive:** Cola-Cola was invented by Dr John Pemberton.

▶▶ **Grammar Reference 11.1 p140**

**2** Don't look at the text! Look at the passive verb forms in the columns above and try to remember the whole sentence.

*Coca-Cola is enjoyed all over …*

*It was invented by …*

# PRACTICE

## Active and passive

**1** Complete these sentences.

| Active | Passive |
|---|---|
| 1 They make Rolls Royce cars in England. | Rolls Royce cars *are made* ________ in England. |
| 2 They ________ rice in China. | Rice is grown in China. |
| 3 Bell invented the telephone in 1876. | The telephone ________ by Bell in 1876. |
| 4 Thieves ________ two pictures from the museum last night. | Two pictures were stolen from the museum last night. |
| 5 They have built three new factories this year. | Three new factories ________ this year. |
| 6 They ________ the picture for £3,000. | The picture has been sold for £3,000. |
| 7 The factory will produce 10,000 cars next year. | 10,000 cars ________ next year. |
| 8 ________ they ________ many cars last year? | Were many cars made last year? |
| 9 Bell didn't invent the television. | The television ________ by Bell. |

**2** Put the verbs in brackets in the correct tense, active or passive.

### The History of the Hamburger

The hamburger is the most eaten food in the whole world. The first hamburgers (1) ________ (make) and sold in Connecticut in 1895 by an American chef called Louis Lassen. Louis (2) ________ (call) them hamburgers because he (3) ________ (give) the recipe by sailors from Hamburg in Germany. Hamburgers (4) ________ (become) a favourite in America in the early part of the twentieth century. Their popularity (5) ________ (grow) even more after the Second World War, when they (6) ________ (buy) in large quantities by teenagers who (7) ________ (prefer) fast food to family meals. In 1948 two brothers, Dick and Mac McDonald (8) ________ (open) a drive-in hamburger restaurant in San Bernardino, California. Since then over 25,000 McDonald's restaurants (9) ________ (open) worldwide and now 35 million McDonald's hamburgers (10) ________ (eat) every day in 115 countries from India to the Arctic Circle.

### Questions and answers

**3** Match the question words and answers.

| | |
|---|---|
| When?<br>Where?<br>Who?<br>Why?<br>How many? | Louis Lassen.<br>In Connecticut.<br>In 1895.<br>In 1948.<br>Because the recipe came from Hamburg.<br>25,000.<br>35 million. |

**4** Complete the questions using the passive. Ask and answer them with a partner.

**T 11.1** Listen and check.

**5** Complete the conversations and practise them with a partner.

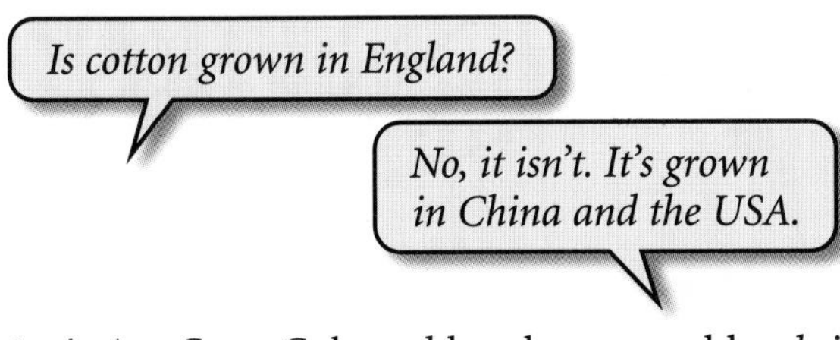


1 **A** Are Coca-Cola and hamburgers sold *only* in America?
**B** No, they aren't. They _______ .
2 **A** Was Cola-Cola invented by Louis Lassen?
**B** No, it _______ .
3 **A** Were the first hamburgers made in 1948?
**B** No, they _______ .
4 **A** Was the first McDonald's restaurant opened in New York?
**B** No, it _______ .
5 **A** Have 2,500 restaurants now been opened worldwide?
**B** No, not 2,500. _______ .

**T 11.2** Listen and check.

### Check it

**6** Underline the correct word or words in each sentence.

1 Where *was / were* these shoes made?
2 I was given this watch *by / from* my aunt.
3 Someone *has stolen / has been stolen* my bag!
4 The newsagent *sells / is sold* stamps.
5 British policemen *don't carry / aren't carried* guns.
6 All the beer was *drank / drunk* by nine o'clock.
7 Have all the sandwiches *eaten / been eaten*?

## VOCABULARY
### Verbs and nouns that go together

**1** In each box below, one noun does *not* go with the verb. Which one?

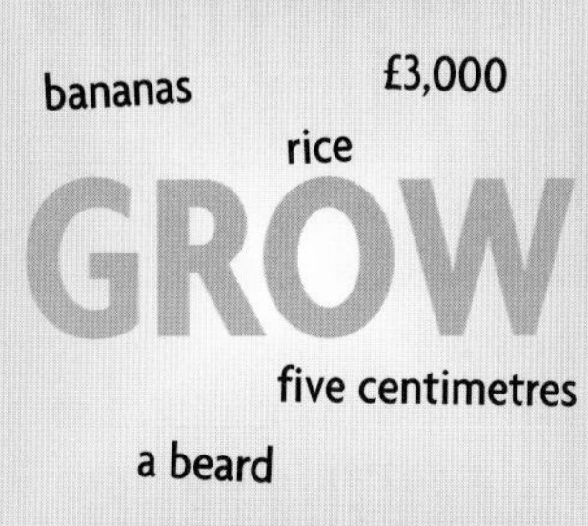


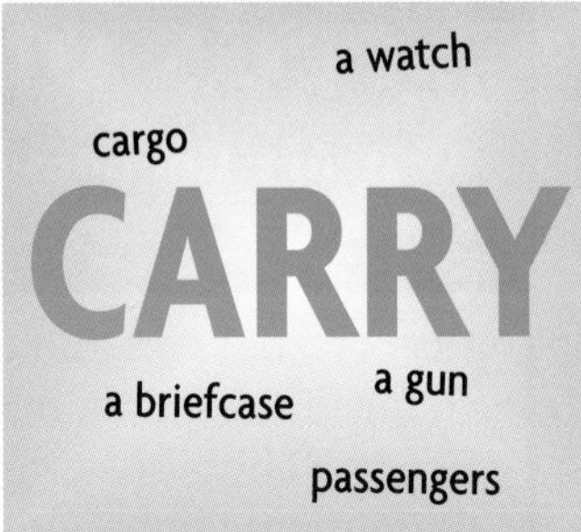


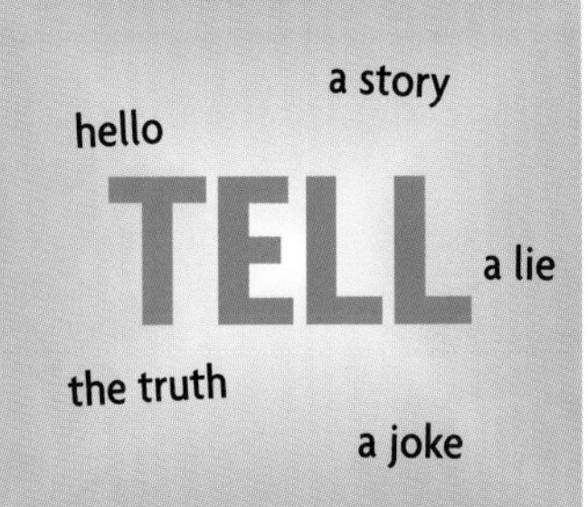

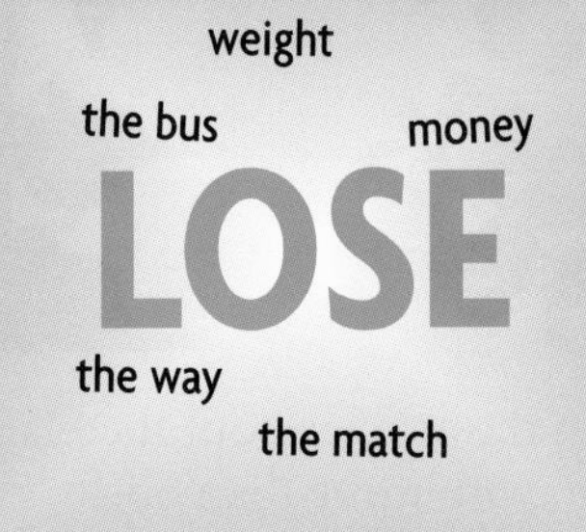

**2** Work with a partner. Choose two nouns from each box, and write two sentences using the verb. Read your sentences to the class.

***Rice is grown in China.***
***The ship carried a cargo of tobacco and cotton.***

**3** Which six nouns do not go with the verbs? Which verbs do they go with? Complete the sentences with the correct verbs.

1 _______ hello to your parents from me when you see them.
2 I was late for work because I _______ the bus.
3 This is my grandfather's watch. He _______ it every day until he died.
4 I _______ just _______ a good idea. Let's eat out tonight.
5 My uncle _______ £500 on the stock exchange.
6 We _______ a complaint to the manager because our meal was so bad.

# READING AND SPEAKING

## Three plants that changed the world

**1** Read the introduction to a book review. What is the book about?

# Seeds of Change

**By Henry Hobhouse**
Reviewed by Donald Crisp

History books are full of the ways in which the actions of men and women have changed the world, but what about plants? Which plants have changed history? Henry Hobhouse, farmer and journalist, discusses this topic in his fascinating and illuminating book *Seeds of Change*.

**2** Look at these drawings. Do you recognize the three plants?

**1**

**2**

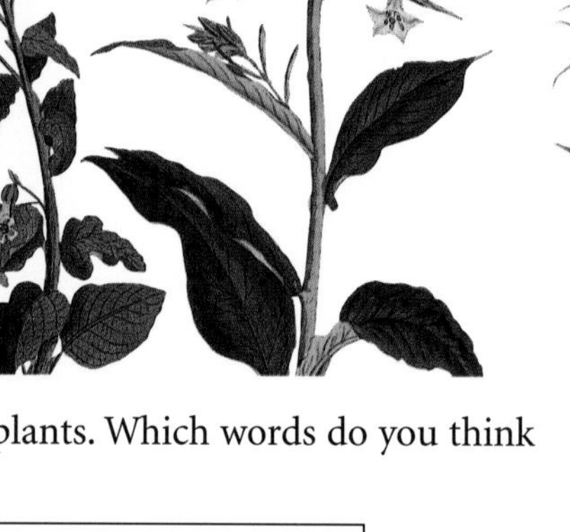

**3**

**3** All the words below appear in the article about the plants. Which words do you think go with which plant? Some go with more than one.

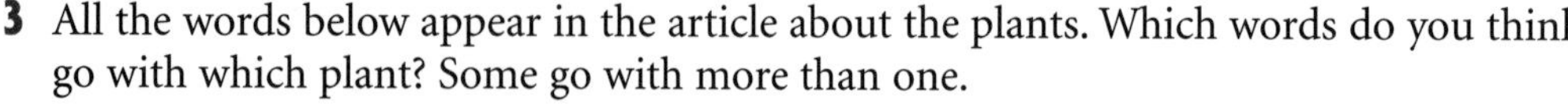

| **nouns:** | addict soil fabric silk plantation slaves lung cancer luxury |
|---|---|
| **verbs:** | chain-smoke inhale ban sweeten refine chew harvest |

**4** Work in three groups.
**Group A** Read about tobacco. **Group B** Read about sugar. **Group C** Read about cotton.

**5** Which words from exercise 3 are in your text? What are the bad effects of the plant? What are the good effects? Discuss in your group.

**6** Compare plants with two students from the other groups. Answer the questions.

**Which plant (or plants) . . .**

- has been grown for thousands of years?
- was known as white gold? Why?
- was once thought to be a luxury?
- caused the American Civil War? Why?
- was the main American export until 1820?
- became the main American export after 1820?
- was harvested by slaves?
- has caused the death of many people?

### What do you think?

- Which of the three plants has *most* changed history? How?
- Which plant has done the greatest good? Which has done the greatest harm?

# Tobacco

For thousands of years **tobacco** was used by the American Indians with no ill-effect. In the 16th century it was brought to Europe. This early tobacco was mixed with soil and rather dirty. It was chewed or smoked in pipes only by men – women thought it smelly and disgusting.

It was first grown commercially in America in the 17th century on slave plantations. In the 18th century new technology refined tobacco and the first cigarettes were produced. By the 1880s huge factories were producing cigarettes which were clean and easy to smoke. Chain-smoking and inhaling became possible and by the middle of the 20th century tobacco addicts, both men and women, were dying of lung cancer in great numbers.

Nowadays cigarette smoking is banned in many places, especially in the USA. But until 1820 tobacco was America's main export, and still today their tobacco industry makes over $4.2 billion a year.

# Sugar

**Sugar** cane was grown in India thousands of years ago. In Roman times it was known in Europe as a great luxury, and it was rare and expensive for many centuries after that. In 1493 Columbus took a sugar plant with him to the West Indies, where it grew so well that huge plantations were started by Europeans and worked on by slaves. The slaves were shipped across the Atlantic from Africa, packed sometimes one on top of the other in chains, on a journey that took six weeks. Many died. The empty ships then carried the sugar back to Europe. So much money was made that sugar was known as 'white gold'.

Sugar is used to sweeten food and make sweets and chocolate. It is addictive but unnecessary. By the 16th century the English were the greatest sugar-eaters in history. Elizabeth I lost *all* her teeth because she ate so much of it.

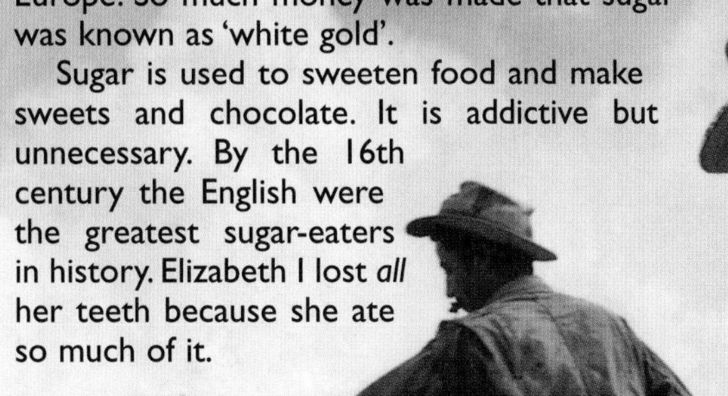

# Cotton

**Cotton** has been grown for over five thousand years in places as far apart as Mexico, China, Egypt, and India. It was first planted in America in 1607. Before 1800 cotton was a great luxury, more expensive than silk, because so many workers were needed to pick it. However, a huge increase in the number of slaves in the American South resulted in much greater cotton production and a fall in the price. This, and the new technology of the industrial revolution, made cotton the cheapest fabric in history. By 1820 cotton was making more money for the USA than tobacco, and more money worldwide than sugar.

The American Civil War of 1861–1865 was fought because the Southern States wanted to form a separate country, so that they could continue to keep slaves on their cotton plantations. Slavery was banned in the Northern States in 1808. 500,000 soldiers were killed in the war.

# LISTENING AND SPEAKING

## The world's most common habit: chewing gum

**1** Do you chew gum? How often? Stand up and ask the students in the class. Complete the chart below.

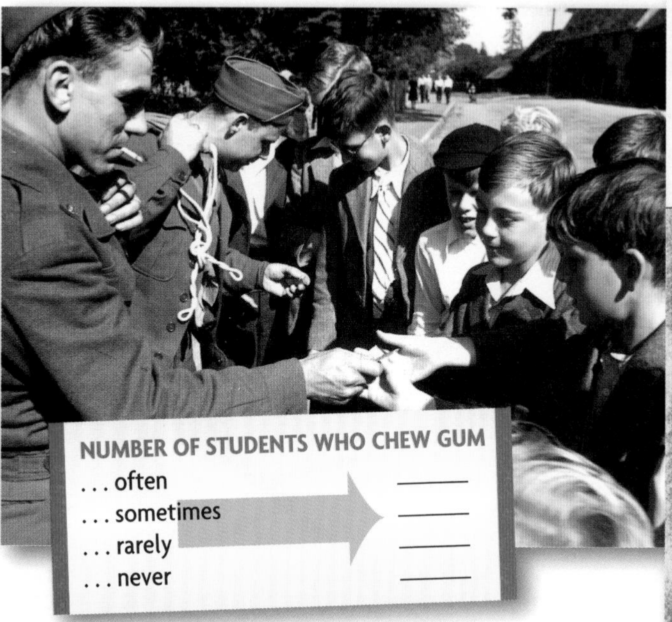


**2** Discuss these questions as a class.

1 Who often chews gum? Who never chews gum?
2 When and where do you chew gum?
3 Where do you put it when it has lost its flavour?

**3** You are going to listen to a radio programme about chewing gum. Check the meaning of these words. Which have an obvious connection with the topic of chewing gum? How?

| | | |
|---|---|---|
| skeleton *(n)* | to freshen (the breath) *(v)* | tree sap *(n)* |
| honey *(n)* | to wrap *(v)* | packet *(n)* |
| to hire *(v)* | billboard *(n) (Am. Eng.)* | |

**4** Read the statements below. Do you think they are true (✓) or false (✗)? Discuss with a partner.

1 ☐ One million tons of gum is chewed every year.
2 ☐ Chewing gum was invented in Sweden.
3 ☐ Chewing gum was found in the mouth of a nine thousand-year-old skeleton.
4 ☐ The first gum was made of tree sap and sugar.
5 ☐ Babies are born wanting to chew gum.
6 ☐ The ancient Greeks believed chewing gum was good for your health.
7 ☐ South American Indians made the first packets of chewing gum.
8 ☐ Chewing gum was taken to North America by the English.

**T 11.3** Listen to part one of the programme and check your ideas. Correct the false sentences.

**5** **T 11.4** Listen to part two of the programme. Answer the questions.

1 Who was William Wrigley?
2 What did he do to advertise chewing gum?
3 When did chewing gum become popular outside the USA?
4 What did the children shout?
5 What is today's chewing gum made of?

### What do you think?

- Is chewing gum a common habit in your country?
- Is it considered a bad habit? Why/Why not?
- Is chewing gum good for you? Why/Why not?

# EVERYDAY ENGLISH
## Notices

**1** When you first go to a foreign country, it can be difficult to understand notices. Here are some typical English notices. Match them with these places.

1 [l] a bank or a post office
2 [ ] a petrol station
3 [ ] a broken drinks machine
4 [ ] a road in a town
5 [ ] an airport
6 [ ] a pub
7 [ ] the Underground
8 [ ] a park
9 [ ] a zoo
10 [ ] a hotel
11 [ ] a railway station
12 [ ] a public toilet
13 [ ] a motorway

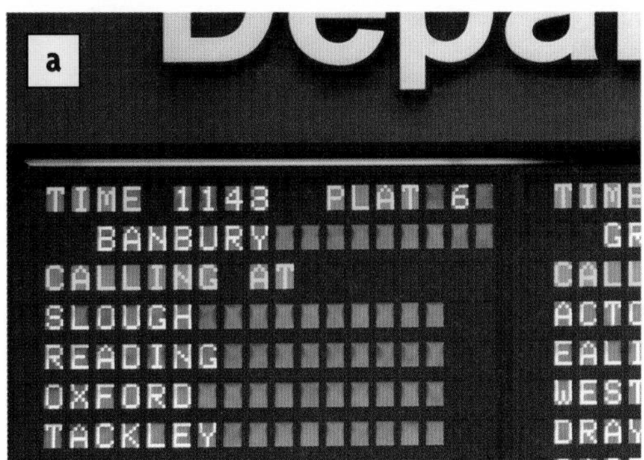

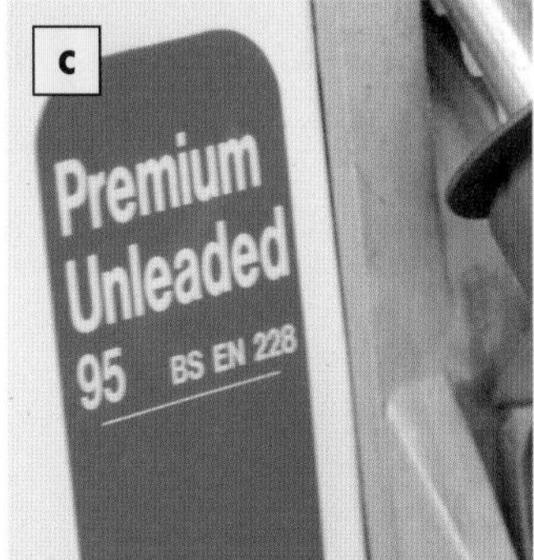

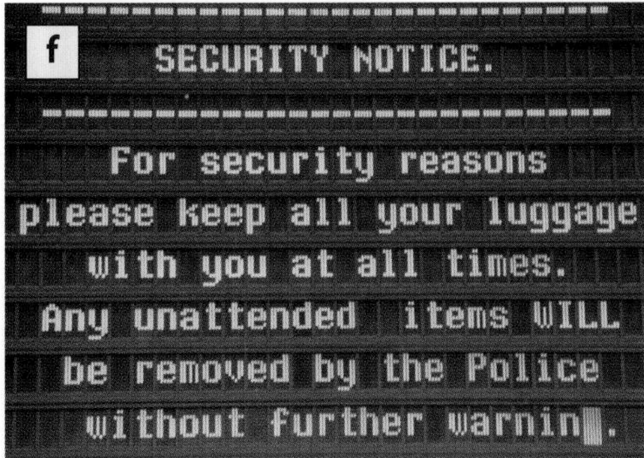

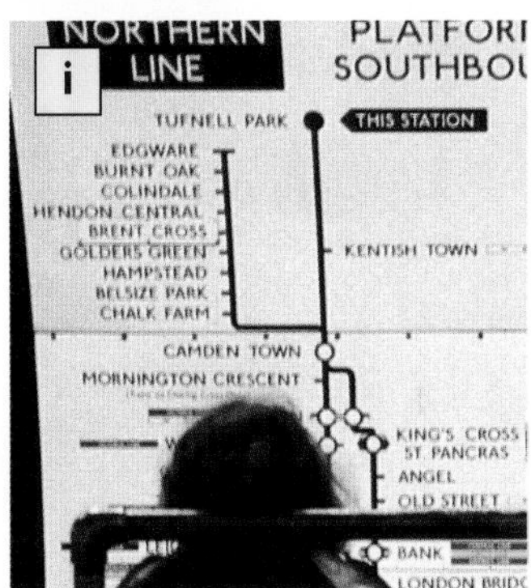

**2** T 11.5 Listen to five conversations. Where are the people?

**3** Work with a partner. Choose two other places, and write conversations that could happen there. Read them to the class, and see if they can guess the place.

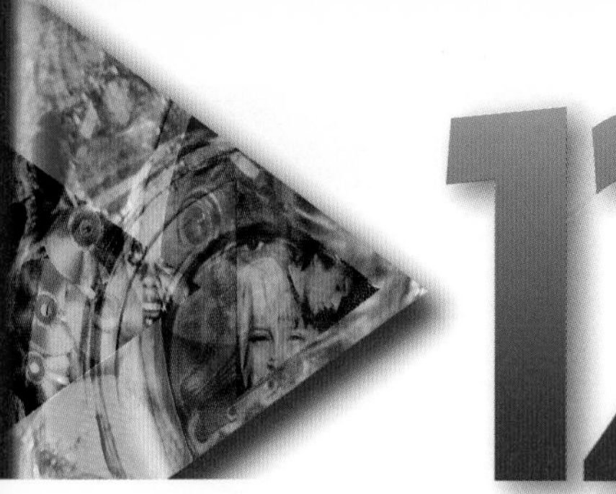

# 12 Dreams and reality

**Second conditional • *might* • Phrasal verbs • Social expressions 2**

**STARTER** 

1. Which famous person would you like to meet? What would you talk about?
2. Which country would you like to visit? What would you do there?
3. If you won a lot of money, what would you buy? How much would you give to friends?

## SWEET DREAMS

### Second conditional

**1** Read about Nicola. Which text describes her life? Which describes her dreams?

I live in a flat with my Mum and my little brother. My Mum works in a hospital, so my Gran often looks after us and she helps my Mum. We have a budgie. I go to St Barnabas School and I wear a green uniform. I can only have sweets on Saturdays.

Nicola, aged 7

If I were a princess, I'd live in a ________ . I'd have ________ to look after me. My Mum would be Queen, and she wouldn't work. I wouldn't go to school. I'd have a private ________ . I'd ride a white ________ , and I'd wear a long ________ . I could have all the ________ I wanted.

**2** Complete the text on the right with these words.

| horse | sweets | palace | dress | teacher | servants |
|---|---|---|---|---|---|

**T 12.1** Listen and check. Then listen and repeat.

## GRAMMAR SPOT

1 What tense describes Nicola's real life?

2 *If I lived in a palace, . . .*
Does she live in a palace? What tense is *lived*?
*. . . I'd have servants.* (I'd = I would)
Is this a dream or reality?

3 Complete the rule.
We make unreal conditional clauses with *if* + the _____ tense.
In the result clause, we use the auxiliary verb _____ + the infinitive.

4 Notice that *was* can change to *were* in the condition clause.
*If I were a princess, . . .*

▶▶ **Grammar Reference 12.1 p141**

**3** Look at the questions and short answers.

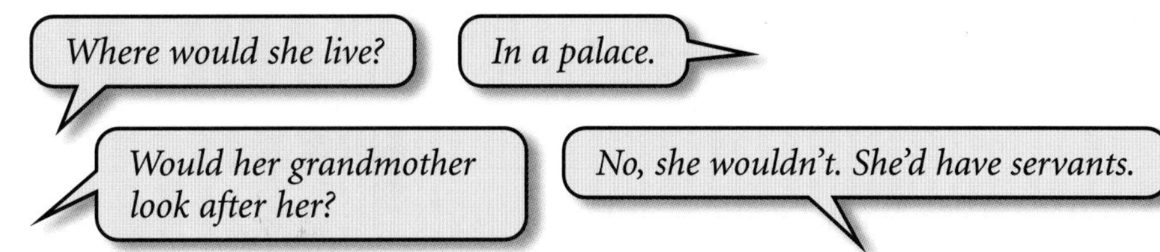


Ask and answer questions about Nicola's dreams with a partner.

- What . . . her mother do?
- . . . work?
- . . . Nicola go to school?
- What pet . . . have?
- What . . . wear?
- . . . have a lot of sweets?

# PRACTICE

## Discussing grammar

**1** Make sentences from the chart.

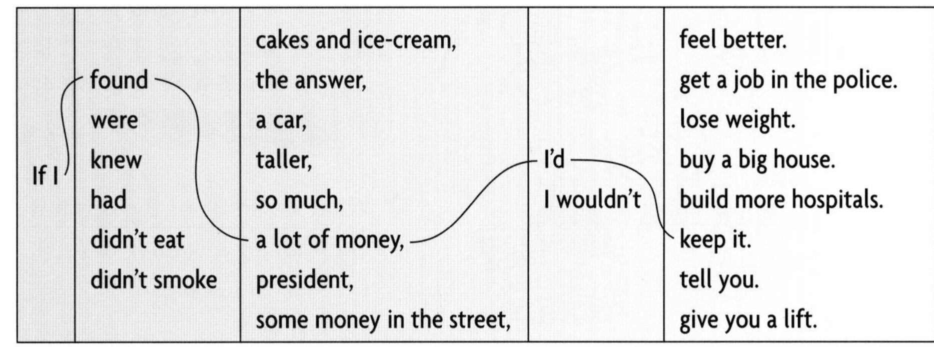

| | | | | |
|---|---|---|---|---|
| If I | found | cakes and ice-cream, | I'd | feel better. |
| | were | the answer, | I wouldn't | get a job in the police. |
| | knew | a car, | | lose weight. |
| | had | taller, | | buy a big house. |
| | didn't eat | so much, | | build more hospitals. |
| | didn't smoke | a lot of money, | | keep it. |
| | | president, | | tell you. |
| | | some money in the street, | | give you a lift. |

**2** Put the verbs in the correct form.

1 If I _____ (be) rich, I _____ (travel) round the world. First I _____ (go) to Canada, then I _____ (go) to New York.
2 If he _____ (work) harder, he _____ (have) more money.
3 I _____ (go) to work if I _____ (feel) better, but I feel terrible.
4 If I _____ (can) speak perfect English, I _____ (not be) in this classroom.
5 'What _____ you _____ (do) if a stranger _____ (give) you £1 million?'

## What would you do?

**3** Discuss what you would do if …

- you came home and found a burglar.
- someone gave you a present that you really didn't like.
- you saw someone shoplifting.
- you found a wallet with a lot of money in it.
- you saw two people fighting in the street.

### *If I were you . . .*

**4** **T 12.2** We can give advice using *If I were you, I'd …*

*I feel terrible! My head hurts, and I feel dizzy.*

*If I were you, I'd go to bed.*

Work with a partner. Give the people advice about their problems.

1 I have no money.
2 My hair's awful.
3 I've got toothache.
4 I've had a row with my boyfriend.
5 My car won't start in the morning.
6 My neighbours make a lot of noise.

**T 12.3** Listen and compare your answers.

## WHO KNOWS?

### *might*

**1** **T 12.4** Listen to two students saying what they're going to do when they leave university. Complete the texts.

I ______ a holiday in Italy for a couple of weeks, staying in a villa in Tuscany. Then I ______ for a job. I ______ in the media – advertising or the BBC would be perfect.

My sister and I ______ a flat together, somewhere central, so we ______ to start looking soon. I'm very excited about the future. And I'm also highly ambitious!

**2** What are some of the certainties in Ruth's life?

*She's having a holiday in Italy.*

- . . . villa in Tuscany.
- . . . for a job.
- . . . flat together.
- . . . start looking soon.

**3** What are some of the possibilities in Henry's life?

*He might go to America.*

- . . . restaurant for a bit.
- . . . Paris for a while.
- . . . French girl . . .

**GRAMMAR SPOT**

1 *Might* means the same as *perhaps . . . will . . . .*

What are you doing tonight?
I don't know. I might go out, or I might stay at home.

2 *Might* is a modal auxiliary.

Ann might come round tonight.
I might not pass my exams.

Do we add *-s* with *he/she/it*?
Do we use *do/does* in the negative?

▶▶ **Grammar Reference 12.2 p141**

# PRACTICE

## Discussing grammar

**1** Choose the correct verb in these sentences.

1. 'What's for supper?' '*We're having / we might have* lamb. It's in the oven.'
2. 'What time are we eating?' 'Don't worry. *It'll be / it might be* ready before your TV programme.'
3. 'Who's eating with us?' 'I've invited Jerry, but *he'll be / he might be* late. It depends on the traffic.'
4. I'm going into town tomorrow. *I'm having / I might have* lunch with Jo at 1.00.
5. 'Are you going to have a winter holiday this year?' '*I am / I might.* I haven't decided yet.'

## Possibilities

**2** Make conversations with a partner about these future possibilities. One of you isn't sure about anything.

*What are you doing tonight?*

*I'm not sure. I might go out or I might stay at home.*

1. What sort/car/buy?
   Fiat/Toyota
2. Where/on holiday?
   Scotland/Spain
3. What/have to eat?
   steak/fish
4. Who/going to the dance with?
   ask Tony/ask Richard

**3** Ask and answer questions with a partner about your possible future plans:

- after the lesson
- at the weekend
- this evening
- for your next holiday

## Check it

**4** Correct the mistakes in these sentences.

1. If I'd have a car, I'd give you a lift.
2. They'll call their baby Lily, but they aren't sure yet.
3. I'd visit you more often if you wouldn't live so far away.
4. I'm playing tennis tomorrow. I'm not sure.
5. If I'm younger, I'll learn to play the piano, but I'm too old now.

# READING AND LISTENING
## Ghost stories

**1** Do you believe in ghosts? What would you do if you saw a ghost? Would you talk to it? Would you run away?

**2** You are going to read about a man called Aelwyn Roberts. He's a ghostbuster.

Do you think he . . . ?
- believes or doesn't believe in ghosts.
- tries to find ghosts.
- tries to get rid of ghosts.

Read the text and find out.

**3** Are the statements true (✓) or false (✗)? Correct the false ones.
1. Mr Roberts is a social worker.
2. He helps to sort out problems for both people and ghosts.
3. He is sure that ghosts exist.
4. The boy knew it was his great-grandfather at the end of his bed.
5. The old man made the boy laugh.
6. Mr Roberts solved the boy's problem easily.
7. Ghosts are not usually members of the family.
8. Mr Roberts says you should never talk firmly to ghosts.

**4** **T 12.5** Look at the newspaper extract on the right, then listen to an interview with Alice Lester.

Check that you know these words.

| brain scan | consultant | tumour | operation |
|---|---|---|---|

**5** Answer the questions.
1. Did Alice Lester know she was ill before she heard the voices?
2. What was she doing when she first heard the voices?
3. What did the first voice tell her?
4. What happened while she was away on holiday?
5. What happened when she returned to London?
6. Did the consultant believe what she told him?
7. What did the voices finally tell her? How is she now?

### What do you think?

- Do you think Alice Lester's story is a ghost story?
- Do you believe that Mr Roberts really gets rid of ghosts?

### Telling stories

Do you know any ghost stories? In small groups, tell your ghost stories. Which is the most frightening?

**Woman heard 'voices' telling her of tumour**

by John Crutchley

The mysterious case of Alice Lester appeared in the British Medical Journal. Alice claims that she heard voices in her head which correctly told her that she had a brain tumour.

# I'M A GHOSTBUSTER, SAYS VICAR

**Aelwyn Roberts**, 79, used to be a vicar. He's retired now, but he still works as a ghostbuster. He helps people who have ghosts in their houses to get rid of them.

'I'm a kind of social worker for ghosts,' he explains. 'Some people die and they still have problems when they leave this world, so they come back again as ghosts to sort them out. I don't think ghosts *might* exist. I know they *do* exist.'

He says he has met thousands of ghosts trapped between this world and the next. He helps them sort out their problems so they can move on to the next world.

One example is typical. At exactly nine every night a three-year-old boy got out of bed and came downstairs. When his parents asked him to explain why, he said that he saw an old man in a funny hat sitting on the end of the bed and the man told him to get out of his bed and go downstairs.

For Mr Roberts this was simple to sort out. He moved the boy's bed from one part of the room to another. 'The ghost was the boy's great-grandfather and the bed was in his way', he explains. The family were never troubled again.

'Eighty per cent of the time the ghosts are members of the family. I tell people that if they want me to get rid of them, I might be throwing their grandmother out of the house. I worry that they might miss her.'

Mr Roberts calls ghosts 'yesterday's people'. His advice is simple. 'You just need to tell them, firmly, to go away and leave you alone.'

# VOCABULARY
## Phrasal verbs

**1** Phrasal verbs consist of a verb + adverb/preposition. Some phrasal verbs are literal.

***Go away** and leave me alone.*
***Take off** your coat and come and **sit down**.*

Complete the sentences with a word from the box.

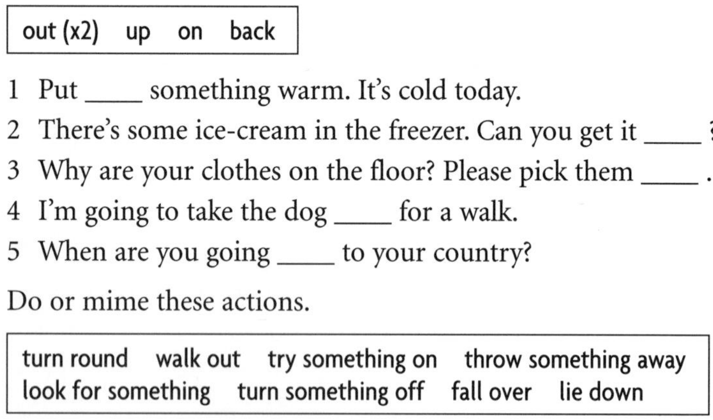

| out (x2) up on back |
|---|

1 Put ____ something warm. It's cold today.
2 There's some ice-cream in the freezer. Can you get it ____ ?
3 Why are your clothes on the floor? Please pick them ____ .
4 I'm going to take the dog ____ for a walk.
5 When are you going ____ to your country?

Do or mime these actions.

| turn round walk out try something on throw something away<br>look for something turn something off fall over lie down |
|---|

**2** Some phrasal verbs aren't literal.

*'Can you **sort out** this problem?'* *The plane **took off**.* *I **gave up** my job.*

Do or mime these actions.

| look after a baby put out a cigarette look up a word ask somebody out<br>we've run out of milk my car broke down Look out! fill in a form |
|---|

**3** Look at the position of the object when it is a pronoun in these sentences.

*Your shoes are dirty. Take **them** off.* *This jumper looks nice. Can I try **it** on?*

Complete the sentences with phrasal verbs from exercises 1–2. Use pronouns.

1 'Where's my tea?' 'Sorry. I threw _______ . It was cold.'
2 You shouldn't smoke in here. Put _______ .
3 We don't need all these lights on. Turn _______ .
4 Leave little Annie with me. I'll look _______ .
5 I haven't got time to fill in this form. I'll fill _______ later.

**4** Complete the sentences with one of these phrasal verbs in the correct form.

| grow up go out with fall out with get on with look forward to |
|---|

1 How do you __________ your parents?
2 Do you ever __________ your brothers and sisters?
3 What are you __________ doing on holiday?
4 Are you __________ anyone at the moment?
5 Where did you __________ ? Or have you always lived here?

In pairs, ask and answer the questions about you.

# EVERYDAY ENGLISH

## Social expressions 2

**1** Complete the conversations with the correct expressions.

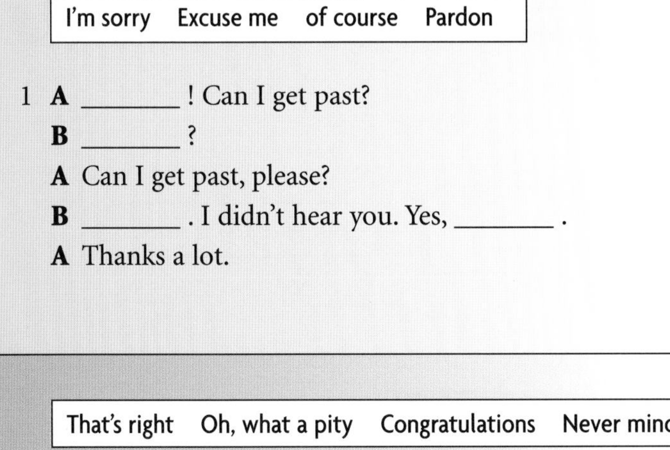

| I'm sorry   Excuse me   of course   Pardon |
|---|

1 **A** _______ ! Can I get past?
**B** _______ ?
**A** Can I get past, please?
**B** _______ . I didn't hear you. Yes, _______ .
**A** Thanks a lot.

| That's right   Oh, what a pity   Congratulations   Never mind   I hear |
|---|

2 **A** _______ you're going to get married soon. _______ !
**B** _______ , next July. July 21. Can you come to the wedding?
**A** _______ ! That's when we're away on holiday.
**C** _______ . We'll send you some wedding cake.
**A** That's very kind.

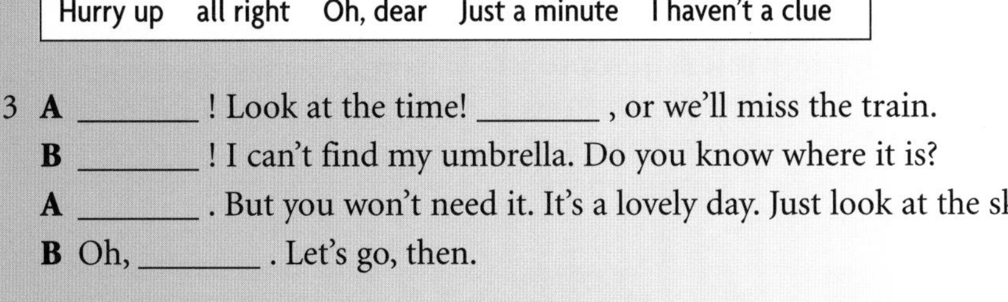

| Hurry up   all right   Oh, dear   Just a minute   I haven't a clue |
|---|

3 **A** _______ ! Look at the time! _______ , or we'll miss the train.
**B** _______ ! I can't find my umbrella. Do you know where it is?
**A** _______ . But you won't need it. It's a lovely day. Just look at the sky!
**B** Oh, _______ . Let's go, then.

| Good luck   See you later   Same to you   Good idea   What about you   No, of course not |
|---|

4 **A** _______ in your exam!
**B** _______ . I hope we both pass.
**A** Did you go out last night?
**B** _______ . I went to bed early. _______ ?
**A** Me, too. _______ after the exam. Let's go for a drink.
**B** _______ .

**2** **T 12.6** Listen and check. Practise the conversations with a partner.

**3** Listen to your teacher. Reply using one of the expressions.

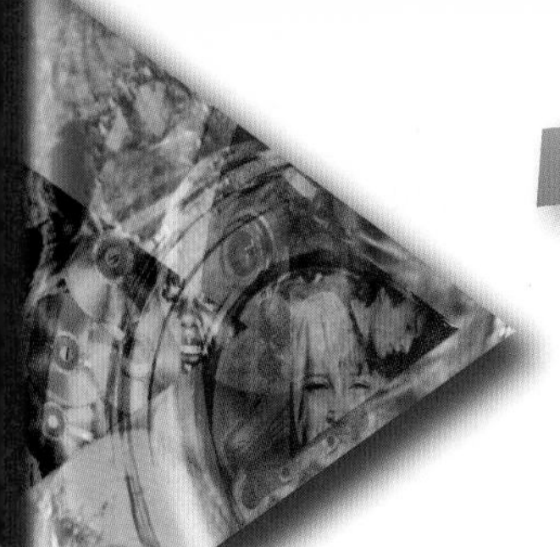

# 13 Earning a living

**Present Perfect Continuous • Word formation • Adverbs • Telephoning**

**STARTER** 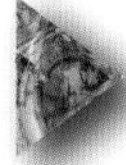

1 Ask and answer these questions.
2 Ask your teacher the same questions about *teaching* English.

*How long have you been learning English?*

*When did you start?*

## STREET LIFE
### Present Perfect Continuous

1 Read Andy's story.
2 Match the questions a–f on p103 with the answers in the text.

**T 13.1** Listen and check. Finish Andy's answer in question 4.

3 With a partner, cover the questions and practise the conversation. Then cover the answers, and practise again.

**GRAMMAR SPOT**

1 Which are the questions in the Present Perfect Continuous? What are the other tenses?
2 Look at these two questions.
How long have you been selling *The Big Issue*?
How many copies have you sold today?
Which question asks about the activity of selling?
Which question asks about the number of magazines sold?
3 Complete these sentences with the Present Perfect Simple or Continuous.
I __________ (smoke) since I was 16.
I __________ (smoke) five cigarettes today.

▶▶ Grammar Reference 13.1 p142

## STREET LIFE

### ANDY'S STORY

**Andy, 28, from Scotland, used to have his own taxi business. When he lost it, he also lost his home and his family. He now sleeps on the streets in London. *The Big Issue* is a magazine sold by homeless people in Britain. This gives them a small income, so they can begin to find somewhere to live.**

**1** ☐ ____________________?

**For a year. It was very cold at first, but you get used to it.**

**2** ☐ ____________________?

**I came here to look for work, and I never left.**

**3** ☐ ____________________?

**For six months. I'm in Covent Garden seven days a week selling the magazine.**

**4** ☐ ____________________?

**Lots. But I can't stand people who think I drink or take drugs. My problem is I'm homeless. I want a job, but I need somewhere to live before I can get a job. So I need money to get somewhere to live, but …**

**5** ☐ ____________________?

**Usually about fifty.**

**6** ☐ ____________________?

**So far, ten. But it's still early.**

**4** Make more questions about Andy.

- How long/trying to find a job?
- How many jobs/had?
- How long/standing here today?
- How/lose your business?
- How long/had your dog?
- Who/best friend?
- Where/meet him/her?
- How long/known each other?

**T 13.2** Listen and check.

**5** Ask and answer the questions with a partner. Invent Andy's answers.

**T 13.3** Listen and compare your answers.

# PRACTICE

## Discussing grammar

**1** Choose the correct tense.

1 How long *have you been living / do you live* in Paris?
2 Anna *has been finding / has found* a good job.
3 Pete and I *have gone out / have been going out* for over six months.
4 I *bought / have bought* a new flat a few months ago.
5 How long *have you had / have you been having* your car?
6 Tom *worked / has been working* as a postman for the past month.
7 I*'ve written / 've been writing* an essay all day.
8 I*'ve written / been writing* six pages.

## Talking about you

**2** Put the verbs in the Present Perfect Simple or Continuous or the Past Simple.

1 How long _____ you _____ (come) to this school?
2 How long _____ you _____ (use) this book?
3 Which book _____ you _____ (have) before this one?
4 How long _____ you _____ (know) your teacher?

## What have they been doing?

**3** Make a sentence about the people using an idea from the box. Add *because* and say what they've been doing.

*He's hot because he's been running.*

| hot back hurts paint on her clothes dirty hands no money tired eyes hurt wet red face |
|---|

**4** Complete these sentences in the Present Perfect Simple about some of the people in exercise 3.

1 He __________ (run) five miles.
2 They __________ (spend) all their money.
3 She __________ (read) five books today.
4 They __________ (play) six games.
5 He __________ (make) a cake and a pie.

## Getting information

**5** Work with a partner. Your teacher will give you different information about the life and career of Steven Spielberg, the movie director. Ask and answer questions to complete the information.

**Student A**
Steven Spielberg was born in . . . *(Where?)* He is one of the most successful filmmakers of the late 20th century, and in his career he has earned millions of dollars.

**Student B**
Steven Spielberg was born in Ohio. He is one of the most successful filmmakers of the late 20th century, and in his career he has earned . . . *(How much?)*

*Where was Steven Spielberg born?*

*He was born in Ohio.*

*How much has he earned?*

*Millions of dollars.*

# VOCABULARY

## Word formation

**1** These words appeared in the last few units. Complete the charts and mark the stress.

| Noun | Verb |
|---|---|
| death | *die* |
| waste | _______ |
| _______ | be'lieve |
| _______ | 'advertise |
| 'promise | _______ |
| _______ | feel |
| ad'vice | _______ |
| _______ | de'scribe |
| in'vention | _______ |
| 'government | _______ |

| Noun | Adjective |
|---|---|
| death | _______ |
| _______ | 'honest |
| va'riety | _______ |
| _______ | mad |
| 'mystery | _______ |
| _______ | 'beautiful |
| _______ | 'wealthy |
| suc'cess | _______ |
| _______ | 'comfortable |
| peace | _______ |

**2** Complete the sentences with a word from exercise 1.

1 _______ me that you'll always love me.
2 He was taken to hospital by ambulance, but he was _______ on arrival.
3 'Are they _______ ?' 'Yes, they're millionaires.'
'Where does their money come from?' 'They have a very _______ business.'
4 I love the _______ and quiet of the countryside.
5 I saw an _______ for a job as a waiter.
6 The sofa was so _______ that I fell asleep.
7 I gave the police a _______ of the man who attacked me.
8 I had a few problems, but Bob gave me some good _______ .
9 I was sitting at home when suddenly I had a funny _______ that I wasn't alone.

## Adverbs

**1** Complete the sentences with the adverbs.

| mainly possibly really nearly |
|---|

1 'Are you going out?' '_______ . I don't know yet.'
2 The exam was _______ difficult. I couldn't do any of it.
3 'How old are you?' 'I'm _______ eight. It's my birthday next week.'
4 I travel a lot in my job, _______ to Europe.

**2** Complete the sentences with the adverbs.

| seriously exactly carefully fluently |
|---|

1 I used to speak French _______ , but I've forgotten it now.
2 Please drive _______ . The roads are so dangerous.
3 I have _______ £3.52 to last until the end of the week.
4 There was an accident, but fortunately no one was _______ injured.

## READING AND SPEAKING

### A funny way to earn a living

**1** Play the alphabet game with jobs.

*architect, accountant, ...*
*businessman, bookseller, ...*

**2** What is considered to be a good job in your country? What's an average salary?

**3** Look at the pictures and the headlines, and look at the three texts for ten seconds only. Answer the questions.

1. Do they have regular jobs?
2. Do they like their job?
3. Each headline contains one of these words. What's the difference between them?

| life lively living |
|---|

**4** Choose one of the texts, and read it more carefully. Answer the questions.

1. Does he/she work indoors or outdoors?
2. How long has he/she been doing this job?
3. What does he/she do in his/her job?
4. What did he/she do before?
5. Does he/she do the same thing every day?
6. How much does he/she earn?
7. Why does he/she like the job?

**5** Find two partners who read the other two texts. Compare the three people. Now answer the questions.

1. Who earns the most?
2. Who earns the least?
3. What sort of things has Terry found?
4. Why do Tesco's employ older people?
5. How long has Cathy been flying balloons?
6. What is Terry's philosophy on life?
7. Why didn't Tom phone when he saw the advertisement?
8. How many hours a day does Cathy work?

#### What do you think?

What is your idea of the best and worst jobs in the world?

#### Language work

Find five adverbs that end in *-ly* in the text about the beachcomber on p107.

# Lively Tom, 69, skates for Tesco

**He gets paid for putting on his roller skates**

Tom Hopperton is one of 1,200 over-65s working for the supermarket, Tesco. He's been working there for fifteen months. Before that he was a plumber for thirty years.

Tom skates about five miles a day around the store fetching things for customers who realize that they've forgotten something only when they've reached the checkout till. He earns £4.50 an hour.

'I just love the job. I help the customers, so they're usually very nice to me. I've always liked meeting people. And it keeps me fit. I can't sit at home doing nothing. I'd just die. I have to keep busy. Time goes really quickly. Every day is different.'

Tesco's made the decision to employ people of all ages. It sees the advantages of older workers who are more calm and authoritative when they are dealing with customers.

'When I saw this job advertised, I didn't believe they'd give it to me,' says Tom. 'I went in to see them because I thought they would be put off by my age if I just phoned. I wanted them to see that I am very lively for my age.'

# Life's a beach

**Is it possible to make a living from what you can find on the beach?**

For 25 years Terry Cemm was a policeman, but for the last seventeen years he has been walking up and down five miles of beach every day, looking for things that might be useful to someone. Terry's a beachcomber.

Nearly everything in his cottage has come from the sea – chairs, tables, even tins of food. What's the most unusual thing he has ever found? 'A barrel of beer just before Christmas. That was nice,' he remembers. He finds lots of bottles with messages in them, mainly from children. They all get a reply if there's an address in the bottle. Shoes? 'If you find one, you'll find the other the next week,' he says.

But does he really make a living? 'Half a living,' he replies. I barter with a lot of things I find, and I have my police pension. But I don't actually need money. My life is rich in variety.'

Terry seems to be a very happy man. 'You have to find a way to live a simple, honest life. People spend all their lives chasing things they don't really need. There's so much waste.'

'Some people say I'm mad,' says Terry. 'But there are a lot more who'd like to do what I do. Look at me. I've got everything that I could possibly want.'

# Flying for a living

**Cathy has made a career out of her passion**

Cathy Moorhead has only ever had one job. She has never wanted to do anything but be in a hot air balloon, going where the wind takes her, listening to the birds, and watching deer and small animals below her.

And she gets paid for it, about £25,000 a year. 'I've been flying balloons since I was 10, and I have done it professionally for twelve years. I fly between 10 and 20 passengers in different balloons.' The flights usually last an hour, and they go early in the morning or just before sunset. 'The trips are always mystery tours,' she says. 'I never know where we're going to land.'

She starts work about 6 am, and works anything from 15 hours a day to nothing, if the weather is bad. 'We can't fly if it's too windy, if visibility is poor, or if it's raining. The balloon gets too heavy and the passengers get wet.' What's the best thing about the job? 'The job itself. I love being out in the countryside and I hate routines. So this is heaven for me.'

# LISTENING AND SPEAKING

## Giving news

**1** Craig has left home and has just started his first job in advertising. He's on the telephone to his mother.

**T 13.4** Listen to his side of the conversation.

Work with a partner and decide if these statements are true (✓) or false (✗).

1 Craig starts work at eight o'clock every morning.
2 His mother is worried that he hasn't been eating well.
3 He goes home immediately after work.
4 Craig's mother has not heard about Tessa before.
5 Craig and Tessa share a flat.
6 Tessa has been working for the advertising agency longer than Craig.
7 Craig's father has been working in Holland.
8 Craig's father has been working hard all day.
9 His mother is coming to London next Thursday.
10 Craig and Tessa are going to cook a meal for his mother.

**2** **T 13.4** Listen to Craig again. Your teacher will stop the recording. What do you think his mother said?

**3** **T 13.5** Listen to the complete conversation and compare your ideas.

### Language work

Read the tapescript on p127. Underline examples of the Present Perfect Simple and Continuous.

### Roleplay

**1** Read Ruth's diary. Work with a partner. One of you is Ruth. It's Friday evening and you have phoned your friend for a chat.

*Hi, there. I'm exhausted. I've had a terrible week!*

*What have you been doing?*

**2** Work with a partner. It is Friday evening. One of you has decided to phone the other for a chat. Ask and answer questions about what you've been doing this week.

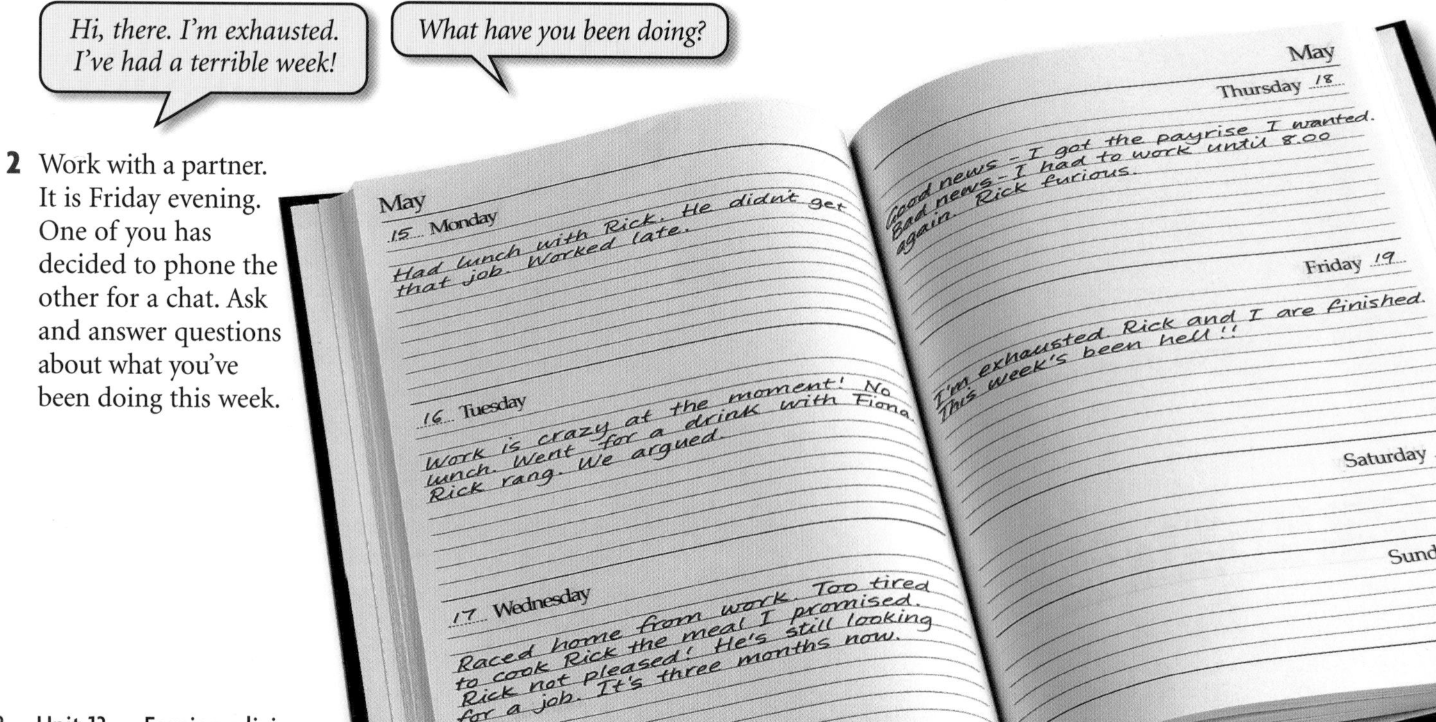

# EVERYDAY ENGLISH

## Telephoning

**1** Practise saying these telephone numbers.

020 7927 4863    01923 272994    0797 0800 994    633488
061 44 501277    07880 705024

**T 13.6** Listen and check.

**2** **T 13.7** Listen to some phone numbers in American English. What differences are there between British and American English?

**3** **T 13.8** Listen to three phone conversations and decide:

- who is speaking to who.
- what about.
- how well they know each other.

**!**

1 Look at these telephone expressions.

Who's speaking?
Is that Mike?
This is John./It's John.
(NOT ~~Here is~~ John, or ~~I'm~~ John.)

2 Complete these expressions from the telephone conversations.

Could I __________ Ann Baker?
I __________ he's out at the moment.
Can I take a __________ ?
I'll __________ later.

3 What do these mean?

Hold on. I'll connect you.
Speaking.

**4** Look at the tapescript on p127/8. Practise the conversations with a partner.

**5** Your teacher will give you a role card. Prepare what you are going to say alone, then be ready to make a call or answer the phone.

# 14 Love you and leave you

**Past Perfect • Reported statements • Saying goodbye**

**STARTER** 

Match the lines about John and Mary.

| | |
|---|---|
| They met each other | every week. |
| They've known each other | when they met. |
| They see each other | for a long time. |
| They were living in New York | a long time ago. |
| They had never been to New York | before. |

## A LOVE STORY
### Past Perfect

**1** Texts **A** and **B** are summaries of a magazine love story. Read and compare them.

One Short Hot Summer by Carmen Day

**A** *The story so far ...*

Saskia met Bradley at a party one Saturday night in June. They fell in love and got married the following Saturday. After the wedding, Bradley moved into Saskia's flat. Saskia rang her parents and told them that she was married. They were furious.

Unfortunately, after a few months, Bradley began to behave very strangely and his marriage to Saskia started to go wrong ...

**B** *The story so far ...*

Saskia and Bradley got married one Saturday in June. They had met only one week earlier at a party and had fallen in love. After the wedding, Saskia rang her parents and told them that she was married, and that Bradley had moved into her flat. They were furious.

Unfortunately, after a few months, their marriage started to go wrong. Bradley had begun to behave very strangely ...

## GRAMMAR SPOT

1 In which text are the events of the story told in chronological order? What tense are *all* the verbs in this text?

2 How is this idea expressed in text **B**?
*They met at a party and fell in love.*
Which two tenses are used in text **B**?

3 What's the difference between these sentences?

| | |
|---|---|
| | they were leaving. |
| When we arrived | they left. |
| | they had left. |

▶▶ **Grammar Reference 14.1 p142**

**2** **T 14.1** Read and listen to text **B** on p110 and underline all the examples of the Past Perfect. Read the text aloud and pay attention to contracted forms.

**3** Are the following statements about Saskia and Bradley true (✓) or false (✗)? Correct the false ones.

1. When Saskia and Bradley got married, they had known each other for a year.
2. When Saskia told her parents about the wedding, Bradley had already moved into her flat.
3. Her parents were angry because she hadn't phoned them for a long time.
4. The marriage started to go wrong, and then Bradley began to behave very strangely.

# PRACTICE

## Speaking

**1** The story continues. Work with a partner. Tell the story in the order of the pictures.

1 On Friday evening when Bradley returned from work, he … his suitcase.

2 Then he …

3 and …

4 Saskia … home.

**2** Which of these sentences is true? Explain why.

| | |
|---|---|
| | was packing. |
| When Saskia arrived home, Bradley | packed. |
| | had packed. |

**3** Tell the story again, but begin at picture 4.
*When Saskia arrived home, Bradley …*

## Grammar and pronunciation

**4** Make sentences from the chart below.

| | | | | | |
|---|---|---|---|---|---|
| I<br>Our teacher<br>My leg<br>The plants<br>The house | was in a mess<br>hurt<br>died<br>was delighted<br>was angry<br>was hungry<br>went to bed early | because | I<br>we | had<br>hadn't | fallen over playing football.<br>done the homework.<br>passed all my exams.<br>had a party the night before.<br>forgotten to water them.<br>had a busy day.<br>had any breakfast. |

**T 14.2** Listen and check. Practice saying the sentences.

**5** The *had* in the Past Perfect tense is often contracted.

*I'd passed my exams.* (The *'d* is sometimes difficult to hear.)

(*'d* is also the contracted form of *would*: *I'd like to come.*)

**T 14.3** Listen to the sentences. Put a tick (✓) if the sentence contains *had*. Put a cross (✗) if it doesn't.

1 ☐ 2 ☐ 3 ☐ 4 ☐ 5 ☐ 6 ☐ 7 ☐ 8 ☐ 9 ☐ 10 ☐

**6** Put the verbs into the correct tense, Past Simple or Past Perfect.

### The story continues ...

Saskia (1) ______ (read) Bradley's letter and then she (2)______ (walk) slowly into the kitchen.

Earlier that day she (3) ______ (buy) his favourite food for dinner, now she (4) ______ (throw) it into the rubbish bin. Why (5)______ he ______ (do) this to her? She remembered how happy they (6) ______ (be) in the beginning. They (7) ______ (laugh) a lot then. Saskia (8) ______ (feel) desperate.

One hour later the phone (9)______ (ring) in the flat ...

**7** Read the end of the story. What happened before? Write your ideas in groups.

### The end of the story

Bradley took Saskia in his arms and said, 'Forgive me, my darling. I'm so happy we're together again – this time it's forever!'

# WHAT DID SHE SAY?

## Reported statements

**1** **T 14.4** Listen and complete what Mary says about John in **A**.

| **A What does Mary say?** |
|---|
| 'I ________ John very much.' |
| 'We ________ six months ago.' |
| 'I ________ in love before.' |
| 'We ________ very happy.' |
| 'I ________ him forever.' |
| 'I ________ him this evening. |

**2** **T 14.5** Read and listen to **B**.

| **B What did Mary tell you?** |
|---|
| **She told me/said that . . .** |
| she loved John very much. |
| they had met six months ago. |
| she had never been in love before. |
| they were very happy. |
| she would love him forever. |
| she was seeing him that evening. |

### GRAMMAR SPOT

1 **A** is direct speech. **B** is reported speech. What are the tense changes from direct to reported speech?

2 How are *say* and *tell* used to introduce reported speech?

▶▶ **Grammar Reference 14.2 p142**

**3** Practise the sentences using contracted forms where possible.

# PRACTICE

## An interview

**1** **T 14.6** Listen to an interview with the writer Carmen Day, who wrote *One Short Hot Summer.*

**2** Complete this report of the interview with the correct verb forms.

In an interview Carmen said she (1) **had written** another romantic novel because she (2) ____________ romantic fiction easy to write, but that her next novel (3) ____________ something different, possibly a detective story.

Carmen said that the character of Bradley (4) ____________ on her first husband, Clive Maingay, the actor, who (5) ____________ her very unhappy. But she added that she (6) ____________ now married to Tony Marsh, the politician. She said that they (7) ____________ married for nearly ten years and that they (8) ____________ very happy together.

She told me that she (9) ____________ now ____________ five novels and also that she (10) ____________ three stories for children. She said she (11) ____________ never stop writing, not even when she (12) ____________ an old lady.

**T 14.7** Listen and check.

## Check it

**3** Report these statements.

1 'I like Anna,' said Jim.
2 'I'm staying with my aunt,' said Anna.
3 'Mr Walker phoned before lunch,' Sue said. 'He didn't leave a message,' she added.
4 'I don't think it'll rain,' said Ken.
5 'Ken's gone home,' Sue said. 'He went early,' she added.
6 'I'll ring you this evening,' Anna told Jim.

# READING AND SPEAKING

## The tale of two silent brothers

**1** Sometimes in families there are arguments and family members don't speak to each other for a long time. Has this ever happened to anyone you know?

**2** You are going to read about two brothers who didn't speak to each other for many years. These expressions are in the text. Match the verbs and phrases.

| | |
|---|---|
| get | a bachelor all his life |
| make | a coin |
| have | revenge |
| see | a will |
| remain | a quarrel |
| toss | and make up |
| kiss | a solicitor about something |

**3** Read the first part of the story.

### PART ONE | A death in the family

There were once two brothers, John and Robert Hessian. John was 52 years old, Robert 49. They had never married and they lived together in a house in Oldcastle in the north of England. They lived together, they ate meals together but they never spoke a single word to each other. They hadn't spoken to each other for ten years, ever since they had had a quarrel. Whenever they wanted to communicate they wrote notes.

One evening the brothers were sitting together after supper. They were both wearing black because their older sister, Mary, had recently died. John wrote a note to Robert: *Mr Liversage is coming to visit.* (Mr Liversage was their solicitor.)
Robert wrote: *Why?*
John wrote: *I don't know. He phoned and said that he wanted to see us.*
At that moment there was a knock at the door. It was the solicitor, Mr Powell Liversage. He had been to school with the brothers and was an old friend. He too was unmarried.
'How are you, Powell?' asked Robert.
'Very well,' he replied. 'I've come to tell you about your sister's will. Did you know that she had left a will?'
'No,' answered John and Robert together. 'How much did she leave?'
'£12,000. But let me read you the will.'

### What do you think?

Discuss these questions with a partner before you read part two.

Why do you think the brothers quarrelled? Do you think they quarrelled about:

- money?
- the house?
- a woman?

What do you think is in the will? Do you think:

- the sister leaves the brothers £6,000 each?
- she leaves all the money to one brother? Which one?
- she leaves them the money on certain conditions? What conditions?

**4** Read part two and find out if your ideas are correct.

### Part Two | The will

Mr Liversage took the will out of his pocket and began to read.

**Last Will and Testament of Mary Hessian**

*To my dear brothers John and Robert:*

*You have both behaved very stupidly. I have never understood why you quarrelled about Annie Emery. You have been cruel and unfair to poor Annie. She has waited ten years for one of you. So, John, if you marry Annie, I'll give all my money to you. And Robert, if you marry her, I'll give it to you. And, if neither of you marries her, all my money will go to Annie, herself.*

*Your ever-loving sister*

## What do you think?

Discuss these questions as a class before you read part three.

- What do you think will happen?
- What will John and Robert do?
- Who will marry Annie?

**5** Read part three and find out if your ideas are correct.

### Part Three | To marry or not to marry?

The two brothers sat and thought for a long time. Ten years ago when Annie was a young woman of 27, both John and Robert had been in love with her. They had had a violent quarrel and some terrible things were said. Afterwards they had both wanted to make up and be friends again but by this time they had stopped speaking to each other, so neither of them learned that the other had decided not to marry Annie.

At two o'clock in the morning John spoke: 'Why don't we toss a coin for Annie? Heads or tails?'

'Tails,' said Robert. But it was heads. The next evening John went round to Annie's house. Powell Liversage was just leaving when he arrived.

So in the end neither brother married Annie. They are still bachelors to this day, but at least they are now talking to each other again. And Annie? Well, she got her revenge and now she's very happily married.

ADAPTED FROM A STORY BY ARNOLD BENNET

## What do you think?

Discuss these questions with a partner. Then tell the class your ideas.

- What happened when John went to Annie's house?
- Why didn't Annie marry either brother?
- Who did she marry?
- Who got the money?

Your teacher will tell you what actually happened.

## Language work

Complete the sentences using the Past Perfect.

1. John and Robert didn't speak to each other because …
2. They were wearing black because …
3. They didn't know that their sister …
4. Mary said in her will that …
5. When Annie was 27, both brothers …
6. Annie told John that she wouldn't marry him or his brother because …

## LISTENING AND VOCABULARY

### Talk to me

**1** **T 14.8** Close your books and your eyes and listen to a song. What is it about?

**2** Work with a partner. Complete the song, choosing the best word on the right for each line.

### Talk to me by Bruce Springsteen

| | | |
|---|---|---|
| Well, every night I see a _______ up in your window | light | man |
| But every night you won't _______ the door | come to | answer |
| But although you won't _______ let me in | never | ever |
| From the street I can see your _______ sitting close to him | silhouette | shadow |

What must I do?
What does it take
To get you to

Talk to me
Until the night is over
Talk to me
Well until the night is over, yeah yeah yeah

| | | |
|---|---|---|
| I got a full week's _______ | pay | stay |
| And baby I've been working hard _______ day | all | each |
| I'm not _______ for the world, you see | asking | looking |

I'm just asking, girl
Talk to me

| | | |
|---|---|---|
| Well late at night I hear music that you're playing _______ and low | soft | loud |
| Yes and late at night I see the two of you _______ , so close | sitting | swaying |
| I don't understand darling, what was my _______ ? | mistake | sin |
| Why am I down here below _______ you're up there with him? | while | when |

What did I do?
What did I say?
What must I pay
to get you to
talk to me

**3** **T 14.8** Listen again and check.

# EVERYDAY ENGLISH

## Saying goodbye

**1** Match the sentences with the correct photos.

a b c d e f

1 [c] 'Goodbye! Have a safe journey. Send us a postcard!'
2 [ ] 'Goodbye. Thank you for a lovely evening.' 'You must come to us next time.'
3 [ ] 'Goodbye. It has been most interesting talking to you. We'll let you know by post.'
4 [ ] 'Bye! See you later. Are you doing anything tonight?'
5 [ ] 'Bye-bye! Thank you very much for having me.'
6 [ ] 'Goodbye. Here's my number. Please get in touch if you have any problems with it.'
7 [ ] 'Goodbye! Drive carefully and call us when you get there!'
8 [ ] 'Goodbye! Good luck in the future. I've really enjoyed our lessons together!'

**2** **T 14.9** Listen and check. Practise saying the sentences.

**3** Make more conversations for these situations:

- parents saying goodbye to son/daughter leaving home to share a flat with friends
- saying goodbye to friends after spending a holiday with them
- saying goodbye to your teacher/boss after finishing school/work on Friday
- saying goodbye to teachers/schoolfriends when you leave school

# Tapescripts

## Unit 1

**T 1.1 Maurizio**

My name's Maurizio Celi. I come from Bologna, a city in the north of Italy. I'm a student at the University of Bologna. I'm studying modern languages – English and Russian. I also know a little Spanish, so I can speak four languages. I'm enjoying the course a lot, but it's really hard work. The course started three years ago.

I live at home with my parents and my sister. My brother went to work in the United States last year.

After I graduate, I'm going to work as a translator. I hope so, anyway.

**T 1.2 Carly**

Hi. My name's Carly and I come from Australia. But I live near London now with my husband Dave and our three children. I came to Britain fifteen years ago when I got married.

I'm a student with the Open University. This means I watch special programmes on the television and work at home. I send my work to my course teacher every week. I'm studying art and the course is really interesting. At the moment, I'm reading about Italian painters in Italian, which is difficult because I only speak a little Italian!

My course started a year ago and it's three years long. After I graduate, I'm going to look for a job in an art gallery or museum.

**T 1.3**

1 I'm reading a good book.
I booked a room at a hotel.
2 What kind of music do you like?
My mother's a very kind person.
3 Can you swim?
I'd like a can of Coke.
4 What does this mean?
Some people are very mean. They don't like spending their money.
5 I live in a flat.
Holland is a flat country.
6 Do you want to play football?
We saw a play at the theatre.
7 The train's coming.
Athletes have to train very hard.
8 The phone's ringing.
What a lovely ring you're wearing!

**T 1.4 Mrs Snell**

I've got a new neighbour. He moved in a few weeks ago. He's got a job, because I see him leaving the house every morning and then coming home in the evening. He's a builder, I think. He wears jeans and a T-shirt, so it can't be a very good job. Sometimes he comes home late.

I've never spoken to him. When he sees me, he says hello, but I don't answer back because nobody has introduced us. How can I speak to him?

His girlfriend is living with him. I know it's not unusual these days, but I still don't like it, boys and girls living together and not married. It's such a small flat. I don't know how two people can live there.

He had a party last week. Forty people! The noise! It went on until two in the morning. He said sorry the next day, but it was a bit late by then. I didn't sleep all night.

Oh, there's the door. I can see him now. He's going out with his girlfriend. I wonder what they're doing tonight. Having a good time. Going to the pub, probably.

**T 1.5 Steve**

I moved into this flat a few weeks ago, and I'm really enjoying living here. There's only one bedroom, and at the moment my sister is staying with me because she's looking for a job.

I work in advertising. It's hard work, and the hours are really long, but I like it. And it's well paid. The office is really relaxed. No one wears a suit or a tie.

The only thing I don't like about this flat is one of the neighbours, Mrs Snell, I think her name is. She's really strange. She never speaks to anyone. I always say hello to her, and 'Are you all right?' and 'What a lovely day today!', but she never says a word. Maybe she doesn't like young people.

I had a party a few days ago. It really wasn't very noisy. About ten of us were here until 11.00 and then we went out to a club. When I saw Mrs Snell the next day, I said I hoped there wasn't too much noise, but as usual she didn't say anything. Funny lady.

This evening my sister and I are going to visit a friend of ours who's in hospital, and then we're going out for a Chinese meal.

**T 1.6**

1 'How are you?' 'Fine, thanks.'
2 'Hello, Jane!' 'Hi, Peter!'
3 'How do you do?' 'How do you do?'
4 'See you tomorrow!' 'Bye!'
5 'Good night!' 'Sleep well!'
6 'Good morning!' 'Good morning!'
7 'Hello, I'm Ela Paul.'
'Pleased to meet you, Ela.'
8 'Cheers!' 'Cheers!'
9 'Excuse me!' 'Yes. Can I help you?'
10 'Bless you!' 'Thanks.'
11 'Have a good weekend!' 'Same to you!'
12 'Thank you very much indeed.'
'Not at all. Don't mention it.'
13 'Make yourself at home.'
'That's very kind. Thank you.'

## Unit 2

**T 2.1**

d Well, my country's got a population of ... er ... about three and a half million, so it's not a big place. Most of the people are from Europe, but about twelve per cent are Maori ... they were the original inhabitants. A lot of people live in bungalows, which are small houses on one floor, and have a pet. It's a very beautiful country. It's got a lot of mountains, and people love the countryside. Oh, and we're very good at rugby and cricket.

e My country is the northern part of a bigger country, but we've got our own parliament. There are just over 5 million of us. We've got a lot of mountains, and there are also lots of rivers, lakes, and islands. People come to my country to fish. Our salmon is famous all over the world. And we also produce a very famous drink called whisky.

f I come from a big country. It has a lot of wide open spaces. We have a population of ... almost 300 million, and these people have come from all over the world. We have big, cosmopolitan cities, but a lot of people live on farms, ranches, and in small towns. We like baseball and football – our kind of football. And we love to eat ... hamburgers with fries, and apple pie and ice-cream.

**T 2.2**

**A** Do you have a car?
**B** Yes, I do.
**C** No, I don't.

**A** Have you got a car?
**B** Yes, I have.
**C** No, I haven't.

**D** I don't have a computer.
**E** I haven't got a computer.

**T 2.3**

Where does he come from?
Is she married?
Does she have any brothers and sisters?
Has he got any children?
How many brothers and sisters has she got?
What does he do?
What does she do in her free time?
Where do they go on holiday?
What's she doing at the moment?

**T 2.4**

have breakfast
wash my hair
watch a film on TV
talk to my friends

make a cup of tea
listen to music
relax on the sofa
do my homework

have a shower
clear up the mess
do the washing-up
have or put posters on the wall

cook a meal
go to the toilet
put on make-up
read magazines

**T 2.5 Home Truths**

**P = Presenter C = Carol M = Mike**
**D = Dave A = Alison**

**P** Hello and welcome to the programme. Today we're going to hear just what couples really think of each other. What drives you mad about your partner? Here's Carol, talking about her husband, Mike.

**C** Well, there are a lot of arguments about television in our house. He gets the remote control and he's always changing channels, so I never see what I want to. All he wants to watch is football, football, football. When I try to talk to him, he doesn't listen because he's watching the TV. And … something else … he never remembers anything – birthdays, when we're going out – nothing. I have to do it all. I decide where we're going on holiday, what car to buy. He can't make a decision to save his life.

**P** So there we have Carol's opinion. What does Mike say about her?

**M** When we're out in the car and she's driving, she doesn't change gears. She's talking about somebody or other, and not thinking about driving at all. I want to shout at her 'Change gear now!' but I don't. When I want to watch something on television, like … the news, she always wants to watch a soap or a film. And another thing. She's always on the phone. She spends hours talking to our daughter, and do you know where she lives? Just round the corner.

**P** But what do they think of their marriage? Here's Carol.

**C** Well, I can't change him now, so I'll just have to put up with him.

**P** And Mike?

**M** We've been married for twenty-five years, and she's the only one for me!

**P** And now we have another couple, Dave and Alison. Oh, and by the way, Dave's an electrician.

**A** What drives me absolutely mad is that he starts a job and never finishes it. At work he's so professional, but at home, if I want a light in the bedroom changed, it takes him months. And he's so untidy. He just drops things on the floor. I keep saying that I don't want to be his mother as well as his wife. When we go out, he looks so scruffy, even when I'm all dressed up. His clothes are so old-fashioned. He never throws anything away.

**P** Oh, dear. Now what does Dave have to say about Alison?

**D** Well, she's never ready on time. She always finds something to do that means we're always late, wherever we go. She's usually doing her hair or her make-up while I'm saying 'Come on love, it's time to go.' And she loses things. She forgets where she parked the car, she leaves the car keys in the most stupid places. But what is most annoying about Alison is that she's always right!

**P** And their final opinions about each other?

**A** He's great. He's good fun, and he's one in a million.

**D** See? As I said, she's always right!

**P** So, there we are. My thanks to Carol and Mike, and Dave and Alison.

**T 2.6**

**J = James M = Maria**

1 **J** Hello. What's your name?
**M** Maria.
**J** I'm … James. I'm a teacher. And … where are you from?
**M** Rome.
**J** Er … What … what do you do?
**M** I'm a student.
**J** Mm. And … how long have you been here in London, Maria?
**M** Two months.
**J** Are you having a good time?
**M** Mm … Yes.
**J** Can I get you a coffee?
**M** No.
**J** Are you missing your family at all?
**M** No.
**J** Have you got any brothers or sisters?
**M** Yes.
**J** Er … Oh! Er … what do they do?
**M** They are students too.
**J** Oh well, I've got a class now. Goodbye, Maria.
**M** Ciao.

**S = Sylvia J-P = Jean-Paul**

2 **S** Hello. What's your name?
**J-P** Jean-Paul. And what's your name?
**S** Sylvia. Where are you from, Jean-Paul?
**J-P** I come from Paris, the most romantic city in the whole world. And you, Sylvia, where do you come from?
**S** I come from Scotland. What do you do in Paris?
**J-P** I'm an architect.
**S** Oh, really?
**J-P** Yeah. I design beautiful buildings for people with lots of money. I'm very expensive.
**S** How interesting.
**J-P** And how long have you been a teacher, Sylvie?
**S** Actually, my name's Sylvia.
**J-P** I am so sorry. Sylvie is the French name. Sylvia, sorry.
**S** Don't worry. I like it. I've been working here for five years.
**J-P** And do you enjoy it?
**S** Yes, very much. You meet a lot of people from all sorts of different countries. I like that very much. Are you enjoying it here?
**J-P** Very, very much. I'm learning a lot of English, I'm making a lot of friends, and even the food's not bad! Well, I'm not dead yet, and I've been here for five weeks. Sylvia, can I get you a coffee?
**S** I've got a few minutes before my next class, so that would be lovely. Thank you very much …
**J-P** Why don't we …

**T 2.7**

1 What a lovely day it is today!
Yes. Beautiful, isn't it?
2 It's very wet today.
Mm. Horrible. Makes you feel miserable, doesn't it?
3 How are you today?
I'm very well, thanks. How about you?
4 Did you have a nice weekend?
Yes, it was lovely. We had a pub lunch and went for a walk.
5 How are you finding living in London?
I'm enjoying it. It was a bit strange at first, but I'm getting used to it.
6 Did you have a good journey?
Yes, no problems. The plane was a bit late, but it didn't matter.
7 Did you watch the football yesterday?
No, I missed it. Was it a good game?
8 What a lovely coat you're wearing!
Thank you. I got it in Paris last year.
9 If you have any problems, just ask me for help.
Thank you very much. That's very kind of you.

# Unit 3

**T 3.1** see p22

**T 3.2**

1 Russell woke up at two o'clock.
2 He woke up because he was thirsty.
3 He heard a noise in the kitchen.
4 He found three men.
5 Russell's mother kept her purse in her handbag.
6 They left at five o'clock.
7 When they left, Russell watched TV.
8 The police caught the burglars the next day.

**T 3.3**

| | |
|---|---|
| asked | carried |
| showed | liked |
| wanted | believed |
| walked | used |
| started | stopped |
| tried | planned |

**T 3.4**

1 I broke a cup, but I mended it with glue.
2 I felt ill, so I went to bed.
3 I made a sandwich because I was hungry.
4 I had a shower and washed my hair.
5 I lost my passport, but then I found it at the back of a drawer.
6 I called the police because I heard a strange noise.
7 I ran out of coffee, so I bought some more.
8 I forgot her birthday, so I said sorry.
9 The phone rang, so I answered it.
10 I told a joke but nobody laughed.

**T 3.5**

**Hands up, I've got a burger!**

Last Tuesday a man armed with just a hot hamburger in a bag stole $1,000 from a bank in Danville, California.

Police Detective Bill McGinnis said that the robber, who was wearing a mask, entered the Mount Diablo National Bank at about 1.30 p.m. and gave the teller a note demanding $1,000. He claimed that he had a bomb in the bag. The teller said she could smell a distinct odour of hamburger coming from the bag. Even so, she handed the money to the man. As he was running out of the bank, he dropped the bag with the hamburger. He escaped in a car that was waiting for him outside.

**Teenage party ends in tears**

When Jack and Kelly Harman went away on holiday, they left their teenage daughter alone in the house. Zoë, aged 16, wanted to stay at home because she was revising for exams. Her parents said she could have some friends to stay. However, Zoë decided to have a party. Everyone was having a good time when suddenly things started to go wrong. Forty uninvited guests arrived, and some of them were carrying knives. They broke furniture, smashed windows, and stole jewellery.

When Mr and Mrs Harman heard the news, they came home immediately.

**T 3.6** **A radio drama – The perfect crime**

**A = Alice  H = Henry  P = Detective Parry**
**T = Sergeant Taylor  F1 and F2 = Friends**

Alice Jackson is a happily married woman. She loves her baby son, and she adores her husband, Henry. Tonight is her tenth wedding anniversary, and some friends are coming round to have a drink. Everything seems perfect ... but ... Alice's life is going to change.

**A** Hello, darling. Have some beer.
**H** Sit down. I've got something to say. ... I'm sorry. I know it's a bad time to tell you. It's our anniversary. But it's just that Kathy and I are in love. Bobby won't miss me, he's too young.
**A** I'll get ready for the party ... .
**H** What on earth ... ?
**A** Hello, police please. Hello, is that the police? Come quickly. It's my husband. Something awful has happened to him.
**P** Detective Parry, Mrs Jackson. Where is he?
**A** In the kitchen. Is he all right?
**P** He's dead.
**A** No, no, not Henry! My Henry! Oh Henry!'
**P** What happened?
**A** I was putting the baby to bed upstairs. And I just came downstairs and found him lying on the kitchen floor.
**T** Burglars.
**P** Sit down, Mrs Jackson. Sergeant Taylor, get Mrs Jackson a drink. A brandy with some ice. Phew! It's hot in this room. I hope you understand, Mrs Jackson, that we have to search the house immediately. We must find the murder weapon.
**A** Yes, yes. Of course.
**P** What was that?
**T** It's this statue, sir. It's melting.
**T** Phew! Can I have a glass of water, Mrs Jackson? It's so hot in here.
**P** I think we all need one. And with ice.
**F1** Poor Alice!
**F2** Poor Henry! I don't believe it. What a shock for you!
**A** Oh thank you, thank you. Please ... stay and have a drink. Help yourselves.
**F1** I wonder what the burglar hit him with.
**F2** Who knows? Mmm.

**T 3.7**

the eighth of January, nineteen ninety-eight
January the eighth, nineteen ninety-eight

the sixteenth of July, nineteen eighty-five
July the sixteenth, nineteen eighty-five

the twenty-fifth of November, two thousand and two
November the twenty-fifth, two thousand and two

**T 3.8**

January eighth, nineteen ninety-eight
July sixteenth, nineteen eighty-five
November twenty-fifth, two thousand and two

**T 3.9**

June the fourth
the fifth of August
the thirty-first of July
March the first
February the third
the twenty-first of January, nineteen eighty-eight
December the second, nineteen ninety-six
the fifth of April, nineteen eighty
June the eleventh, nineteen sixty-five
the eighteenth of October, two thousand
January the thirty-first, two thousand and five

# Unit 4

**T 4.1** see p30

**T 4.2** see p31

**T 4.3**

1 'Did you meet anyone nice at the party?'
'Yes. I met someone who knows you!'
2 'Ouch! There's something in my eye!'
'Let me look. No, I can't see anything.'
3 'Let's go somewhere hot for our holidays.'
'But we can't go anywhere that's too expensive.'
4 'I'm so unhappy. Nobody loves me.'
'I know somebody who loves you. Me.'
5 I lost my glasses. I looked everywhere, but I couldn't find them.
6 'Did you buy anything at the shops?'
'No, nothing. I didn't have any money.'
7 I'm bored. I want something interesting to read, or someone interesting to talk to, or somewhere interesting to go.
8 It was a great party. Everyone loved it.

**T 4.4** see p33

**T 4.5**

1 **A** Hello. Can I help you?
**B** I'm just looking, thanks.
**B** I'm looking for a jumper like this, but in blue. Have you got one?
**A** I'll just have a look. What size are you?
**B** Medium.
**A** Here you are.
**B** That's great. Can I try it on?
**A** Of course. The changing rooms are over there.
**B** I like it.
**A** It fits you very well.
**B** How much is it?
**A** £39.99.
**B** OK. I'll have it.
**A** How would you like to pay?
**B** Cash.

2 **A** Could you help me? I'm looking for this month's edition of *Vogue*. Can you tell me where it is?
**B** Over there. Middle shelf. Next to *She*.

3 **A** Hello. I wonder if you could help me. I've got a bad cold and a sore throat. Can you give me something for it?
**B** OK. You can take these three times a day.
**A** Thank you. Could I have some tissues as well, please?
**B** Sure. Anything else?
**A** No, that's all, thanks.

4 **A** Good morning. Can I have a black coffee, please?
**B** Espresso?
**A** Yes, please. Oh, and a doughnut, please.
**B** I'm afraid there aren't any left. We've got some delicious carrot cake, and chocolate cake.
**A** OK. Carrot cake, then.
**B** Certainly. Is that all?
**A** Yes, thanks.
**B** That'll be £1.85, please.
**A** Thank you.

**T 4.6**

1 **A** A book of ten first class stamps, please.
**B** Two pounds eighty, please.
2 **A** How much is this jumper?
**B** Twenty-eight pounds fifty.
3 **A** A white loaf and three rolls, please.
**B** That'll be one pound eighty-two p.
4 **A** How much do I owe you?
**B** Twelve dollars and twenty cents.
5 **A** How much was your car?
**B** Fifteen thousand dollars.
6 **A** What a fantastic house!
**B** Darling! It cost half a million pounds!
7 **A** Just this book, please.
**B** Five pounds ninety-nine, then.
8 **A** How much was the cheque for?
**B** A hundred and sixty dollars.

# Unit 5

**T 5.1**

1 **Sean**
When I grow up, I want to be a footballer and play for Manchester United, because I want to earn lots of money. After that, I'm going to be an astronaut, and fly in a rocket to Mars and Jupiter. And I'd like all the people in the world and all the animals in the world to be happy.

2 **Mel**
I've finished my first year at Bristol University, and now I'm going to have a year off. My boyfriend and I are going round the world. We hope to find work as we go. I really want to meet people from all over the world, and see how different people live their lives.

3 **Justin**
What I'd really like to do, because I'm mad about planes and everything to do with flying, is to have my own business connected with planes, something like a flying school. I'm getting married next June, so I can't do anything about it yet, but I'm going to start looking this time next year.

4 **Martyn**
My great passion is writing. I write plays. Three have been perfomed already, two in Edinburgh and one in Oxford. But my secret ambition ... and this would be the best thing in my life ... I would love to have one of my plays performed on the London stage. That would be fantastic.

5 **Amy**
We're thinking of moving, because the kids are leaving home soon. Meg's eighteen, she's doing her A levels this year, so with a bit of luck, she'll be off to university next year. And Kate's fifteen. Jack and I both enjoy walking,

and Jack likes fishing, so we're going to move to the country.

5 **Alison**
Well, I've just broken my arm, so what I really want to do is to go back to the health club as soon as possible. I really enjoy swimming. At my age, it's important to stay physically fit, and I want to be able to go off travelling without feeling unwell. I'm going to retire next year, and I'm looking forward to having more time to do the things I want to do.

**T 5.2**

1 **A** I hope to go to university.
**B** What do you want to study?
2 **A** One of my favourite hobbies is cooking.
**B** What do you like making?
3 **A** I get terrible headaches.
**B** When did you start getting them?
4 **A** We're planning our summer holidays at the moment.
**B** Where are you thinking of going?
5 **A** I'm tired.
**B** What would you like to do tonight?

**T 5.3**

1 'What are the lads doing this afternoon?'
'They're going to watch a football match. Arsenal are playing at home.'
2 'Damn! I've dropped one.'
'I'll pick it up for you.'
'Thank you. That's very kind.'
3 'What's Ali doing next year?'
'She's going to travel round the world.'
'Oh, lucky her!'
4 'The phone's ringing.'
'It's OK. I'll answer it. I'm expecting a call.'
5 'I haven't got any money.'
'Don't worry. I'll lend you some.'
'Thanks. I'll pay you back tomorrow. I won't forget.'
6 'What are you and Pete doing tonight?'
'We're going out to have a meal. It's my birthday.'

**T 5.4**

1 'My bag is so heavy.' 'Give it to me …'
2 I bought some warm boots because …
3 'Tony's back from holiday.'
'Is he? I …'
4 What are you doing tonight?
5 You can tell me your secret.
6 Congratulations! I hear …
7 I need to post these letters.
8 Now, holidays. Where …

**T 5.5** **A song**

***You've got a friend***
When you're down and troubled
And you need a helping hand
And nothing, but nothing is going right
Close your eyes and think of me
And soon I will be there
To brighten up even your darkest nights.
*(Chorus)*
You just call out my name,
and you know wherever I am
I'll come running to see you again.
Winter, spring, summer, or fall
All you have to do is call
And I'll be there, yeah, yeah, yeah,
You've got a friend.

If the sky above you
Turns dark and full of clouds
And that old north wind begins to blow
Keep your head together
And call my name out loud
And soon I'll be knocking on your door.
Hey, ain't it good to know that you've got a friend?
People can be so cold.
They'll hurt you and desert you.
Well, they'll take your soul if you let them.
Oh, yeah, but don't you let them.
*(Chorus)*

**T 5.6**

1 'I feel nervous. I've got an exam today.'
'Good luck! Do your best.'
2 'I don't feel very well. I think I'm getting the 'flu.'
'Why don't you go home to bed?'
3 'I'm feeling a lot better, thanks. I've got a lot more energy.'
'That's good. I'm pleased to hear it.'
4 'I'm really excited. I'm going on holiday to Australia tomorrow.'
'That's great. Have a good time.'
5 'I'm fed up with this weather. It's so wet and miserable.'
'I know. We really need some sunshine, don't we?'
6 'I'm really tired. I couldn't get to sleep last night.'
'Poor you! That happens to me sometimes. I just read in bed.'
7 'I'm a bit worried. My grandfather's going into hospital for tests.'
'I'm sorry to hear that, but I'm sure he'll be all right.'
8 'I feel really depressed at the moment. Nothing's going right in my life.'
'Cheer up! Things can't be that bad!'

# Unit 6

**T 6.1** **Todd's tennis tour**

**T** = **Todd** **E** = **Ellen**
**E** You're so lucky, Todd. You travel all over the world. I never leave Chicago!
**T** Yeah – but it's hard work. I just practise, practise, practise and play tennis all the time. I don't get time to see much.
**E** What about last year? Where did you go? Tell me about it.
**T** Well – in January I was in Melbourne, for the Australian Open. It's a beautiful city, sort of big and very cosmopolitan, like Chicago. There's a nice mixture of old and new buildings. January's their summer so it was hot when I was there.
**E** And what's Dubai like? When were you there?
**T** In February. We went from Australia to Dubai for the Dubai Tennis Open. Boy is Dubai hot! Hot, very dry, very modern. Lots of really modern buildings, white buildings. Interesting place, I enjoyed it.
**E** And Paris! That's where I want to go! What's Paris like?
**T** Everything that you imagine! Very beautiful, wonderful old buildings but lots of interesting modern ones too. And of course very, very romantic, especially in May. Maybe I can take you there sometime.
**E** Yeah?

**T 6.2** **What's Chicago like?**

**T** = **Todd** **F** = **Todd's English friend**
1 **F** What's the weather like?
**T** Well, Chicago's called 'the windy city' and it really can be windy!
2 **F** What are the people like?
**T** They're very interesting. You meet people from all over the world.
3 **F** What are the buildings like?
**T** A lot of them are very, very tall. The Sears Tower is 110 storeys high.
4 **F** What are the restaurants like?
**T** They're very good. You can find food from every country in the world.
5 **F** What's the night-life like?
**T** Oh, it's wonderful. There's lots to do in Chicago.

**T 6.3** **Todd's world tour**

Melbourne was interesting, but, for me, Paris was more interesting than Melbourne, and in some ways Dubai was the most interesting of all because it was so different from any other place I know. It was also the hottest, driest, and most modern. It was hot in Melbourne but not as hot as in Dubai. Dubai was much hotter! Melbourne is much older than Dubai but not as old as Paris. Paris was the oldest city I visited, but it has some great modern buildings, too. It was the most romantic place. I loved it.

**T 6.4** see p48

**T 6.5** see p48

**T 6.6** **Conversations**

1 **A** I moved to a new flat last week.
**B** Oh, really? What's it like?
**A** Well, it's bigger than my old one but it isn't as modern, and it's further from the shops.
2 **A** I hear Sandy and Al broke up.
**B** Yeah. Sandy's got a new boyfriend.
**B** Oh, really? What's he like?
**A** Well, he's much nicer than Al and much more handsome. Sandy's happier now than she's been for a long time.
3 **A** We have a new teacher.
**B** Oh, really? What's she like?
**A** Well, I think she's the best teacher we've ever had. Our last teacher was good but she's even better and she works us much harder.
4 **A** Is that your new car?
**B** Well, it's second-hand, but it's new to me.
**A** What's it like?
**B** Well, it's faster than my old car and more comfortable, but it's more expensive to run. I love it!

**T 6.7**

**Jane Bland talks about living in Sweden**
**J** = **Jane** **F** = **Fran, a friend**
**J** When I say that I live in Sweden, everyone always wants to know about the seasons …
**F** The seasons?
**J** Yeah … you know, how cold it is in winter – what it's like when the days are so short.
**F** So what *is* it like?

**J** Well, it *is* cold, very cold in winter, sometimes as cold as –26° and of course when you go out you wrap up warm, but inside, in the houses, it's always very warm, much warmer than at home. Swedish people always complain that when they visit England the houses are cold even in a good winter. In Sweden the houses are much better insulated than in Britain and they always have the heating on very high.

**F** And what about the darkness?

**J** Well, yeah, around Christmas time, in December, there's only *one* hour of daylight – so you really look forward to the spring. It is sometimes a bit depressing but you see the summers are amazing – from May to July, in the north of Sweden, the sun never sets, it's still light at midnight, you can walk in the mountains and read a newspaper.

**F** Oh, yeah – the land of the midnight sun.

**J** That's right. But it's wonderful, you want to stay up all night and the Swedes make the most of it. Often they start work earlier in summer and then leave at about two or three in the afternoon, so that they can really enjoy the long summer evenings. They like to work hard but play hard too. I think Londoners work longer hours, but I'm not sure this is a good thing.

**F** So what about free time? Weekends? Holidays? What do Swedish people like doing?

**J** Well, every house in Sweden has a sauna …

**F** *Every* house!?

**J** Well, every house I've been to. And most people have a country cottage, so people like to leave the town and get back to nature at weekends. These cottages are sometimes quite primitive, – no running water or not even toilets and …

**F** No *toilet*?

**J** Well, *some* don't have toilets but they *all* have a sauna and all the family sit in it together, then run and jump into the lake to get cool.

**F** What!? Even in winter?

**J** Yeah – Swedish people are very healthy.

**F** Brrr! Or mad!

### T 6.8 Synonyms

1 'Mary's family is very rich.'
'Well, I knew her uncle was very wealthy.'
2 'Look at all these new buildings!'
'Yes. Paris is much more modern than I expected.'
3 'Wasn't that film wonderful!'
'Yes, it was brilliant.'
4 'George doesn't earn much money, but he's so kind.'
'He is, isn't he? He's one of the most generous people I know.'
5 'Ann's bedroom's really untidy again!'
'Is it? I told her it was messy yesterday, and she promised to clean it.'
6 'I'm bored with this lesson!'
'I know, I'm really fed up with it, too!'

### T 6.9 Antonyms

1 'London's such an expensive city.'
'Well, it's not very cheap.'
2 'Paul and Sue are so mean.'
'They're certainly not very generous.'
3 'Their house is always so messy.'
'Mmm … it's not very tidy.'
4 'Their children are so noisy.'
'Yes, they're certainly not very quiet.'
5 'John looks so miserable.'
'Hmm, he's not very happy.'
6 'His sister's so stupid.'
'Well, she's certainly not very clever.'

### T 6.10 Giving directions

You go down the path, past the pond, over the bridge, and out of the gate. Then you go across the road and take the path through the wood. When you come out of the wood you walk up the path and into the church. It takes five minutes.

## Unit 7

### T 7.1

1 He wrote novels about Victorian life. She writes novels about modern people and their relationships.
2 He wrote 47 novels, travel books, biographies, and short stories. She has written over twenty novels. She started writing in her thirties.
3 She has lived in the west of England for forty years. He lived in Ireland for eighteen years.
4 She has been married twice, and has two daughters. She married for the first time in 1966. He was married and had two sons.

### T 7.2

1 Anthony Trollope travelled to South Africa, Australia, Egypt, and the West Indies. Joanna Trollope has travelled to many parts of the world.
2 She has won many awards, and several of her stories have appeared on TV.
3 Her first book came out in 1980. Since then, she has sold more than 5 million copies.
4 She went to school in the south of England, and studied English at Oxford University, but she has lived in the country for most of her life.
5 She writes her books by hand. She has had the same pen since 1995.

### T 7.3

1 How long has she lived in the west of England?
For forty years.
2 What did she study at university?
English.
3 How many novels has she written?
More than twenty.
4 How many books has she sold?
Over five million.
5 When did her first novel come out?
In 1980.
6 How many times has she been married?
Twice.
7 Has she got any children?
Yes, two daughters.
8 How long has she had her pen?
Since 1995.

### T 7.4

1 I've known my best friend for years. We met when we were 10.
2 I last went to the cinema two weeks ago. The film was rubbish.
3 I've had this watch for three years. My Dad gave it to me for my birthday.
4 We've used this book since the beginning of term. It's not bad. I quite like it.
5 We lived in our old flat from 1988 to 1996. We moved because we needed somewhere bigger.
6 We haven't had a break for an hour. I really need a cup of coffee.
7 I last had a holiday in 1999. I went camping with some friends.
8 This building has been a school since 1985. Before that it was an office.

### T 7.5

**A** Where do you live, Olga?
**B** In a flat near the park.
**A** How long have you lived there?
**B** For three years.
**A** And why did you move?
**B** We wanted to live in a nicer area.

### T 7.6

**An interview with the band *Style***
**I = Interviewer S = Suzie G = Guy**

**I** … and that was the latest record from *Style* called *Give it to me*. And guess who I've got sitting right next to me in the studio? I've got Suzie Tyler and Guy Holmes, who are the two members of *Style*. Welcome to the programme!

**S** Thanks a lot.

**I** Now you two have been very busy this year, haven't you? You've had a new album out, and you've been on tour. How are you feeling?

**S** Pretty tired. We've just got back from Holland, and in April we went to Japan and Australia, so yeah … we've travelled a lot this year.

**G** But we've made a lot of friends, and we've had some fun.

**I** Tell us something about your background. What did you do before forming *Style*?

**G** Well, we both played with a lot of other bands before teaming up with each other.

**I** Who have you played with, Suzie?

**S** Well, over the years I've sung with Lionel Richie and Phil Collins, and a band called *Ace*.

**I** And what about you, Guy?

**G** I've recorded with *Genesis* and *UB40*, and of course, *Happy Mondays*.

**I** Why is *Happy Mondays* so important to you?

**G** Because I had my first hit record with them. The song was called *Mean Street*, and it was a hit all over the world … that was in 1995.

**I** So how long have you two been together as *Style*?

**S** Since 1997. We met at a recording studio while I was doing some work with *Bon Jovi*. We started chatting and Guy asked me if I'd like to work with him, and it all started from there.

**I** Suzie, you're obviously the vocalist, but do you play any music yourself?

**S** Yes, I play keyboards.

**I** And what about you, Guy?

**G** I play guitar and harmonica. I can play the drums, but when we're doing a concert we have a backing group.

**I** So where have you two travelled to?

**S** Well, I … er … I sometimes think that we've

been everywhere, but we haven't really. We've toured in Europe, Italy, Holland, and we've done Japan and Australia, but we've never been to America. That's the next place we'd like to go. And then Eastern Europe. I'd love to play in these places.

**G** You forgot Sweden. We went there two years ago.
**S** Oh yeah.
**I** Over the years you've made a lot of records. Do you know exactly how many?
**G** That's a difficult question, erm …
**I** Well, about how many?
**S** Oh, I don't know. Perhaps about twenty-five.
**G** Yeah, something like that.
**I** And how long have you been in the music business?
**G** I guess about fifteen years. I've never had another job. I've only ever been a musician, since I was seventeen.
**S** I've had all sorts of jobs. When I left college, I worked as a waitress, a shop assistant, a painter, a gardener … I could go on and on …
**I** Well, stop there, because now you're a member of a band. Suzie and Guy, it was great to talk to you. Good luck with the new record.
**S/G** Thanks.
**I** And now for something different. We're …

**T 7.7**

1 'Do you still play tennis?'
'Not regularly. Just now and then, when I have time.'
2 This is a pretty relaxed place to work. There aren't many do's and don'ts.
3 Here you are at last! I've been so worried! Thank goodness you've arrived safe and sound.
4 'Do you like your new job?'
'Yes and no. The money's OK, but I don't like the people.'
5 Sometimes there are too many people in the house. I go into the garden for a bit of peace and quiet.
6 Good evening, ladies and gentlemen. It gives me great pleasure to talk to you all tonight.
7 'How's your Gran?'
'Up and down. There are good days, and then not such good days.'
8 'Here's supper. Careful! It's hot.
'Fish and chips! Yummy!'

**T 7.8**

1 'Do you like learning English, Elsa?'
'Yes.'
'Do you like learning English, Elsa?'
'Yes, I do. I love it. It's the language of Shakespeare.'
2 'Are those new jeans you're wearing?'
'No.'
'Are those new jeans you're wearing?'
'No, they aren't. I've had them for ages.'
3 'Have you got the time, please?'
'No.'
'Have you got the time, please?'
'No, I haven't. I'm so sorry.'
4 'Can you play any musical instruments?'
'Yes.'
'Can you play any musical instruments?'
'Yes, I can, actually. I can play the violin.'

# Unit 8

**T 8.1** **Steven's job**

**I = Interviewer S = Steven**
**I** What sort of hours do you work, Steven?
**S** Well, I have to work very long hours, about eleven hours a day.
**I** What time do you start?
**S** I work nine till three, then I start again at five thirty and work until eleven. Six days a week. So I have to work very unsocial hours.
**I** And do you have to work at the weekend?
**S** Oh, yes. That's our busiest time. I get Wednesdays off.
**I** What are some of the things you have to do, and some of the things you don't have to do?
**S** Er … I don't have to do the washing-up, so that's good! I have to wear white, and I have to be very careful about hygiene. Everything in the kitchen has to be totally clean.
**I** What's hard about the job?
**S** You're standing up all the time. When we're busy, people get angry and shout, but that's normal.
**I** How did you learn the profession?
**S** Well, I did a two-year course at college. In the first year we had to learn the basics, and then we had to take exams.
**I** Was it easy to find a job?
**S** I wrote to about six hotels, and one of them gave me my first job, so I didn't have to wait too long.
**I** And what are the secrets of being good at your job?
**S** Attention to detail. You have to love it. You have to be passionate about it.
**I** And what are your plans for the future?
**S** I want to have my own place. When the time's right.

**T 8.2**

1 I have a good job.
I have to work hard.
2 He has a nice car.
She has to get up early.
3 I had a good time.
I had to take exams.

**T 8.3**

1 'I'm working 16 hours a day'.
'I think you should talk to your boss.'
2 'I can't sleep.'
'You shouldn't drink coffee at night.'
3 'My ex-boyfriend's getting married.'
'I don't think you should go to the wedding.'
4 'I've had a terrible toothache for weeks.'
'You must go to the dentist!'

**T 8.4** **Holidays in January**

1 **Silvia**
In January the weather is wonderful. It's the most perfect time of year, not too hot, not too cold, but the temperature can change a lot in just one day. It can go from quite chilly to very warm, so you should perhaps bring a jacket but you don't need any thick winter clothes. The capital city is the most populated city in the world and there are lots of things to see and do there. We have lots of very old, historic buildings. We are very proud of our history, with Mayan and Aztec temples. But you should also go to the coast. We have beautiful beaches. Perhaps you've heard of Acapulco.

You don't need a lot of money to enjoy your holiday. There are lots of good cheap hotels and restaurants, and of course you must visit the markets. You can buy all kinds of pottery and things quite cheaply, and don't forget our wonderful fruit and vegetables. We have one hundred different kinds of pepper. You should try tacos, which are a kind of bread filled with meat, beans, and salad. And our beer is very good, especially if you add lemon and salt. Or, of course, you can always drink *tequila*.

2 **Fatima**
It's usually quite mild in January, and it doesn't often rain, so you don't have to bring warm clothes. But you'll need a light coat or a jumper because it can get cool in the evenings.

There is so much to see and do. We have some wonderful museums, especially the museum of Islamic Art and the mosques are beautiful, but of course what everyone wants to see is the Pyramids. You must visit the pyramids. Go either early in the morning or late in the afternoon, the light is much better then. And if you have time you should take a cruise down the Nile, that's really interesting, you can visit all sorts of places that are difficult to get to by land.

The best place to try local food is in the city centre. You should try *koftas* and *kebabs*, which are made of meat, usually lamb. You should also try *falafel*, which is a kind of ball made of beans mixed with herbs, it's fried until it's crispy. It's delicious. One of the nicest things to drink is tea, mint tea. It's especially good if the weather is very hot, it's really refreshing.

3 **Karl**
Well, of course in January in my country it can be very cold, with lots of snow everywhere, so you must bring lots of warm clothes, coats and woolly hats, and, if you can, snow boots.

Many people go skiing in the mountains at the weekends and when you are up so high and the sky is blue, the sun can feel really quite hot - warm enough to have lunch outside. You can even sunbathe, so you should bring sun cream! But you don't have to go skiing, there are lots of other things to do and see. A lot of our towns are very pretty. They look exactly the same today as they did four hundred years ago. And we have beautiful lakes. If the weather's fine you can go for a boat trip and you can get really wonderful views of the mountains all around, from Lake Geneva you can sometimes see as far as Mont Blanc.

The food you must try is *fondue* , which is cheese melted in a pot. You put pieces of bread on long forks to get it out. Also you could try *rösti* made with potatoes and cream – mmm! They're both delicious.

**T 8.5**

1 Children always need the support of their parents, whether they're four or 24. I think you should pay for him to get some qualifications, and when he's ready, you

should help him to find somewhere to live. Meanwhile, you've got to give him all the love that he needs.
**Jenny Torr**
**Brighton**

2 I decided to give it all up and change my life dramatically three years ago. Since then, I have had the most exciting three years of my life. It can be scary, but if you don't do it, you won't know what you've missed. I don't think she should worry. Go for it.
**Mike Garfield**
**Manchester**

3 He's using you. I think you should tell him to leave home. It's time for him to go. Twenty-four is too old to be living with his parents. He's got to take responsibility for himself. And you must tell the police about his drug-taking. Sometimes you have to be cruel to be kind.
**Tony Palmer**
**Harrow**

4 Why should he accept it? He isn't their slave, they don't own him. And I too can't stand the way people use their mobiles in restaurants, on trains and buses. They think that the people around them are invisible and can't hear. It is so rude.
**Jane Sands**
**London**

5 I think she should be very careful before she gives up her job and goes to live abroad. Does she think that the sun will always shine? If there is something in her life that makes her unhappy now, this will follow her. She should take her time before making a decision.
**Nigella Lawnes**
**Bristol**

6 He must keep it! He should have a word with his company and come to an arrangement with them. Why can't he turn it off sometimes? Mobile phones are great, and if he's got one for free, he's very lucky. They are one of the best inventions ever.
**Pete Hardcastle**
**Birmingham**

**T 8.6**

| | |
|---|---|
| alarm clock | hairdrier |
| car park | sunset |
| traffic lights | earring |
| credit card | signpost |
| ice-cream | bookcase |
| sunglasses | rush hour |
| timetable | cigarette lighter |
| raincoat | earthquake |

**T 8.7**

**D = Doctor M = Manuel**

**D** Hello. Come and sit down. What seems to be the matter?
**M** Well, I haven't felt very well for a few days. I've got a bit of a temperature, and I just feel terrible. I've got stomach ache as well.
**D** Have you felt sick?
**M** I've been sick a few times.
**D** Mm. Let me have a look at you. Your glands aren't swollen. Have you got a sore throat?
**M** No, I haven't.
**D** Have you had diarrhoea at all?
**M** Yes, I have, actually.
**D** Have you had anything to eat recently which might have disagreed with you?
**M** No, I don't think … Oh! I went to a barbecue a few days ago and the chicken wasn't properly cooked.
**D** It could be that, or just something that was left out of the fridge for too long.
**M** Yes, I started being ill that night.
**D** Well, you should have a day or two in bed, and I'll give you something that will look after the stomach ache and diarrhoea. Drink plenty of liquids, and just take things easy for a while. I'll write you a prescription.
**M** Thank you. Do I have to pay you?
**D** No, no. Seeing me is free, but you'll have to pay for the prescription. It's £6.
**M** Right. Thanks very much. Goodbye.
**D** Bye-bye.

# Unit 9

**T 9.1**

1 We're travelling round the world before we go to university.
2 We're going to leave as soon as we have enough money.
3 When we're in Australia, we're going to learn to scuba dive on the Great Barrier Reef.
4 If we get ill, we'll look after each other.
5 After we leave Australia, we're going to the USA.
6 We can stay with my American cousins while we're in Los Angeles.
7 Our parents will be worried if we don't keep in touch.
8 We'll stay in the States until our visa runs out.

**T 9.2**

1 When I get home, I'm going to have a bath.
2 As soon as this lesson finishes, I'm going home.
3 If I win, I'll buy a new car.
4 After I leave school, I want to go to college.
5 While I'm in New York, I'll do some shopping.
6 I'm going to travel the world before I get too old.

**T 9.3**

**P = Paul M = Mary**

**P** Bye, darling. Have a good trip to New York.
**M** Thanks. I'll ring you as soon as I arrive at the hotel.
**P** Fine. Remember I'm going out with Henry tonight.
**M** Well, if you're out when I ring, I'll leave a message on the answer phone, so you'll know I've arrived safely.
**P** Great. What time do you expect you'll be there?
**M** If the plane arrives on time, I'll be at the hotel about 10.00.
**P** All right. Give me a ring as soon as you know the time of your flight back, and I'll pick you up at the airport.
**M** Thanks, darling. Don't forget to water the plants while I'm away.
**P** Don't worry. I won't. Bye!

**T 9.4** **An interview with Michio Kaku**

**I = Interviewer MK = Michio Kaku**

**I** Are you optimistic about the future?
**MK** Generally, yeah. If we go back to 1900, most Americans didn't live after the age of 50. Since then we've had improvements in healthcare and technology. There's no reason why these won't continue far into the 21st century.
**I** Are we ready for the changes that will come?
**MK** Changes are already happening. The future is here now. We have DNA, microchips, the Internet. Some people's reaction is to say 'We're too old, we don't understand new technology.' My reaction is to say 'We must educate people to use new technology now.'
**I** Is world population going to be a big problem?
**MK** Yes and no. I think that world population will stop increasing as we all get richer. If you are part of the middle class, you don't want or need twelve children.
**I** What will happen to people who don't have computers?
**MK** Everyone will have computers. The Internet will be free and available to everyone.
**I** Will there be a world government?
**MK** Very probably. We will have to manage the world and its resources on a global level, because countries alone are too small. We already have a world language called English, and there is the beginning of a world telephone system, and that's called the Internet.
**I** Will we have control of everything?
**MK** I think we'll learn to control the weather, volcanoes and earthquakes. Illness won't exist. We will grow new livers, kidneys, hearts, and lungs like spare parts for a car. People will live till about 130 or 150. For two thousand years we have tried to understand our environment. Now we will begin to control it.
**I** What are your reasons for pessimism?
**MK** People will still fundamentally be the same, with all their intelligence and stupidity. There will still be cruel people, people who want to fight wars against other races and religions, people who don't see that we have to look after our forests, our oceans, our atmosphere, people who think that money is everything. We will have the technology. The question is, will we have the wisdom to use the technology to our advantage?

**T 9.5**

1 I did some shopping while I was in town. I bought myself a new jumper.
2 'I don't know if I love Tom or Henry.'
'Make up your mind. You can't marry both of them.'
3 Bye-bye! See you soon. Take care of yourself.
4 Aachoo! Oh dear. I think I'm getting a cold.
5 'Are the doors locked?'
'I think so, but I'll just make sure.'

**T 9.6**

**R = Receptionist C = Client**

**R** Hello, the Grand Hotel. Cathy speaking. How can I help you?
**C** I'd like to make a reservation, please.
**R** Certainly. When is it for?
**C** It's for two nights, the thirteenth and the fourteenth of this month.
**R** And do you want a single or a double room?

C A single, please.
R OK. Yes, that's fine. I have a room for you. And your name is?
C Robert Palmer. Can you tell me how much it is?
R Yes. That's £95 a night. Can I have a credit card number, please?
C Yes, sure. It's a Visa. 4929 7983 0621 8849.
R Thank you. And could I have a phone number?
C Uh huh. 01727 489962.
R That's fine. We look forward to seeing you on the thirteenth. Bye-bye.
C Thanks a lot. Goodbye.

# Unit 10

**T 10.1** **Don't look down**

**Paul Lay dances with death in the mountains of southern Spain**

I have always enjoyed walking. When I was a boy, I used to go walking at weekends with my father. We went camping and climbing together.

I try to visit a new place every year. Last year I decided to walk a path in Spain called *El Camino del Rey*, which means the King's Way. It is one of the highest and most dangerous footpaths in Europe. It used to be very safe, but now it is falling down.

I took a train to the village of El Chorro and started to walk towards the mountains. I was very excited.

Then the adventure began. The path was about three feet wide and there were holes in it. It used to have a handrail, but not any more. I didn't know what to do – should I go on my hands and knees, or stand up? I decided to stand up and walk very slowly. At times the path was only as wide as my two boots. I stopped to have a rest, but there was nowhere to sit.

I began to feel very frightened. It was impossible to look down or look up. I was concentrating so hard that my body started aching. There was no thrill of danger, no enjoyment of the view. I thought I was going to die.

I finally managed to get to the end. I was shaking, and I was covered in sweat from heat and fear. I fell to the ground, exhausted.

**T 10.2**

1 Now I usually go shopping on Saturday, and on Sunday morning I play tennis. When I was a child, I used to go to school on Saturday morning. On Sunday all the family used to get together for Sunday lunch.
2 In the evening I used to watch TV and do my homework. Now I read, or go out with friends.
3 We go to a hotel somewhere hot and just do nothing. When I was young, we used to go camping in Europe. We went everywhere – France, Italy, Austria, Germany.
4 I was very sporty. I used to play everything. Rugby, tennis, swimming, hockey. Now I just play tennis. Oh, and walk the dog!
5 I like documentaries and sport. When I was a kid, I used to like cartoons, comedies, action films, you know, like James Bond.
6 I liked all the things that kids like. Beans, pizza, fizzy drinks. I used to love chips. Still do. Now I eat everything. Except peppers. Really don't like peppers.

**T 10.3**

1 'I'm hungry. I need something to eat.'
'Have a sandwich.'
2 'I'm going to a posh party, but I don't know what to wear.'
'I think you should wear your black dress.'
3 'My CD player's broken. Can you show me how to repair it?'
'I'm sorry. I haven't a clue.'
4 'Don't talk to me. I have nothing to say to you.'
'Oh, dear! What have I done wrong?'
5 'Do I turn left or right? I don't know where to go.'
'Go straight on.'
6 'I'm bored. I haven't got anything to do.'
'Why don't you read the dictionary?'
7 'Can you get some meat?'
'Sure. Tell me how much to buy.'
'A kilo.'
8 'I feel lonely. I need somebody to talk to.'
'Come and talk to me. I'm not doing anything.'

**T 10.4**

frightened terrified
excited bored
surprised exhausted

**T 10.5**

1 I met a famous film star today.
2 I spent four hours going round a museum.
3 I haven't heard from my parents for two months.
4 Wow, Maria! What are you doing here?
5 I failed my exam. I worked …
6 A man started to follow me home last night.
7 My computer's broken, and …

**T 10.6** **It was just a joke**

**I = Interviewer J = Jamie**

I So you decided to kidnap this boy, Tom, for his eighteenth birthday?
J Yeah, just for a joke. We wanted to give him a real scare.
I So how did you organize it?
J About eight of us planned it. Tom thought he was going round to Richard's house, and Dave was driving him there. They came to a place which is quite dark, and there in the middle of the road was this body, this … dead body.
I And this was one of you?
J Yeah, it was Andrew. Dave stopped the car and got out, and then said to Tom, 'Hey, Tom, come and help. This looks really serious.' So Tom got out. I was hiding behind a tree, and I jumped on him. There were about six of us, all dressed in black with balaclavas on our heads. And I had this gun, well, a toy gun, and I put it in his face and started screaming at him to lie on the ground. Then we tied him up, put a blindfold on him, and threw him in the back of the car.
I Did anyone see you doing this?
J Well, yeah, but I'll tell you about that later.
I And how was Tom? Wasn't he terrified?
J Yeah, it was all so real. Tom started to say things like 'Please, I haven't seen your faces. Please let me go.' We were all so worried … you know, that it was getting too real, but we couldn't stop. 'Please,' he said, 'don't kill me!' Anyway, we got him to Richard's house and put him in a room with just a chair in the middle and all these lights pointing at him, so we could see him but he couldn't see us, and then we all started singing Happy Birthday.
I That's amazing!
J Tom tried to say that he knew it was us from the start, but that's just not true. He was so terrified.
I So what about these people who saw the kidnap?
J Well, someone saw what was happening from a bedroom window and called the police, and soon there were police cars and armed police everywhere, dogs, and a police helicopter all looking for terrorists. And that was us!
I And they found you?
J We were driving past later that evening, and the police were stopping everyone and asking if they knew anything about a kidnap, and we had to confess that it was just a joke.
I Weren't they angry with you for wasting so much police time?
J Yeah, well. We're still waiting to hear if we're going to be taken to court.
I And has Tom forgiven you?
J Oh, yeah. He'll never forget his eighteenth birthday, though.

**T 10.7** **see p85**

**T 10.8**

1 Their house is such a mess! I don't know how they live in it.
2 There were so many people at the party! There was nowhere to dance.
3 I'm so hungry! I could eat a horse.
4 Jane and Pete are such nice people! But I can't stand their kids.
5 I've spent so much money this week! I don't know where it's all gone.
6 A present! For me? You're so kind! You really didn't have to.
7 We've had such a nice time! Thank you so much for inviting us.
8 Molly's such a clever dog! She understands every word I say.

# Unit 11

**T 11.1** **Questions and answers**

1 When was the first hamburger made?
In 1895.
2 When was the first McDonald's opened?
In 1948.
3 Where were the first hamburgers made?
In Connecticut.
4 Who were they made by?
Louis Lassen.
5 Why were they called hamburgers?
Because the recipe came from Hamburg.
6 How many McDonald's restaurants have been opened since 1948?
25,000.
7 How many hamburgers are eaten every day?
35 million.

**T 11.2**

1 **A** Are Coca-Cola and hamburgers sold *only* in America?
**B** No, they aren't. They're sold all over the world.

2 **A** Was Coca-Cola invented by Louis Lassen?
**B** No, it wasn't. It was invented by John Pemberton.

3 **A** Were the first hamburgers made in 1948?
**B** No, they weren't. They were made in 1895.

4 **A** Was the first McDonald's restaurant opened in New York?
**B** No, it wasn't. It was opened in San Bernadino, in California.

5 **A** Have 2,500 restaurants now been opened worldwide?
**B** No, not 2,500. 25,000 have been opened worldwide.

**T 11.3 The history of chewing gum**

**P = Presenter I = Interviewer**
**LW = Leanne Ward, chewing gum expert**
**AB = Interviewees**

**Part one**

**P** Today in Worldly Wise, the world's most common habit … .
Yes, chewing gum. We chew 100,000 tons of it every year but how many of us actually know what it's made of?

**I** Excuse me, I see you're chewing gum …
**A** Yeah.
**I** Have you got any idea what it's made of?
**A** Nah – no idea. Never thought about it.
**I** Have *you* any idea what chewing gum is made of?
**B** … Er no, not a clue. Rubber maybe?
**I** And do you have any idea who invented it?
**A** The Americans?
**B** Yeah – sure – I reckon it was invented in America, yeah.

**P** Well no. It wasn't the Americans who invented chewing gum. It was the Swedes. The Swedes, I hear you say? But listen to Leanne Ward, a chewing gum expert.
**LW** The history of chewing goes back thousands of years. In Sweden in 1993, the skeleton of a teenager was found, he was nine thousand years old. And in his mouth was a gum made of tree sap and sweetened with honey – the first known chewing gum.
**P** It seems we've always chewed things of no real food value. Babies are born wanting to chew. Everything goes straight into their mouths. So why do we chew? Here's Leanne again.
**LW** We chew to clean our teeth and freshen our breath but also because we just like chewing. The ancient Greeks chewed a gum called *mastica*, which is a type of tree sap. They thought it was good for their health and women really enjoyed chewing it as a way to sweeten their breath. Then in the first century AD we know that the Mayan Indians in South America liked to chew a tree sap, called *chiclay*. They wrapped it in leaves and put it in their mouths so this was, if you like, the first packet of chewing gum. The American Indians also chewed tree sap – they gave it to the English when they arrived, but it wasn't until a few hundred years after, that it became really popular in America.

**T 11.4 Part two**

**P** The history of modern chewing gum begins in 19th century America. In 1892 a clever young salesman called William Wrigley decided that chewing gum was the thing of the future. Wrigley was a business genius. He was the first to use advertising to sell in a big way. Here's Leanne.
**LW** William Wrigley was really an advertising genius. He hired hundreds of pretty girls, who he called 'the Wrigley girls'. They walked up and down the streets of Chicago and New York City handing out free gum. Millions of pieces were given away. He also had huge electric signs and billboards – one billboard was a mile long, it ran along the side of the train track. So with all this, chewing gum became very popular all over the USA.
**P** So how did the world get to know and love chewing gum? Leanne again.
**LW** Well, during the Second World War American soldiers were given Wrigley gum to help them relax. In 1944 *all* gum production went to the US Army and they took their gum overseas and gave it to children. Soon they were followed everywhere by the cry: 'Got any gum, chum?'.
**P** And so the popularity of gum spread to other countries. After the war sales of gum exploded worldwide. Chewing gum was even taken into space by the first astronauts. So what exactly *is* it made of?
**LW** Well, the strangest thing about gum today is that nobody knows what it's made of. Nobody will tell you. The chewing gum industry keeps the recipe top secret.

**T 11.5**

1 'Are we nearly there yet, Dad?'
'No. It's miles to go, but we'll stop soon and have something to eat.'
'All right. I need the toilet, anyway.'

2 'How much is it to send this letter to Australia?'
'Give it to me and I'll weigh it. That's … £1.20.'
'OK. That's fine. And a book of ten first-class stamps, please.'
'All right.'

3 'Hi. Can I pay for my petrol, please?'
'Which pump?'
'Er … pump number … five.'
'Forty-one pounds 78p, please.'

4 The 7.56 from Bristol is now arriving at platform 4. Virgin Rail would like to apologize for the late arrival of this service. This was due to circumstances beyond our control.

5 'A vodka and orange, please.'
'How old are you?'
'Eighteen.'
'Hmm. Have you got any identification on you?'
'No.'

# Unit 12

**T 12.1**

If I were a princess, I'd live in a palace. I'd have servants to look after me. My Mum would be Queen, and she wouldn't work. I wouldn't go to school. I'd have a private teacher. I'd ride a white horse, and I'd wear a long dress. I could have all the sweets I wanted.

**T 12.2** **see p96**

**T 12.3**

1 'I have no money. What am I going to do?'
'If I were you, I'd try to spend less.'
'What do you mean?'
'Well, you buy a lot of clothes, designer clothes. Stop buying such expensive clothes.'
'But I like them!'

2 'My hair's awful. I can't do anything with it.'
'It's not that bad.'
'It is, really. Just look at it.'
'Well, if I were you, I'd try that new hairdresser, Antonio. He's supposed to be very good, and not that expensive.'
'Mmm. OK, I'll try it. Thanks.'

3 'I've got toothache.'
'Have you seen a dentist?'
'No.'
'Well, if I were you, I'd make an appointment right now.'

4 'I've had a row with my boyfriend.'
'What about?'
'Oh, the usual thing. He gets jealous if I just look at another boy.'
'And did you?'
'No, of course not!'
'Well, if I were you, I'd love him and leave him. He won't ever change, you know.'
'Oh, I couldn't do that.'

5 'My car won't start in the morning.'
'If I were you, I'd buy a new one. Yours is so old.'
'I know it's old, but I can't afford a new one.'
'Well, take it to a garage. Let them have a look at it.'
'All right.'

6 'My neighbours make a lot of noise.'
'Do they? That's awful.'
'Mmm. We can't get to sleep at night.'
'Have you spoken to them about this?'
'No, we're too frightened.'
'If I were you, I'd invite them round to your flat for coffee and say that you're having problems.'
'That's probably a good idea. I'm not sure they'll come, but I'll try it.'

**T 12.4**

**Ruth**

I'm having a holiday in Italy for a couple of weeks, staying in a villa in Tuscany. Then I'm going to look for a job. I want to work in the media – advertising or the BBC would be perfect.

My sister and I are going to buy a flat together, somewhere central, so we'll have to start looking soon. I'm very excited about the future. And I'm also highly ambitious!

**Henry**

I'm not sure yet. Some friends have invited me to go to Long Island with them, so I might go to

America. I'll have to earn some money, so I might work in a restaurant for a bit.

I don't know what I want to do. I love France, so I might live in Paris for a while. I could earn some money painting portraits in Montmartre. Who knows? I might meet a beautiful French girl and fall in love! Wouldn't that be wonderful!

**T 12.5**

**I = Interviewer A = Alice Lester**

**I** When did you first hear these voices, Alice?
**A** Well, I was at home, sitting and reading.
**I** And what did they say?
**A** The first time, there was just one voice. It said, 'Don't be afraid, I just want to help you.'
**I** But it didn't say how it wanted to help you?
**A** No, it didn't. It just went away.
**I** And what about the second time?
**A** It was while I was away on holiday, but this time there were two voices. They told me to go back home immediately, because there was something wrong with me.
**I** So is that what you did?
**A** Yes. And when I was back in London, the voices gave me an address to go to.
**I** And what was the address?
**A** Well, now it starts to get very strange. The address was the brain scan department of St Mary's Hospital. I went there and I met Mr Abrahams, who is a consultant. As I was meeting him, the voices said to me, 'Tell him you have a tumour in your brain, and that you're in a lot of danger.' I said this to Mr Abrahams, but I know he didn't believe me. Anyway, he gave me a scan, and I did have a tumour!
**I** What an incredible story? Did you have an operation?
**A** Yes, I did. And after the operation, the voices came back again, and they said 'We're pleased we were able to help you. Goodbye.' And I've been in good health ever since. Now, what do you think of that?

**T 12.6**

1 **A** Excuse me! Can I get past?
**B** Pardon?
**A** Can I get past, please?
**B** I'm sorry. I didn't hear you. Yes, of course.
**A** Thanks a lot.

2 **A** I hear you're going to get married soon. Congratulations!
**B** That's right, next July. July 21. Can you come to the wedding?
**A** Oh, what a pity! That's when we're away on holiday.
**C** Never mind. We'll send you some wedding cake.
**A** That's very kind.

3 **A** Oh, dear! Look at the time! Hurry up, or we'll miss the train.
**B** Just a minute! I can't find my umbrella. Do you know where it is?
**A** I haven't a clue. But you won't need it. It's a lovely day. Just look at the sky!
**B** Oh, all right. Let's go, then.

4 **A** Good luck in your exam!
**B** Same to you. I hope we both pass.
**A** Did you go out last night?
**B** No, of course not. I went to bed early. What about you?
**A** Me, too. See you later, after the exam. Let's go out for a drink.
**B** Good idea.

# Unit 13

**T 13.1**

1 How long have you been sleeping on the streets?
For a year. It was very cold at first, but you get used to it.
2 Why did you come to London?
I came here to look for work, and I never left.
3 How long have you been selling *The Big Issue*?
For six months. I'm in Covent Garden seven days a week selling the magazine.
4 Have you made many friends?
Lots. But I can't stand people who think I drink or take drugs. My problem is I'm homeless. I want a job, but I need somewhere to live before I can get a job. So I need money to get somewhere to live, but I can't get money because I can't get a job, and I can't get a job because I haven't got somewhere to live. So I'm trapped.
5 How many copies do you sell a day?
Usually about fifty.
6 How many copies have you sold today?
So far, ten. But it's still early.

**T 13.2**

How long have you been trying to find a job?
How many jobs have you had?
How long have you been standing here today?
How did you lose your business?
How long have you had your dog?
Who's your best friend?
Where did you meet him?
How long have you known each other?

**T 13.3**

**A** How long have you been trying to find a job?
**B** For three years. It's been really difficult.
**A** How many jobs have you had?
**B** About thirty, maybe more. I've done everything.
**A** How long have you been standing here today?
**B** Since 8.00 this morning, and I'm freezing.
**A** How did you lose your business?
**B** I owed a lot of money in tax, and I couldn't pay it.
**A** How long have you had your dog?
**B** I've had her for about two months, that's all.
**A** Who's your best friend?
**B** A chap called Robbie, who's also from Scotland, like me.
**A** Where did you meet him?
**B** I met him here in London.
**A** How long have you known each other?
**B** About ten months. I met him soon after I came to London.

**T 13.4** **see T13.5**

**T 13.5 Phoning home**

**C = Craig M = His mother**

**C** Hi Mum. It's me, Craig.
**M** Craig! Hello! How lovely to hear from you. How are you? How's the new job going?
**C** Work's OK – I think. I'm just … so …
**M** Tired? You sound tired. Are you tired? What have you been doing?
**C** I *am* tired, really tired. I've been working so hard and everything's so new to me. I'm in the office until eight o'clock every night.
**M** Eight o'clock! Every night? That's terrible. And when do you eat? Have you been eating well?
**C** Yes, yes – I've been eating OK. After work, Tessa and I go out for a drink and something to eat in the pub round the corner. We're too tired to cook.
**M** Tessa? Who's Tessa?
**C** Tessa? Yes, Tessa. I'm sure I've told you about Tessa. We work together in the same office – she's been working here for a while, so she's been helping me a lot. She's really nice. You'd like her, Mum, if you met her. She lives near me.
**M** Mmm. Maybe you told your father about her, but not me. I've certainly never heard you talk about Tessa before.
**C** Ah yes. Dad. How is he? What's he been doing recently?
**M** Well, he's just returned from a business trip to Holland, so he hasn't been to work today, he's … he's been relaxing.
**C** Oh, yes of course. He's been working in Amsterdam, hasn't he? Well, I'm glad he's relaxing now. And what about you, Mum?
**M** Well, I was going to ring you actually. You see I'm coming to London next Tuesday. I'm going to a teachers' conference at the university, and I wondered if I could stay at your flat.
**C** Next Tuesday. That's great! Of course you can stay at my flat. I'll try to leave work earlier that day and I'll meet you after the conference. You can meet Tessa, too. We'll go out for a meal.
**M** Lovely! I'm looking forward to it already.
**C** Me too. See you next week. Bye for now. Love to Dad!
**M** Bye, Craig. Take care.

**T 13.6** **See p109**

**T 13.7**

307 4922
1-800-878-5311
315 253 6031
517 592 2122
212 726 6390

**T 13.8**

**P = Peter J = John**

1 **P** Hello. 793422.
**J** Hello, Peter. This is John.
**P** Hi, John. How are you?
**J** Fine, thanks. And you?
**P** All right. Did you have a nice weekend? You went away, didn't you?
**J** Yes, we went to see some friends who live in the country. It was lovely. We had a good time.
**P** Ah, good.
**J** Peter, could you do me a favour? I'm playing squash tonight, but my racket's broken. Could I borrow yours?
**P** Sure, that's fine.
**J** Thanks a lot. I'll come and get it in half an hour, if that's OK.
**P** Yes, I'll be in.
**J** OK. Bye.
**P** Bye.

**A = Receptionist B = Student**
**C = Ann, a teacher.**

2 **A** Good morning. International School of English.
**B** Hello, could I speak to Ann Baker, please?
**A** Hold on. I'll connect you.
**C** Hello.
**A** Hello. Can I speak to Ann Baker, please?
**C** Speaking.
**A** Ah, hello. I saw your advertisement about English classes in a magazine. Could you send me some information, please?
**C** Certainly. Can I just take some details? Could you give me your name and address, please?

**A = Mike's flatmate B = Jim**

3 **A** Hello.
**B** Hello. Is that Mike?
**A** No, I'm afraid he's out at the moment. Can I take a message?
**B** Yes, please. Can you say that Jim phoned, and I'll try again later. Do you know what time he'll be back?
**A** In about an hour, I think.
**B** Thanks. Goodbye.
**A** Goodbye.

# Unit 14

### T 14.1 see p111

### T 14.2 Listen and check

I was delighted because I'd passed all my exams.
I was hungry because I hadn't had any breakfast.
I went to bed early because I'd had a busy day.
Our teacher was angry because we hadn't done the homework.
My leg hurt because I'd fallen over playing football.
The plants died because I'd forgotten to water them.
The house was in a mess because we'd had a party the night before.

### T 14.3 Which sentences contain *had*?

1 When we arrived she left.
2 When we arrived she'd left.
3 She'd like to leave now.
4 We'd stopped playing when the rain started.
5 We stopped playing when the rain started.
6 We'd play tennis if the rain stopped.
7 He checked that he'd turned off his mobile phone.
8 He turned off the television and went to bed.
9 I couldn't believe that I'd lost my passport again.
10 If I lost my passport, I'd be very upset.

### T 14.4 What does Mary say?

I love John very much.
We met six months ago.
I've never been in love before.
We're very happy.
I'll love him forever.
I'm seeing him this evening.

### T 14.5 What did Mary tell you?

Mary told me that she loved John very much. She said that they'd met six months ago and that she'd never been in love before. She told me that they were very happy and that she'd love him forever. She said that she was seeing him that evening.

### T 14.6 An interview with Carmen Day

**I = Interviewer CD = Carmen Day**

**I** Carmen, why have you written another romantic novel?
**CD** Because I find romantic fiction easy to write, but my next novel won't be a romance. I'm hoping to write something different, perhaps a detective story.
**I** In *One Short Hot Summer*, who is the character of Bradley based on?
**CD** Ah, well he's based on my first husband, Clive Maingay the actor. Clive made me very unhappy, very unhappy indeed.
**I** You say 'your first husband' – have you then remarried?
**CD** Yes, indeed. I've been married for nearly ten years to Tony Marsh, you know, the politician.
**I** Yes, I know him. Are you happy now?
**CD** Oh, yes. I can honestly say that I've found happiness again. Tony and I are very happy indeed.
**I** Carmen, how many novels have you written so far?
**CD** Well, I've written five novels now, and three stories for children.
**I** And when do you think you'll stop writing?
**CD** Never. I'll never stop. I'll continue to write even when I'm an old lady.

### T 14.7

In an interview Carmen said she had written another romantic novel because she found romantic fiction easy to write, but that her next novel would be something different, possibly a detective story.

Carmen said that the character of Bradley was based on her first husband, Clive Maingay, the actor, who had made her very unhappy. But she added that she was now married to Tony Marsh, the politician. She said that they had been married for nearly ten years and that they were very happy together.

She told me that she had now written five novels, and also that she had written three stories for children. She said she would never stop writing, not even when she was an old lady.

### T 14.8 A song

***Talk to me***

Well every night I see a light up in your window
But every night you won't answer the door
But although you won't ever let me in
From the street I can see your silhouette sitting close to him

What must I do?
What does it take
To get you to
Talk to me
Until the night is over
Talk to me
Well until the night is over, yeah yeah yeah
I got a full week's pay
And baby I've been working hard all day
I'm not asking for the world, you see
I'm just asking girl
Talk to me

Well late at night I hear music that you're playing soft and low
Yes and late at night I see the two of you swaying so close
I don't understand darling what was my sin?
Why am I down here below while you're up there with him?

What did I do?
What did I say?
What must I pay
To get you to
Talk to me
Until the night is over
Talk to me
Well until the night is over, yeah yeah yeah
I've got a full week's pay
And baby I've been working hard all day
I'm not asking for the world, you see
I'm just asking girl
Talk to me.

### T 14.9 Saying goodbye

a Goodbye! Drive carefully and call us when you get there!
b Bye! See you later. Are you doing anything tonight?
c Goodbye! Have a safe journey. Send us a postcard!
d Goodbye. Here's my number. Please get in touch if you have any problems with it.
e Goodbye. It has been most interesting talking to you. We'll let you know by post.
f Goodbye! Good luck in the future. I've really enjoyed our lessons together!
g Bye-bye! Thank you for a lovely evening. You must come to us next time.
h Goodbye. Thank you for a lovely evening. You must come to us next time.

# Grammar Reference

## Unit 1

### 1.1 Tenses

This unit has examples of the Present Simple and Present Continuous, the Past Simple, and two future forms: *going to* and the Present Continuous for the future.
All these tenses are covered again in later units.

| | |
|---|---|
| Present tenses | Unit 2 |
| Past tenses | Unit 3 |
| Future forms | Units 5 and 9 |

The aim in this unit is to revise what you know.

**Present tenses**

He **lives** with his parents.
She **speaks** three languages.
I'**m enjoying** the course.
They'**re studying** at university.

**Past tense**

He **went** to America last year.
She **came** to England three years ago.

**Future forms**

I'**m going to work** as an interpreter.
What **are** you **doing** tonight?

### 1.2 Questions

**Questions with question words**

1 Questions can begin with a question word.

| | | | |
|---|---|---|---|
| what | where | which | how |
| who | when | why | whose |

**Where**'s the station?
**Why** are you laughing?
**Whose** is this coat?
**How** does she go to work?

2 *What, which,* and *whose* can be followed by a noun.

**What size** do you take?
**What sort** of music do you like?
**Which coat** is yours?
**Whose book** is this?

3 *Which* is generally used when there is a limited choice.

**Which** is your husband? The blond one or the dark one?

This rule is not always true.

**What** / **Which** newspaper do you read?

4 *How* can be followed by an adjective or an adverb.

**How big** is his new car?
**How fast** does it go?

*How* can also be followed by *much* or *many.*

**How much** is this sandwich?
**How many** brothers and sisters have you got?

**Questions with no question word**

The answer to these questions is *Yes* or *No.*

| | |
|---|---|
| Are you hot? | Yes, I am./No, I'm not. |
| Is she working? | Yes, she is./No, she isn't. |
| Does he smoke? | Yes, he does./No, he doesn't. |
| Can you swim? | Yes, I can./No, I can't. |

**Form**

**Verb forms with an auxiliary verb**

| Positive | Question |
|---|---|
| She is reading.<br>They are watching a film.<br>She can drive. | Is she reading?<br>What are they watching?<br>Can she drive? |

**Verb forms with no auxiliary verb**

In the Present Simple and the Past Simple there is no auxiliary verb in the positive.

They **live** in London.
He **arrived** yesterday.

*Do/does/did* is used in the question.

**Do** they live in London?
Where **does Bill come from?**
**When did he arrive?**

# Unit 2

## 2.1 Present Simple

### Form

**Positive and negative**

<table>
<tr><td>I<br>We<br>You<br>They</td><td>live<br>don't live</td><td rowspan="2">near here.</td></tr>
<tr><td>He<br>She<br>It</td><td>lives<br>doesn't live</td></tr>
</table>

**Question**

<table>
<tr><td rowspan="2">Where</td><td>do</td><td>I<br>we<br>you<br>they</td><td rowspan="2">live?</td></tr>
<tr><td>does</td><td>he<br>she<br>it</td></tr>
</table>

**Short answer**

| Do you like Peter?<br>Does she speak French? | Yes, I do.<br>No, she doesn't. |
|---|---|

### Use

The Present Simple is used to express:

1 a habit.
I **get up** at 7.30.
Cinda **smokes** too much.

2 a fact which is always true.
Vegetarians **don't eat** meat.
We **come** from Spain.

3 a fact which is true for a long time.
I **live** in Oxford.
She **works** in a bank.

## 2.2 Present Continuous

### Form

*am/is/are* + *-ing* (present participle)

**Positive and negative**

<table>
<tr><td>I</td><td>'m (am)<br>'m not</td><td rowspan="3">working.</td></tr>
<tr><td>He<br>She<br>It</td><td>'s (is)<br>isn't</td></tr>
<tr><td>We<br>You<br>They</td><td>'re (are)<br>aren't</td></tr>
</table>

**Question**

<table>
<tr><td rowspan="3">What</td><td>am</td><td>I</td><td rowspan="3">wearing?</td></tr>
<tr><td>is</td><td>he<br>she<br>it</td></tr>
<tr><td>are</td><td>we<br>you<br>they</td></tr>
</table>

**Short answer**

| Are you going?<br>Is Anna working? | Yes, I am./No, I'm not.<br>Yes, she is./No, she isn't. |
|---|---|

NOT Yes, ~~I'm~~.
Yes, ~~she's~~.

### Use

The Present Continuous is used to express:

1 an activity happening now.
They**'re playing** football in the garden.
She can't answer the phone because she**'s washing** her hair.

2 an activity happening around now, but perhaps not at the moment of speaking.
She**'s studying** maths at university.
I**'m reading** a good book by Henry James.

3 a planned future arrangement.
I**'m meeting** Miss Boyd at ten o'clock tomorrow.
What **are** you **doing** this evening?

## 2.3 Present Simple and Present Continuous

1 Look at the wrong sentences, and compare them with the correct sentences.

| | |
|---|---|
| ✗<br>✓ | Hans is coming from Germany.<br>Hans comes from Germany. |
| ✗<br>✓ | This is a great party. Everyone has a good time.<br>This is a great party. Everyone is having a good time. |
| ✗<br>✓ | I read a good book at the moment.<br>I'm reading a good book at the moment. |

2 There are some verbs that are usually used in the Present Simple only. They express a state, not an activity.

| | |
|---|---|
| ✓<br>✗ | I like Coke.<br>I'm liking Coke. |

Other verbs like this are *think, agree, understand, love.*

## 2.4 *have/have got*

### Form

**Positive**

| | | |
|---|---|---|
| I<br>We<br>You<br>They | have<br>'ve got | two sisters. |
| He<br>She | has<br>'s got | |

**Negative**

| | | |
|---|---|---|
| I<br>We<br>You<br>They | don't have<br>haven't got | any money. |
| He<br>She | doesn't have<br>hasn't got | |

**Question**

| | | |
|---|---|---|
| Do | I<br>we<br>you<br>they | have a car? |
| Does | he<br>she | |

| | | |
|---|---|---|
| Have | I<br>we<br>you<br>they | got a car? |
| Has | he<br>she | |

**Short answer**

| | |
|---|---|
| Do you have a camera?<br>Have you got a camera? | Yes, I do./No, I don't.<br>Yes, I have./No, I haven't. |

We can use contractions (*'ve* and *'s*) with *have got*, but not with *have*.

**I've got** a sister.

I **have** a sister. NOT ~~I've~~ a sister.

### Use

1 *Have* and *have got* mean the same. *Have got* is informal. We use it a lot when we speak, but not when we write.

**Have** you **got** a light?

The Prime Minister **has** a meeting with the President today.

In American English, *have + do/does* is much more common.

2 *Have* and *have got* express possession.

| | |
|---|---|
| I have<br>I've got | a new car.<br>three children.<br>blond hair. |
| She has<br>She's got | |
| He has<br>He's got | |

3 When *have* + noun expresses an activity or a habit, *have* and the *do/does/don't/doesn't* forms are used. *Have got* is not used. Compare these sentences.

| | |
|---|---|
| ✗<br>✓ | I've got a shower in the morning.<br>I have a shower in the morning. |
| ✗<br>✓ | What time have you got lunch?<br>What time do you have lunch? |
| ✗<br>✓ | He has never got milk in his coffee.<br>He never has milk in his coffee. |

4 In the past tense, the *got* forms are unusual. *Had* with *did* and *didn't* is much more common.

I **had** a bicycle when I was young.

My parents **had** a lot of books in the house.

**Did** you **have** a nice weekend?

I **didn't have** any money when I was a student.

# Unit 3

## 3.1 Past Simple

### Spelling

1 The normal rule is to add *-ed.*

work**ed** start**ed**

If the verb ends in *-e*, add *-d*.

live**d** love**d**

2 If the verb has only one syllable + one vowel + one consonant, double the consonant.

sto**pp**ed pla**nn**ed

3 If the verb ends in a consonant + *-y*, change the *-y* to *-ied.*

stud**ied** carr**ied**

There are many common irregular verbs. See the list on p143.

### Form

The form of the Past Simple is the same for all persons.

**Positive**

| | | |
|---|---|---|
| I<br>He/She/It<br>We<br>You<br>They | finished<br>arrived<br>went | yesterday. |

**Negative**

The negative of the Past Simple is formed with *didn't.*

He walk[ed].

He [**didn't**] walk[ ].

| | | |
|---|---|---|
| I<br>He/She/It<br>We<br>You<br>They | didn't (did not) | arrive yesterday. |

**Question**

The question in the Past Simple is formed with *did.*

She finish[ed].

When [**did**] she finish[ ]?

| | | |
|---|---|---|
| When did | she<br>you<br>they<br>etc. | arrive? |

**Short answer**

| | |
|---|---|
| Did you go to work yesterday?<br>Did it rain last night? | Yes, I did.<br>No, it didn't. |

### Use

1 The Past Simple expresses a past action that is now finished.
   We **played** tennis last Sunday.
   I **worked** in London from 1994 to 1999.
   John **left** two minutes ago.

2 Notice the time expressions that are used with the Past Simple.

| | |
|---|---|
| I did it | last year.<br>last month.<br>five years ago.<br>yesterday morning.<br>in 1985. |

## 3.2 Past Continuous

### Form

*was/were* + *-ing*
(present participle)

**Positive and negative**

| | | |
|---|---|---|
| I<br>He<br>She<br>It | was<br>wasn't (was not) | working. |
| We<br>You<br>They | were<br>weren't (were not) | |

**Question**

| | | | |
|---|---|---|---|
| What | was | I<br>he<br>she<br>it | doing? |
| | were | we<br>you<br>they | |

**Short answer**

| | |
|---|---|
| Were you working yesterday? | Yes, I was. |
| Was she studying when you arrived? | No, she wasn't. |

### Use

1 The Past Continuous expresses a past activity that has duration.
   I met her while I **was living** in Paris.
   You **were making** a lot of noise last night.
   What **were** you **doing**?

2 The activity began *before* the action expressed by the Past Simple.
   She **was making** coffee when we arrived.
   When I phoned Simon he **was having** dinner.

3 The Past Continuous expresses an activity in progress before, and probably after, a time in the past.
   When I woke up this morning, the sun **was shining**.
   What **were** you **doing** at 8.00 last night?

## 3.3 Past Simple and Past Continuous

1 The Past Simple expresses past actions as simple facts.
   I **did** my homework last night.
   'What **did** you **do** yesterday evening?' 'I **watched** TV.'

2 The Past Continuous gives past activities time and duration. The activity can be interrupted.
   'What **were** you **doing** at 8.00?' 'I **was watching** TV.'
   I **was doing** my homework when Jane arrived.

3 In stories, the Past Continuous can describe the scene. The Past Simple tells the action.
   It **was** a beautiful day. The sun **was shining** and the birds **were singing**, so we **decided** to go for a picnic. We **put** everything in the car …

4 The questions below refer to different time periods. The Past Continuous asks about activities before, and the Past Simple asks about what happened after.

| | | |
|---|---|---|
| What were you doing<br>What did you do | when it started to rain? | We were playing tennis.<br>We went home. |

## 3.4 Prepositions in time expressions

| at | in | no preposition |
|---|---|---|
| at six o'clock<br>at midnight<br>at Christmas<br>at the weekend | in the morning/afternoon/evening<br>in December<br>in summer<br>in 1995<br>in two weeks' time | today<br>yesterday<br>tomorrow<br>the day after tomorrow<br>the day before yesterday<br>last night<br>last week<br>two weeks ago<br>next month<br>yesterday evening<br>tomorrow evening<br>this evening<br>tonight |
| **on** | | |
| on Saturday<br>on Monday morning<br>on Christmas Day<br>on January 18 | | |

# Unit 4

## 4.1 Expressions of quantity

**Count and uncount nouns**

1 It is important to understand the difference between count and uncount nouns.

| Count nouns | Uncount nouns |
|---|---|
| a cup | water |
| a girl | sugar |
| an apple | milk |
| an egg | music |
| a pound | money |

We can say *three cups, two girls, ten pounds.* We can count them. We cannot say ~~two waters~~, ~~three musics~~, ~~one money~~. We cannot count them.

2 Count nouns can be singular or plural.
This **cup is** full.
These **cups are** empty.
Uncount nouns can only be singular.
The **water is** cold.
The **weather was** terrible.

### *much* and *many*

1 We use *much* with uncount nouns in questions and negatives.
How **much money** have you got?
There isn't **much milk** left.

2 We use *many* with count nouns in questions and negatives.
How **many people** were at the party?
I didn't take **many photos** on holiday.

### *some* and *any*

1 *Some* is used in positive sentences.
I'd like **some** sugar.

2 *Any* is used in questions and negatives.
Is there **any** sugar in this tea?
Have you got **any** brothers and sisters?
We don't have **any** washing-up liquid.
I didn't buy **any** apples.

3 We use *some* in questions that are requests or offers.
Can I have **some** cake?
Would you like **some** tea?

4 The rules are the same for the compounds *someone, anything, anybody, somewhere,* etc.
I've got **something** for you.
Hello? Is **anybody** here?
There isn't **anywhere** to go in my town.

### *a few* and *a little*

1 We use *a few* with count nouns.
There are **a few cigarettes** left, but not many.

2 We use *a little* with uncount nouns.
Can you give me **a little help**?

### *a lot/lots of*

1 We use *a lot/lots of* with both count and uncount nouns.
There's **a lot of butter**.
I've got **lots of friends**.

2 *A lot/lots of* can be used in questions and negatives.
Are there **lots of tourists** in your country?
There isn't **a lot of butter**, but there's enough.

## 4.2 Articles – *a* and *the*

1 The indefinite article *a* or *an* is used with singular, countable nouns to refer to a thing or an idea for the first time.
We have **a cat** and **a dog**.
There's **a supermarket** in Adam Street.

2 The definite article *the* is used with singular and plural, countable and uncountable nouns when both the speaker and the listener know the thing or idea already.
We have a,cat and a dog. **The cat** is old, but **the dog** is just a puppy.
I'm going to **the supermarket**. Do you want anything? (We both know which supermarket.)

**Indefinite article**

The indefinite article is used:

1 with professions.
I'm **a teacher**.
She's **an architect**.

2 with some expressions of quantity.
**a pair of  a little  a couple of  a few**

3 in exclamations with *what* + a count noun.
**What a** lovely **day**!
**What a pity**!

**Definite article**

The definite article is used:

1 before seas, rivers, hotels, pubs, theatres, museums, and newspapers.
**the Atlantic  the British Museum**
***The Times*  the Ritz**

2 if there is only one of something.
**the sun  the Queen  the Government**

3 with superlative adjectives.
He's **the richest man** in the world.
Jane's **the oldest** in the class.

**No article**

There is no article:

1 before plural and uncountable nouns when talking about things in general.
I like potatoes.
Milk is good for you.

2 before countries, towns, streets, languages, magazines, meals, airports, stations, and mountains.
I had lunch with John.
I bought *Cosmopolitan* at Paddington Station.

3 before some places and with some forms of transport.

| at home | in/to bed | at/to work | at/to school/university |
|---|---|---|---|
| by bus | by plane | by car | by train | on foot |

She goes to work by bus.
I was at home yesterday evening.

4 in exclamations with *what* + an uncount noun.
**What** beautiful **weather**!
**What** loud **music**!

**Note**

In the phrase *go home*, there is no article and no preposition.
I **went home** early.  NOT  ~~I went to home~~.

# Unit 5

## 5.1 Verb patterns 1

Here are four verb patterns. There is a list of verb patterns on p143.

1 Verb + *to* + infinitive
They **want to buy a** new car.
I'd **like to go** abroad.

2 Verb + *-ing*
Everyone **loves going** to parties.
He **finished reading** his book.

3 Verb + *-ing* or + *to* + infinitive with no change in meaning
It **began to rain/raining.**
I **continued to work/working** in the library.

4 Verb + preposition + *-ing*
We**'re thinking of moving** house.
**I'm looking forward to having** more free time.

## 5.2 *like doing* and *would like to do*

1 *Like doing* and *love doing* express a general enjoyment.
I **like working** as a teacher. = I am a teacher and I enjoy it.
I **love dancing.** = This is one of my hobbies.

2 *Would like to do* and *would love to do* express a preference now or at a specific time.
**I'd like to be** a teacher. = When I grow up, I want to be a teacher.
Thank you. **I'd love to dance.** = We're at a disco. I'm pleased that you asked me.

| **Question** | **Short answer** |
|---|---|
| Would you like to dance?<br>Would you like to come for a walk? | Yes, I would./Yes, I'd love to.<br>Yes, I would./No, thank you. |

**Note**
*No, I wouldn't* is not common because it is impolite.

## 5.3 *will*

### Form

*will* + infinitive without *to*
*Will* is a modal auxiliary verb. There is an introduction to modal auxiliary verbs on p137 of the Grammar Reference. The forms of *will* are the same for all persons.

**Positive and negative**

| | | |
|---|---|---|
| I<br>He/She/It<br>We/You/They | 'll (will)<br>won't | come.<br>help you.<br>invite Tom. |

**Question**

| | | |
|---|---|---|
| When will | he<br>you<br>they | help me? |

**Short answer**

| | |
|---|---|
| Will you help me? | Yes, I will. |

**Note**
*No, I won't* is not common because it is impolite. It means 'I don't want to help you.'
A polite way of saying 'no' here is 'I'm afraid I can't.'

### Use

*Will* is used:

1 to express a future decision or intention made *at* the moment of speaking.
'It's Jane's birthday.' 'Is it? **I'll buy** her some flowers.'
**I'll give** you my phone number.
'Which do you want? The blue or the red?'
'**I'll take** the red, thank you.'

2 to express an offer.
**I'll carry** your suitcase.
We**'ll do** the washing-up.

Other uses of *will* are covered in Unit 9.

## *going to*

### Form

*am/is/are* + *going* + *to* + infinitive

**Positive and negative**

| | | |
|---|---|---|
| I | 'm (am)<br>'m not | going to work. |
| He<br>She<br>It | 's (is)<br>isn't | |
| We<br>You<br>They | 're (are)<br>aren't | |

**Question**

| | | | |
|---|---|---|---|
| When | am | I | going to arrive? |
| | is | he<br>she<br>it | |
| | are | we<br>you<br>they | |

**Short answer**

| | |
|---|---|
| Are they going to get married? | Yes, they are./No, they aren't. |

### Use

*Going to* is used:

1 to express a future decision, intention, or plan made *before* the moment of speaking.
How long **are** they **going to stay** in Rome?
She **isn't going to have** a birthday party.

**Note**
The Present Continuous can be used in a similar way for a plan or arrangement, particularly with the verbs *go* and *come.*
She**'s coming** on Friday.
**I'm going** home early tonight.

2 when we can see or feel now that something is certain to happen in the future.
Look at these clouds! It**'s going to rain.**
Watch out! That box **is going to fall.**

***will* or *going to*?**
Look at the use of *will* and *going to* in these sentences.
I'm **going to make** a chicken casserole for dinner.
(I decided this morning and bought everything for it.)
What shall I cook for dinner? Er ... I know! **I'll make** chicken casserole! That's a good idea!
(I decided at the moment of speaking.)

# Unit 6

## 6.1 *What . . . like?*

### Form

*what* + *to be* + subject + *like?*

| What | 's (is) your teacher<br>are his parents<br>was your holiday<br>were the beaches | like? | She's very patient.<br>They're very kind.<br>Wonderful. We swam a lot.<br>OK, but some were dirty. |
|---|---|---|---|

**Note**

We don't use *like* in the answer.

She's patient. NOT ~~She's like patient~~.

### Use

*What ... like?* means 'Describe somebody or something. Tell me about them. I don't know anything about them.'

*Like* in this question is a preposition, not a verb:

'What's Jim **like?**' 'He's intelligent and kind, and he's got lovely blue eyes.'

In the following sentences *like* is a verb:

'What does Jim **like?**' 'He **likes** motorbikes and playing tennis.'

**Note**

*How's your mother?* asks about health. It doesn't ask for a description.

'How's your mother?' 'She's very well, thank you.'

## 6.2 Comparative and superlative adjectives

### Form

1 Look at the chart.

| | | **Comparative** | **Superlative** |
|---|---|---|---|
| **Short adjectives** | cheap<br>small<br>*big | cheaper<br>smaller<br>bigger | cheapest<br>smallest<br>biggest |
| **Adjectives that end in *-y*** | funny<br>early<br>heavy | funnier<br>earlier<br>heavier | funniest<br>earliest<br>heaviest |
| **Adjectives with two syllables or more** | careful<br>boring<br>expensive<br>interesting | more careful<br>more boring<br>more expensive<br>more interesting | most careful<br>most boring<br>most expensive<br>most interesting |
| **Irregular adjectives** | far<br>good<br>bad | further<br>better<br>worse | furthest<br>best<br>worst |

* Short adjectives with one vowel + one consonant double the consonant: *hot/hotter/hottest, fat/fatter/fattest.*

2 *Than* is often used after a comparative adjective.

I'm **younger than** Barbara.

Barbara's **more intelligent than** Sarah.

*Much* can come before the comparative to give emphasis.

She's **much nicer than** her sister.

Is Tokyo **much more modern than** London?

3 *The* is used before superlative adjectives.

He's **the funniest** boy in the class.

Which is **the tallest** building in the world?

### Use

1 We use comparatives to compare one thing, person, or action with another.

She's **taller** than me.

London's **more expensive** than Rome.

2 We use superlatives to compare somebody or something with the whole group.

She's the **tallest** in the class.

It's the **most expensive** hotel in the world.

3 *As ... as* shows that something is the same or equal.

Jim's **as tall as** Peter.

I'm **as worried as** you are.

4 *Not as/so ... as* shows that something isn't the same or equal.

She **isn't as tall as** her mother.

My car **wasn't so expensive as** yours.

# Unit 7

## 7.1 Present Perfect

### Form

*have/has* + *-ed* (past participle)
The past participle of regular verbs ends in *-ed*. There are many common irregular verbs. See the list on p143.

**Positive and negative**

| | | |
|---|---|---|
| I<br>We/You/They | 've (have)<br>haven't | worked in a factory. |
| He/She/It | 's (has)<br>hasn't | |

**Question**

| | | |
|---|---|---|
| Have | I<br>we/you/they | been to the United States? |
| Has | he/she/it | |

**Short answer**

| | |
|---|---|
| Have you been to Egypt?<br>Has she ever written poetry? | Yes, I have./No, I haven't.<br>Yes, she has./No, she hasn't. |

**Note**
We cannot use *I've, they've, he's*, etc. in short answers.
Yes, I **have**. NOT ~~Yes, I've~~.
Yes, we **have**. NOT ~~Yes, we've~~.

### Use

1 The Present Perfect looks back from the present into the past, and expresses what has happened before now. The action happened at an indefinite time in the past.
I**'ve met** a lot of famous people. (before now)
She **has won** awards. (in her life)
She**'s written** twenty books. (up to now)
The action can continue to the present, and probably into the future.
She**'s lived** here for twenty years. (she still lives here)

2 The Present Perfect expresses an experience as part of someone's life.
I**'ve travelled** a lot in Africa.
They**'ve lived** all over the world.
*Ever* and *never* are common with this use.
Have you **ever** been in a car crash?
My mother has **never** flown in a plane.

3 The Present Perfect expresses an action or state which began in the past and continues to the present.
I**'ve known** Alice for six years.
How long **have** you **worked** as a teacher?
Note that the time expressions *for* and *since* are common with this use. We use *for* with a period of time, and *since* with a point in time.
We've lived here **for** two years. (a period of time)
I've had a beard **since** I left the army. (a point in time)

**Note**
In many languages, this use is expressed by a present tense. But in English, we say:
Peter **has been** a teacher for ten years.
NOT ~~Peter is a teacher for ten years.~~

4 The Present Perfect expresses a past action with results in the present. It is often a recent past action.
I**'ve lost** my wallet. (I haven't got it now.)
The taxi**'s arrived**. (It's outside the door now.)
**Has** the postman **been**? (Are there any letters for me?)
The adverbs *just, already*, and *yet* are common with this use. *Yet* is used in questions and negatives.
She's **just** had some good news.
I've **already** had breakfast.
Has the postman been **yet**?
It's 11.00 and she hasn't got up **yet**.

## 7.2 Present Perfect and Past Simple

1 Compare the Past Simple and Present Perfect.

**Past Simple**
1 The Past Simple refers to an action that happened at a definite time in the past.
He **died** in 1882.
She **got** married when she was 22.
The action is finished.
I **lived** in Paris for a year (but not now).
2 Time expressions + the Past Simple

| | |
|---|---|
| I did it | **in** 1999.<br>last week.<br>two months **ago**.<br>**on** March 22.<br>**for** two years. |

**Present Perfect**
1 The Present Perfect refers to an action that happened at an indefinite time in the past.
She **has won** awards.
She**'s written** twenty books.
The action can continue to the present.
She**'s lived** there for twenty years (and she still does.)
2 Time expressions + the Present Perfect

| | |
|---|---|
| I've worked here | **for** twenty years.<br>**since** 1995.<br>**since** I left school. |

We've **never** been to America.

2 Compare these sentences.

| | |
|---|---|
| ✗<br>✓ | I've broken my leg last year.<br>I broke my leg last year. |
| ✗<br>✓ | He works as a musician all his life.<br>He has worked as a musician all his life. |
| ✗<br>✓ | When have you been to Greece?<br>When did you go to Greece? |
| ✗<br>✓ | How long do you have your car?<br>How long have you had your car? |

# Unit 8

## 8.1 *have to*

### Form

*has/have* + *to* + infinitive

**Positive and negative**

| | | | |
|---|---|---|---|
| I<br>We<br>You<br>They | have<br>don't have | to | work hard. |
| He<br>She<br>It | has<br>doesn't have | | |

**Question**

| | | | |
|---|---|---|---|
| Do | I<br>we<br>you<br>they | have to | work hard? |
| Does | he<br>she<br>it | | |

**Short answer**

| | |
|---|---|
| Do you have to wear a uniform?<br>Does he have to go now? | Yes, I do.<br>No, he doesn't. |

**Note**

1 The past tense of *have to* is *had to*, with *did* and *didn't* in the question and the negative.
   I **had to** get up early this morning.
   Why **did** you **have to** work last weekend?
   They liked the hotel because they **didn't have to** do any cooking.
2 The forms of *have got to* + infinitive are the same as *have got* + noun. See p131.

### Use

1 *Have to* expresses strong obligation. The obligation comes from 'outside' – perhaps a law, a rule at school or work, or someone in authority.
   You **have to** have a driving licence if you want to drive a car. (That's the law.)
   I **have to** start work at 8.00. (My company says I must.)
   The doctor says I **have to** do more exercise.
2 *Don't/doesn't have to* expresses absence of obligation (it isn't necessary).
   You **don't have to** do the washing-up. I've got a dishwasher.
   She **doesn't have to** work on Monday. It's her day off.

## 8.2 Introduction to modal auxiliary verbs

### Form

These are modal auxiliary verbs.

| | | | |
|---|---|---|---|
| can | could | might | must |
| shall | should | will | would |

They are looked at in different units of *Headway*.

They have certain things in common:

1 They 'help' another verb. The verb form is the infinitive without *to*.
   She **can** drive.
   I **must get** my hair cut.
2 There is no *do/does* in the question.
   **Can she sing?**
   **Should I go** home now?
3 The form is the same for all persons. There is no *-s* in the third person singular:
   He **can dance** very well.
   She **should try** harder.
   It **will rain** soon.
4 To form the negative, add *n't*. There is no *don't/doesn't*.
   I would**n't** like to be a teacher.
   You must**n't** steal.

   **Note**
   *will not* = *won't*.
   It **won't** rain tomorrow.
5 Most modal verbs refer to the present and future. Only *can* has a past tense form, *could*.
   I **could** swim when I was three.

## 8.3 *should*

### Form

*should* + infinitive without *to*
The forms of *should* are the same for all persons.

**Positive and negative**

| | |
|---|---|
| I<br>He<br>We<br>They | should do more exercise.<br>shouldn't tell lies. |

**Question**

| | | |
|---|---|---|
| Should | I<br>she<br>they | see a doctor? |
| Do you think | I<br>he<br>we | should see a doctor? |

**Short answer**

| | |
|---|---|
| Should I phone home?<br>Should I buy a Mercedes Benz? | Yes, you should.<br>No, you shouldn't. |

### Use

*Should* is used to express what the speaker thinks is right or the best thing to do. It expresses mild obligation, or advice.
   I **should** do more work. (This is my opinion.)
   You **should** do more work. (I'm telling you what I think.)
   Do you think we **should** stop here? (I'm asking you for your opinion.)
*Shouldn't* expresses negative advice.
   You **shouldn't** sit so close to the TV. It's bad for your eyes.

**Note**
*Should* expresses the opinion of the speaker, and it is often introduced by *I think* or *I don't think*.
   **I think** politicians **should** listen more.
   **I don't think** people **should** get married until they're 21.

## 8.4 *must*

### Form

*must* + infinitive without *to*
The forms of *must* are the same for all persons.

**Positive and negative**

| | |
|---|---|
| I<br>He<br>We<br>They | must try harder.<br>mustn't steal. |

Questions with *must* are possible, but the use of *have to* is more common.

| Question | Short answer |
|---|---|
| **Must** I take exams?<br>Do I **have to** take exams? | Yes, you must.<br>Yes, you do. |

### Use

1 *Must* expresses strong obligation. Generally, this obligation comes from 'inside' the speaker.
 I **must** get my hair cut. (I think this is necessary.)
2 Because *must* expresses the authority of the speaker, you should be careful of using *You must* … . It sounds very bossy!
 You **must** help me. (I am giving you an order.)
 *Could you help me?* is much better.
3 *You must* … can express a strong suggestion.
 **You must** see the Monet exhibition. It's wonderful.
 **You must** give me a ring when you're next in town.

# Unit 9

## 9.1 Time clauses

1 Look at this sentence.
 *I'll give her a ring when I get home.*
 It consists of two clauses: a main clause *I'll give her a ring* and a secondary clause *when I get home.*
2 These conjunctions of time introduce secondary clauses.

| when while as soon as after before until |
|---|

 They are not usually followed by a future form. They refer to future time, but we use a present tense.
 **When** I get home, I'll …
 **While** we're away, …
 **As soon as** I hear from you, …
 Wait here **until** I get back.

## 9.2 *will*

### Form

For the forms of *will*, see p134.

### Use

1 *Will* expresses a decision or intention made at the moment of speaking.
 Give me your case. **I'll** carry it for you.
2 It also expresses a future fact. The speaker thinks 'This action is sure to happen in the future'.
 Manchester **will** win the cup.
 Tomorrow's weather **will** be warm and sunny.
 This use is like a neutral future tense. The speaker is predicting the future, without expressing an intention, plan, or personal judgement.

## 9.3 First conditional

### Form

*if* + Present Simple, *will* + infinitive without *to*

**Positive and negative**

| | | | |
|---|---|---|---|
| **If** | I work hard, I<br>she has enough money, she<br>we don't hurry up, we<br>you're late, I | 'll (will)<br>won't | pass my exams.<br>buy a new car.<br>be late.<br>wait for you. |

**Question**

| | | | | |
|---|---|---|---|---|
| What<br>Where | will | you do<br>she go | **if** | you don't go to university?<br>she can't find a job? |

**Short answer**

| | |
|---|---|
| Will you go to university if you pass your exams? | Yes, I will.<br>No, I won't. |
| If we look after the planet, will we survive? | Yes, we will.<br>No, we won't. |

**Note**
The condition clause *if* … can come at the beginning of the sentence or at the end. If it comes at the begining, we put a comma at the end of the clause. If it comes at the end, we do not use a comma.
 **If** I work hard**,** I'll pass my exams.
 I'll pass my exams **if** I work hard.

### Use

1 The first conditional is used to express a possible condition and a probable result in the future.
 **If** my cheque **comes**, **I'll buy** us all a meal.
 You**'ll get** wet if you **don't take** an umbrella.
 What**'ll happen** to the environment if we **don't look after** it?

**Note**
1 English uses a present tense in the condition clause, not a future form.
 If it **rains** … NOT If it ~~will rain~~ …
 If I **work** hard … NOT If ~~I'll work~~ hard …
2 *If* expresses a possibility that something will happen; *when* expresses what the speaker sees as certain to happen.
 **If** I find your book, I'll send it to you.
 **When** I get home, I'll have a bath.

# Unit 10

## 10.1 Verb patterns 2

Verb patterns were first covered in Unit 5. There is a list of verb patterns on p143.

1 Verb + *to* + infinitive
 They **managed to escape**.
 I **try to visit** somewhere new.
 We **decided to go** abroad.

2 *go* + *-ing* for sports and activities
 Let's **go skiing**.
 We **went dancing**.

3 Verb + sb + infinitive without *to*
 My teachers **made** me **work** hard.
 My parents **let** me **go out** when I want.

## 10.2 *used to*

### Form

*used* + *to* + infinitive
*Used to* is the same in all persons.

**Positive and negative**

| I<br>She<br>We<br>They | used to<br>didn't use to | smoke.<br>like cooking. |
|---|---|---|

**Question**

| What did you use to do? |
|---|

**Short answer**

| Did you use to smoke a lot? | Yes, I did./No, I didn't. |
|---|---|

**Note**

1 The question form is not often used. We ask a question in the Past Simple, and reply using *used to.*
 Where **did** you **go** on holiday when you were young?
 We **used to go** camping in France.

2 *Never* is often used.
 I **never** used to watch TV.

3 Be careful not to confuse to *use* (e.g. *I **use** a knife to cut an apple.*) and *used to.*
The pronunciation is also different.
to use /ju:z/ used to /ju:stu:/ or /ju:stə/

### Use

*Used to* is used:

1 to express a past habit.
 He **used to** play football every Saturday, but now he doesn't.

2 to express a past state.
 They **used to** be happy together, but now they fight all the time.

## 10.3 *used to* and the Past Simple

1 The Past Simple can also be used to express a past habit or state.
 He **played** football every Sunday when he **was** a boy.
 They **were** happy together when they **were** first married.

2 Only the Past Simple can be used for actions which happened once in the past.
 We used to go to France every summer, but once, in 1987, we **went** to Greece.
 Last night I **drank** champagne.

**Note**

*Used to* has no equivalent in the present. The Present Simple is used for present habits and states.
 She **lives** in New York.
 She sometimes **comes** to London on business.

## 10.4 Infinitives

1 Infinitives are used to express purpose. They answer the question *Why ... ?* This use is very common in English.
 I'm learning English **to get** a good job.
 She's saving her money **to buy** a car.
 I'm going to Scotland **to visit** my parents.

**Note**

Some languages express this idea of purpose with a translation of *for* + infinitive. English does not use *for.*
 I came here **to learn** English.
 NOT I came here ~~for to~~ learn English.
 I came here ~~for~~ learn English.

2 Infinitives are used after certain adjectives.

| I'm | pleased<br>surprised | to see you. |
|---|---|---|
| It's | hard<br>important<br>impossible | to learn Chinese. |

3 Infinitives are used after the question words *who, what, where, how,* etc.
 Can you tell me **how to get** to the station?
 I don't know **who to speak** to.
 Show me **what to do**.

4 Infinitives are used after the compounds *something, nothing, nowhere, anybody,* etc.
 Have **something to eat**!
 I've got **nothing to do**.
 There's **nowhere to hide**.
 Is there **anyone to talk** to?

# Unit 11

## 11.1 The passive

### Form

| | |
|---|---|
| *am/is/are*<br>*was/were*<br>*has/have been*<br>*will* | + *-ed* (past participle) |

The past participle of regular verbs ends in *-ed*. There are many common irregular verbs. See the list on p143.

**Present**

**Positive and negative**

English **is spoken** all over the world.
Renault cars **are made** in France.
My children **aren't helped** with their homework.
Coffee **isn't grown** in England.

**Question**

Where **is** rice **grown**?
**Are** cars **made** in your country?

**Past**

**Positive and negative**

My car **was stolen** last night.
The animals **were frightened** by a loud noise.
He **wasn't injured** in the accident.
The thieves **weren't seen** by anyone.

**Question**

How **was** the window **broken**?
**Were** the plants **watered** last night?

**Present Perfect**

**Positive and negative**

**I've been robbed**!
Diet Coke **has been made** since 1982.
They **haven't been invited** to the party.

**Question**

How many times **have** you **been hurt** playing football?
**Has** my car **been repaired**?

***will***

**Positive and negative**

10,000 cars **will be produced** next year.
The cars **won't be sold** in the UK.

**Question**

**Will** the children **be sent** to a new school?

**Short answer**

| | |
|---|---|
| Are cars made in your country? | Yes, they are./No, they aren't. |
| Were the plants watered last night? | Yes, they were./No, they weren't. |
| Has my car been repaired? | Yes, it has./No, it hasn't. |
| Will these cars be produced next year? | Yes, they will./No, they won't. |

**Note**

1 The rules for tense usage in the passive are the same as in the active.
Present Simple to express habit:
My car **is serviced** regularly.
Past Simple to express a finished action in the past:
America **was discovered** by Christopher Columbus.
Present Perfect to express an action which began in the past and continues to the present:
Diet Coke **has been made** since 1982.

2 The passive infinitive (*to be* + *-ed*) is used after modal auxiliary verbs and other verbs which are followed by an infinitive.
Driving should **be banned** in city centres.
The house is going **to be knocked down**.

### Use

1 The object of an active verb becomes the subject of a passive verb. Notice the use of *by* in the passive sentence.

| | | |
|---|---|---|
| | | **Object** |
| **Active** | Shakespeare wrote *Hamlet*. | |
| **Passive** | *Hamlet* was written by Shakespeare. | |
| | **Subject** | |

2 The passive is not another way of expressing the same sentence in the active. We choose the active or the passive depending on what we are more interested in.
*Hamlet* **was written** in 1600. (We are more interested in *Hamlet*.)
Shakespeare **wrote** comedies, histories, and tragedies. (We are more interested in Shakespeare.)

**Note**

Some verbs, for example, *give, send, show*, have two objects, a person and a thing.
She **gave me** a **book** for my birthday.
In the passive, we often make the person the subject, not the thing.
**I** was given a book for my birthday.
**She** was sent the information by post.
**You**'ll be shown where to sit.

# Unit 12

## 12.1 Second conditional

### Form

*if* + Past Simple, *would* + infinitive without *to*
*Would* is a modal auxiliary verb. There is an introduction to modal auxiliary verbs on p137.
The forms of *would* are the same for all persons.

**Positive and negative**

| | | | |
|---|---|---|---|
| If | I had more money, I<br>she knew the answer, she<br>we lived in Russia, we<br>I didn't have so many debts, I | 'd (would)<br><br>wouldn't | buy a CD player.<br>tell us.<br>soon learn Russian.<br>have to work so hard. |

**Question**

| | | | | |
|---|---|---|---|---|
| What<br>Which countries | would | you do<br>you go to | if | you had a year off?<br>you travelled round the world? |

**Short answer**

| | |
|---|---|
| Would you travel round the world?<br>If they had the money, would they buy a new car? | Yes, I would./No, I wouldn't.<br>Yes, they would./No, they wouldn't. |

**Note**

1 The condition clause can come at the beginning or the end of the sentence. If it comes at the beginning, we put a comma at the end of the clause. If it comes at the end, we do not use a comma.
   **If** I had more time**,** I'd help.
   I'd help **if** I had more time.
2 *Were* is often used instead of *was* in the condition clause.
   If I **were** you, I'd go to bed.
   If he **were** cleverer, he'd know he was making a mistake.

### Use

The second conditional is used to express an unreal or improbable condition and its probable result in the present or future.
The condition is unreal because it is different from the facts that we know. We can always say 'But … '.
   **If I were** Prime Minister, **I'd increase** tax for rich people. (But I'm not Prime Minister.)
   **If I lived** in a big house, **I'd have** a party. (But I live in a small house.)
   What **would** you **do if you saw** a ghost? (But I don't expect that you will see a ghost.)

**Note**

1 The use of the past tense (If I had) and *would* does not refer to past time. Both the first and second conditional refer to the present and the future. The past verb forms are used to show 'This is different from reality'.
   **If I win** the tennis match, **I'll be** happy. (I think I have a good chance.)
   **If I won** a thousand pounds, **I'd …** (But I don't think I will.)
2 We do not use *would* in the condition clause.
   If the weather **was** nice … NOT If the weather ~~would be~~ nice …
   If I **had** more money … NOT If I ~~would have~~ more money …

## 12.2 *might*

### Form

*might* + infinitive without *to*
*Might* is a modal auxiliary verb. For an introduction to modal auxiliary verbs, see p137.
The forms of *might* are the same for all persons.

**Positive and negative**

| | | |
|---|---|---|
| I<br>He<br>It<br>We | might<br>might not | go to the party.<br>be late.<br>rain tomorrow.<br>go out for a meal tonight. |

**Question**

The inverted question *Might you … ?* is unusual.
It is very common to ask a question with *Do you think … + will … ?*

| | |
|---|---|
| Do you think | you'll get here on time?<br>it'll rain?<br>they'll come to our party? |

**Short answer**

| | |
|---|---|
| Do you think he'll come?<br>Do you think it'll rain? | He might.<br>It might. |

### Use

1 *Might* is used to express a future possibility. It contrasts with *will*, which, in the speaker's opinion, expresses a future certainty.
   England **will** win the match.
   (I am sure they will.)
   England **might** win the match.
   (It's possible, but I don't know.)
2 Notice that, in the negative, these sentences express the same idea of possibility.
   It **might not** rain this afternoon.
   I **don't think it'll** rain this afternoon.

# Unit 13

## 13.1 Present Perfect Continuous

### Form

*has/have* + *been* + *-ing* (present participle)

**Positive and negative**

| | | |
|---|---|---|
| I<br>We<br>You<br>They | ve (have)<br>haven't | been working. |
| He<br>She<br>It | 's (has)<br>hasn't | |

**Question**

| | | | |
|---|---|---|---|
| How long | have | I<br>we<br>you<br>they | been working? |
| | has | he<br>she<br>it | |

**Short answer**

| | |
|---|---|
| Have you been running?<br>Has he been shopping? | Yes, I have./No, I haven't.<br>Yes, he has./No, he hasn't. |

### Use

The Present Perfect Continuous is used:

1 to express an activity which began in the past and continues to the present.
 We**'ve been waiting** here for hours!
 It**'s been raining** for days.

2 to refer to an activity with a result in the present.
 I'm hot because **I've been running**.
 I haven't got any money because **I've been shopping**.

**Note**

1 Sometimes there is little or no difference in meaning between the Present Perfect Simple and Continuous.
 How long **have you worked** here?
 How long **have you been working** here?

2 Think of the verbs that have the idea of a long time, for example, *wait, work, learn, travel, play*.
These verbs can be found in the Present Perfect Continuous.
 **I've been playing** tennis since I was a boy.
Think of the verbs that don't have the idea of a long time, for example, *find, start, buy, die, lose, break, stop*. It is unusual to find these verbs in the Present Perfect Continuous.
 **I've bought** a new dress.
 My cat **has died**.
 My radio**'s broken**.

3 Verbs that express a state, for example, *like, love, know, have* for possession, are not found in the Present Perfect Continuous.
 We**'ve known** each other for a few weeks.
 NOT We've ~~been knowing~~ each other for a few weeks.
 How long **have** you had your car?
 NOT How long have you ~~been having~~ your car?

4 The Present Perfect Simple looks at the completed action. This is why, if the sentence gives a number or a quantity, the Present Perfect Simple is used. The Continuous is not possible.
 **I've written** three letters today.
 NOT I've ~~been writing~~ three letters today.

# Unit 14

## 14.1 Past Perfect

### Form

*had* + *-ed* (past participle)
The past participle of regular verbs ends in *-ed*. There are many common irregular verbs. See the list on p143.

**Positive and negative**

| | | |
|---|---|---|
| I<br>He/She/It<br>We/You/They | 'd (had)<br>hadn't | arrived before 10.00. |

**Question**

| | | |
|---|---|---|
| Had | I<br>he/she/it<br>we/you/they | left? |

**Short answer**

| |
|---|
| Yes, he had.<br>No, they hadn't. |

### Use

The Past Perfect is used to express an action in the past which happened before another action in the past.

Action 2 Action 1

When I got home, John **had cooked** a meal.

**Note**

Notice the use of the Past Perfect and the Past Simple in the following sentences.
 When I got home, John **cooked** a meal. (First I got home, then John cooked.)
 When I got home, John **had cooked** a meal. (John cooked a meal before I got home.)

## 14.2 Reported statements

### Form

The usual rule is that the verb form moves 'one tense back'.

| **Direct speech** | **Reported speech** |
|---|---|
| **Present**<br>'I love you.'<br>'I'm going out now.' | **Past**<br>He said he loved me.<br>Ann said she was going out. |
| **Present Perfect**<br>'We've met before.' | **Past Perfect**<br>She said they'd met before. |
| **Past Simple**<br>'We met in 1987.' | **Past Perfect**<br>He said they'd met in 1987. |
| **will**<br>'I'll mend it for you.' | **would**<br>She said that she would mend it for me. |
| **can**<br>'I can swim.' | **could**<br>She said she could swim. |

**Note**

Notice the use of *say/tell*.
*Say* + *(that)*
 She **said** (**that**) they were happy together.
*Tell* + *person (that)*
 He **told me** (**that**) he loved Mary.

# Appendix 1

## IRREGULAR VERBS

| Base form | Past Simple | Past Participle |
|---|---|---|
| be | was/were | been |
| become | became | become |
| begin | began | begun |
| break | broke | broken |
| bring | brought | brought |
| build | built | built |
| buy | bought | bought |
| can | could | been able |
| catch | caught | caught |
| choose | chose | chosen |
| come | came | come |
| cost | cost | cost |
| cut | cut | cut |
| do | did | done |
| drink | drank | drunk |
| drive | drove | driven |
| eat | ate | eaten |
| fall | fell | fallen |
| feel | felt | felt |
| fight | fought | fought |
| find | found | found |
| fly | flew | flown |
| forget | forgot | forgotten |
| get | got | got |
| give | gave | given |
| go | went | gone/been |
| grow | grew | grown |
| have | had | had |
| hear | heard | heard |
| hit | hit | hit |
| keep | kept | kept |
| know | knew | known |
| learn | learnt/learned | learnt/learned |
| leave | left | left |
| lose | lost | lost |
| make | made | made |
| meet | met | met |
| pay | paid | paid |
| put | put | put |
| read /ri:d/ | read /red/ | read /red/ |
| ride | rode | ridden |
| run | ran | run |
| say | said | said |
| see | saw | seen |
| sell | sold | sold |
| send | sent | sent |
| shut | shut | shut |
| sing | sang | sung |
| sit | sat | sat |
| sleep | slept | slept |
| speak | spoke | spoken |
| spend | spent | spent |
| stand | stood | stood |
| steal | stole | stolen |
| swim | swam | swum |
| take | took | taken |
| tell | told | told |
| think | thought | thought |
| understand | understood | understood |
| wake | woke | woken |
| wear | wore | worn |
| win | won | won |
| write | wrote | written |

# Appendix 2

## VERB PATTERNS

| **Verb + *-ing*** | |
|---|---|
| like<br>love<br>enjoy<br>hate<br>finish<br>stop | swimming<br><br>cooking |

**Note**

We often use the verb *go* + *-ing* for sports and activities.

I **go swimming** everyday.

I **go shopping** at the weekend.

| **Verb + *to* + infinitive** | |
|---|---|
| choose<br>decide<br>forget<br>promise<br>manage<br>need<br>help<br>hope<br>try<br>want<br>would like<br>would love | to go<br><br>to work |

| **Verb + *-ing* or *to* + infinitive** | |
|---|---|
| begin<br>start | raining/to rain |

| **Verb + sb + infinitive without *to*** | | |
|---|---|---|
| let<br>make | somebody | go<br>do |

| **Modal auxiliary verbs** | |
|---|---|
| can<br>could<br>shall<br>will<br>would | go<br><br>arrive |

OXFORD
UNIVERSITY PRESS

Great Clarendon Street, Oxford OX2 6DP

Oxford University Press is a department of the University of Oxford. It furthers the University's objective of excellence in research, scholarship, and education by publishing worldwide in

Oxford New York

Auckland Cape Town Dar es Salaam Hong Kong Karachi Kuala Lumpur Madrid Melbourne Mexico City Nairobi New Delhi Shanghai Taipei Toronto

With offices in

Argentina Austria Brazil Chile Czech Republic France Greece Guatemala Hungary Italy Japan South Korea Poland Portugal Singapore Switzerland Thailand Turkey Ukraine Vietnam

OXFORD and OXFORD ENGLISH are registered trade marks of Oxford University Press in the UK and in certain other countries



The moral rights of the author have been asserted

Database right Oxford University Press (maker)

First published 2000
2009 2008 2007 2006
20 19 18 17 16



ISBN-13: 978 0 19 436670 0 (International edition)
ISBN-10: 0-19-436670-7

ISBN-13: 978 0 19 437876 5 (German edition)
ISBN-10: 0-19-437876-4

Bestellnummer 118 223

Printed and bound in China

ACKNOWLEDGEMENTS

**The authors and publisher are grateful to those who have given permission to reproduce the following extracts and adaptations of copyright material:**

p22 'The burglars' friend' The Daily Mail 5 February 1996 © *The Daily Mail*/Solo Syndication.
p34 'The best shopping street in the world' by Anne Applebaum, *The London Evening Standard* 27 October 1998 © *The London Evening Standard*/Solo Syndication.
p42 'The kids from fame' by Carrie Fisher, *Observer Life Magazine* 13 April 1997 © *The Observer*.
p44 *You've Got a Friend* Words and music by Carole King © 1971 Screen Gems-EMI Music Ltd, London WC2H 0EA. Reproduced by permission of IMP Ltd.
p50 'The man who gave his money away' by Tony Burton, *Mail Weekend Magazine* 31 December 1994 © *The Daily Mail Weekend Magazine*/Solo Syndication
p51 'Hetty Green' from *Virtual Vermont Internet Magazine* www.virtualvermont.com Reproduced by permission of *Virtual Vermont Internet Magazine*.
p73 'Future tense? No, the future will be perfect' interview with Michio Kaku, *Focus Magazine* October 1998. Reproduced by permission of Michio Kaku.
p74 'One day all this will be offices' by Jonathon Glancey, *The Guardian* 11 July 1998 © *The Guardian*.
p78 'All alone with my rocky horrors' by Paul Lay, *The Telegraph* 3 October 1998 reproduced by permission of Paul Lay.
p82 'Into the wild' by Jon Krakauer, published by Macmillan Publishers Ltd, reproduced by permission of John A Ware Literary Agency.
p99 'Reverend ghostbuster faces another haunting hallowe'en' by Martin Wroe, The Observer 26 October 1997 © *The Observer*.
p106 'Tom, 69, skates on for Tesco' *The Daily Mail* 18 February 1999 © *The Daily Mail*/Solo Syndication.
p107 'Life's a beach patrol' by Cordell Marks, *The Weekend Telegraph* September 9 1995 reproduced by permission of Cordell Marks.
p114 'The tale of two silent brothers' from Oxford Bookworms: *Stories From The Five Towns*. Reproduced by permission of Jennifer Bassett.
p116 *Talk to me* by Bruce Springsteen. Copyright © Bruce Springsteen (ASCAP) Administered by Zomba Music Publishers Ltd. In UK & Eire Only. Reproduced by permission of Zomba Music Publishers Ltd.

**Although every effort has been made to trace and contact copyright holders before publication, this has not been possible in some cases. We apologize for any apparent infringement of copyright and if notified, the publisher will be pleased to rectify any errors or omissions at the earliest opportunity.**

p26 'The Perfect Crime' This story is based on Roald Dahl's *Lamb to the Slaughter* but was written without the knowledge or approval of the Dahl estate. The publishers apologize to the Estate for this oversight and are grateful to the Estate for their understanding in allowing them to include the story nevertheless. You can read Roald Dahl's original story in his short story collection *Someone Like You*, published by Penguin Books.

**Illustrations by:**
Kathy Baxendale p30 (list), 108 (diary writing); CartoonStock/Larry p24; Rowie Christopher pp56, 61, 116; Martin Cottam pp114, 115; Paul Dickinson p111; Jessie Eckel, New Division p32; Tim Kahane p14; Ian Kellas pp12, 20, 21, 28, 40, 52, 71, 85, 100; Beverly Levy pp110, 111, 112; Gone Loco, Debut Art p29; Mark Olroyd p84; Pierre Paul Pariseau pp25, 68; Andy Parker p26; Oxford University Press TechGraphics pp74, 79; Debbie Ryder p53; Harry Venning pp10, 60, 64, 69, 72, 78, 96, 104; Azélie Williams pp94, 95

**Commissioned photography by:**
**Gareth Boden** pp6, 7, 21, 37, 38, 58–9, 66, 69, 70, 72, 93 (out of order, this room is ready, engaged), 94, 96–7, 101, 103, 108, 117 **Haddon Davies** pp12, 30 **Mark Mason** pp9, 26–7, 30, 36, 54–5, 73 (Visions), 90, 93 (under 18), 108
**photo 58–9:**
Location: Mr and Mrs M Stewart, Wytham Abbey, Oxford
Hair by Seed, Oxford
Make-up by Sarah Heap, The Make-up Place
Clothes from Allders of Oxford
Glasses from Boots the Optician

**Locations provided by:**
Gareth Boden pp101 (entrance hallway), 108 (living room) Boots p37 (chemist); Café Rouge, Hertford p37 (café); Censored p37 (clothes shop), Countryside Residential Properties pp7, 108 (kitchen), 117 (exterior of house & entrance hallway); Goldsmiths p101 (jewellers); Harlow College p96–7; Antonia Jack pp38, 72, 117 (kitchen & birthday); Post Office Counters p37 (post office); Studio Cambridge pp21, 101 (school), 117 (classroom); Thaxted Surgery p69; WAGN p117 (train station); Waitrose p101 (supermarket)

**We would also like to thank the following for permission to reproduce photographs:**
**The Advertising Archives** pp87 (1908 Coke advertisment), 92 (Wrigley's pixie at bottom), (girl with pixies), (women in white hats); **AKG London** p87 (sailor girl), 90 (tobacco), (cotton); **The Ancient Art & Architecture Collection** pp11 (Greek theatre masks); **The Art Archive** pp11 (Archaelogical Museum, Naples/man reading scroll), (Egyptian Museum, Cairo/ Egyptian papyrus); **The Anthony Blake Photo Library** pp65 (fondue), (A Sydenham/Mexican food), (G Buntrock/mint tea); **The Bridgeman Art Library** p90 (Royal Asiatic Society/sugar cane); **Bubbles Photo Library** pp8 (F Rombout/family by river), 17 (L Tizard), 107 (J Woodcock/ Cathy); **J Allan Cash** p93 (feeding of animals, one way); **Anthony Coleman** p107 (Terry Cemm both); **Collections** pp38 (B Shuel/ Justin), 93 (B Wells/keep off the grass); **Colorific!** pp14 (T Graham/Maori), (B Backman/sheep), 49 (J Tove Johansson/cottage), 51 (C Bernson/Milton Petrie); **Comstock** pp63 (all); **Corbis** pp6 (S Maze/ Bologna), 10 (R Holmes/conversation), 16 (B Krist/ barbecue), 20 (D Modricker/COR/older couple), 45 (Picture Press/man at desk), (Wartenberg/Picture Press/man smiling), 47 (C Osborne/Melbourne), 51 (Bettmann/Hetty Green *both*), 66 (D Katzenstein), 80 (D Gluckstein/middle-aged man), 81 (B Varie/man in office), (F Wartenberg/couple with gift), (L Manning/girl on steps), (Bettmann/man and pipe), (C Garratt/Milepost 92?/security notice); **Corbis Sygma** pp42–3 (L Greenfield), 74 (J van Hasselt/poster); **Digital Vision** p19 (New York); **Fortean Picture Library** p98 (J & C Bord/ghost); **Agencja Gazeta**, Warsaw pp34, 35 (M Mutor); **Getty One Stone** pp10 (W Kaehler/monkeys), 13 (K Fisher/mother and child), (PBJ Pictures/college students), (PBJ Pictures/business people), 15 (S Jauncey/ fishing), (L Adamski Peek/ice hockey), (D Madison/ football), (D Balfour/giraffe), 16 (A Sacks/girls hairstyling), 18 (Rohan), 19 (D Durfee/Roberto Solano), (S Cohen/ Yuet Tung), 20 (B Thomas/young couple), 23 (F Alison), 38 (P Cade/Sean), (M Douet/Martyn), 39 (T Reynolds/ Mel), 45 (I O'Leary/ill woman), (L Monneret/girl with presents), (R E Daemrich/yawning boy), 46 (B Thomas), 47 (R La Salle/Chicago), (D Armand/Dubai), (H Pfeiffer/ Paris), 48 (S Grandadam/Stockholm, Brazilia), 49 (C Ehlers/girls fishing), 57 (H Camille/Guy and Suzie), 65 (R Elliot/Alpine restaurant), (R During/Acapulco beach), 81 (D Day/woman and spider), (D Stewart/man and knife), (C Slattery/rollercoaster), 84 (P Lee Harvey/man), 107 (D Ham/balloon), 109 (L Dutton), 113 (L Monneret); **Sally & Richard Greenhill** pp13 (elderly couple talking); **Robert Harding Picture Library** pp19 (© Noble Stock/ Int'l Stock/Endre Boros), 49 (midnight sun), 76 (N Boyd/ hotel exterior), (F Jalain/swimming pool), (P Langone/ Int'l Stock/conference room and bar), (D Dickinson/Int'l Stock/gym), 93 (S Harris/train departures); **Hulton Getty** pp54 (Anthony Trollope), 80 (boy), 91 (Office of Information for Puerto Rico/sugar cane), (Evans/woman and cotton), 92 (Reiss/American soldiers), (Wrigley's pixie at top); **The Image Bank** pp13 (M Romanelli/men talking in café), 62 (R Mancini), 65 (G A Rossi/market stall); **Images Colour Library** pp82–3 (Panoramic Images); **Impact Photos** p93 (S Shepheard/Undergound); **The Kobal Collection** pp104 (TM & © 1993 Universal City Studios and Amblin Entertainment. All Rights Reserved/ *Schindler's List*), 105 (Lucasfilm/Paramount '81/ Raiders *of the Lost Ark*), (David James 1998 TM & Dreamworks LLC Paramount Pictures Amblin Entertainment. All Rights Reserved/*Saving Private Ryan*), (Warner Bros/Steven Spielberg); **Magnum Photos** pp74 (I Berry/Shenzen building site), 75 (Hong Kong cityscape); **Oxford Picture Library** p33; Oxford University Press p73 (Michio Kaku); **PhotoDisc** p41; **Photofusion** pp45 (M Campbell/woman in car), 98 (B Apicella/woman); **Photographers International** p99 (T Fincher); **Pictorial Press** pp104 (Columbia/*Close Encounters of the Third Kind*), 105 (UPI/ *Jurassic Park*); **Redferns** pp57 (M Hutson/concert); **Ringway Signs Ltd** p93 (services); **Science Photo Library** pp10 (M Agliolo/computer screens), (D Ducros/satellite), 73 (A Pasieka/DNA fingerprinting *background*), (P Plailly/ boy and hologram), (B Edmaier/lava); **John & Liz Soars** p8 (Joy Darling); **Solo Syndication Ltd** p106; **Frank Spooner Pictures** pp50 (Jordan/Gamma), 55 (P Massey/ Joanna Trollope), 86 (N Reynard/Kenyan man drinking), 87 (G Fonluft/Coke bottles), 88 (A Hernandez-Liaison/ MacDonalds); **Still Pictures** p73 (H Schwarzbach/solar panels in Sudan); **The Stock Market** pp38 (A Skelley/ Amy), 48 (D Croucher/Paris), 73 (Zefa/medical scanner); **Stock Shot** p79 (D Willis/El Chorro Gorge); **The Telegraph** p78 (P Lay/Paul Lay); **Telegraph Colour Library** pp8 (R Gage/family portrait), 10 (J Danielsky/ mobile phone), (F Delva/film), 24 (R Chapple/Zoe), (S Miller/police detective), 44 (J P Fruchet), 48 (T Chevassut/ Beijing), 65 (S Adams/snowboarding), (P Scholey/Nile cruise), (K Ross/pyramids), 88 (hamburger); **Tesco Photo Library** p93 (unleaded)